D0856175

Doctor Sócrates

Doctor Sócrates

FOOTBALLER, PHILOSOPHER, LEGEND

Andrew Downie

**SIMON &
SCHUSTER**

London · New York · Sydney · Toronto · New Delhi

A CBS COMPANY

First published in Great Britain by Simon & Schuster UK Ltd, 2017
A CBS COMPANY

Copyright © 2017 by Andrew Downie

1 3 5 7 9 10 8 6 4 2

Simon & Schuster UK Ltd
1st Floor
222 Gray's Inn Road
London WC1X 8HB

www.simonandschuster.co.uk

Simon & Schuster Australia, Sydney
Simon & Schuster India, New Delhi

A CIP catalogue record for this book
is available from the British Library.

ISBN: 978-1-4711-5407-2
Ebook ISBN: 978-1-4711-5409-6

Typeset and designed in the UK by M Rules
Printed and bound by CPI Group (UK) Ltd, Croydon, CR0 4YY

MIX
Paper from
responsible sources
FSC® C020471

Simon & Schuster UK Ltd are committed to sourcing paper that is made
from wood grown in sustainable forests and support the Forest Stewardship
Council, the leading international forest certification organisation. Our
books displaying the FSC logo are printed on FSC certified paper.

For
Mari, Pinky and Sho Jo

'The unexamined life is not worth living.'

Socrates, circa 5th century BC

FOREWORD

by Johan Cruyff

After the 1970 World Cup, the world was focused on Brazil and their attack. But that changed in 1974. Brazil didn't play beautiful football; in fact, they were quite the opposite. The game they played was physical. But in 1982 Brazil happily returned to form at the World Cup in Spain. That was the first time I saw Sócrates play and I paid him special attention. It was thanks to him that I followed the seleção with a special interest. First of all, Sócrates stood out because of his height. He was noticeably tall and came across as elegant, a person who was fleet of foot. There were others in midfield, of course, but I could see very clearly that it was he who gave form to that national side. It's funny that he called me the orchestra conductor because that is exactly how I saw him. Sócrates reminded me of my hero as a boy, Faas Wilkes, a man who also played elegant and beautiful football that was above all technical, for teams that included Inter Milan and Valencia.

Just like him, Sócrates could do what he wanted with the ball thanks to his enormous skill and vision. He knew where to position himself on the field of play. Sócrates wasn't quick, he didn't cross much and he wasn't a great header of the ball, but he made up for it with lots of other qualities. He was one of those players who did a little bit of everything, in the best sense of the word. Sócrates scored a lot of goals. In that sense he reminded me of Di Stéfano, who also scored a lot and was good in many other ways. If he was playing today, Sócrates would, in many respects, be the opposite of Messi, who is small and quick. Sócrates did not need speed to control the game. Like Pep Guardiola, I also see a lot of similarities between the Brazil side of 1982 and Spain in 2010.

With so many players ready to attack, you are simply obliged to keep possession. It's an undeniable fact that this is the case in both those teams as well as at Barcelona. It was a great shame that the beautiful Brazil team were eliminated by a destructive Italy in 1982. It was a huge disappointment for the whole of football because after that World Cup teams started to play like Italy did. No one knows what would have happened had Brazil triumphed. I also think it is a great shame that Sócrates played only one season in Europe, with Fiorentina in 1984/85. It was precisely in that season that football the world over began to improve a little following the 1982 World Cup. If Sócrates had stayed longer in Europe, he would perhaps have become an even bigger star. We saw that happen with the Netherlands. We had already played well at the start of the 1970s, but our football was only recognised by the rest of the world at the 1974 tournament. It's funny that Sócrates had a project in 1982, Corinthians Democracy. I also had a project that came after, my Cruyff Foundation. I understood that Sócrates' main objective was to give players more responsibility. I also fought for that. If you give players more responsibility off the field, they are going to want it on the field too.

I even heard that Sócrates proposed that football change from being 11 against 11 to nine against nine. After thinking about his proposal, I came to the conclusion that I disagreed. If you do that then you change the essence of the game. They tried to abolish offside. The idea was to make football more attacking, but the opposite happened and so it never stuck. Sócrates believed that football had become too physical and on that point I agree. We are on the right track now and Barcelona is a great example of that. Even in Holland we are getting better, with Ajax and Feyenoord leading the way.

Sócrates was obviously an intelligent man. A top sportsman has to be intelligent, there is no way of escaping it. It's also incredible that he graduated in medicine. And in politics he made a difference. We could say that Romário is a substitute for Sócrates, albeit with a very different vision. What I never understood is why Sócrates drank so much. I hope it wasn't because he fell into a black hole when his career ended. He was a man with enormous authority. I would like to know why he did it. I would love to have chatted with him about football. We met on a few occasions and we said hello but it never went further than that. What a shame.

NOTES ON THE TEXT

When Sócrates made his professional debut, football in Brazil was run by the Confederação Brasileira de Desportos (CBD). In 1979, the CBD split into separate units and the Confederação Brasileira de Futebol (CBF) took over the running of the game.

Brazil's first national league began in 1971, but it had different names and different formats, usually culminating in knockout stages and even best-of-three finals, until the current European-style system was introduced in 2003. For reasons of simplicity, I have referred to the national championship by its current name, the Brasileiro, throughout the text.

State leagues were much more important than the national league throughout Sócrates' career. The national league was new and state rivalries were keen and long-standing. Reflecting that importance, the São Paulo state championship and the Rio de Janeiro state championship took up more of the season. Every year the formats and dates changed. Sometimes, the state leagues would begin at the start of the year and be followed by the national league; in other years the order was reversed. The state tournaments could last up to nine months, while the Brasileiro took no more than four.

The southern hemisphere's seasons are opposite to those in

the north and all references to seasons are specific to Brazil. For example, winter refers to the months of June, July and August.

The Brazilian national side is referred to throughout as the seleção.

Brazilian currency values have their US dollar equivalents at the time.

1

'Ever since he was about 11 or 12 years old, wherever he went people knew him, people could see he was different. People who knew football could see he was going places.'

Sócrates' brother Sóstenes

Brazil pushed nine men into the Italian box and the clock read 90:02 when Éder ran to the far side of the field to take the last corner of the game. One of the greatest teams in history desperately needed a goal to take them into the semi-finals of the 1982 World Cup. Éder hauled the advertising boards off the ground to get position and then stepped forward to curl the ball left-footed straight into the goal. Dino Zoff scrambled to punch it out from under his crossbar and then breathed a huge sigh of relief when the whistle went for a foul. The veteran keeper wasted as much time as he could before tapping the ball to a defender and then picking up the back pass and launching it down the field. It was the last kick of the match. Seconds later, the referee blew his whistle and one of the most exciting football matches ever played was over. It was Italy 3 Brazil 2 and the favourites were out. Brazil were going home.

Giuseppe Bergomi ran towards Sócrates to get his shirt and, as the Italian substitutes streamed on to the field to mob the victors, a beaming Bergomi danced around the midfield with his yellow prize scrunched in his hand. The Brazil captain threw Bergomi's shirt over his shoulder and walked dejectedly to the dressing room. His face was a blank and Éder, Paulo Isidoro and Waldir Peres all trooped down the tunnel ahead of him, their faces also a picture of stunned disbelief.

In the bowels of the Sarrià stadium, the Brazil dressing room was like a morgue. Many of the players wept uncontrollably. Paulo Isidoro kept repeating, 'We lost to Italy, we fucking lost to Italy,' like it was something too freaky to have actually happened. Trainer Gilberto Tim punched a door, putting his fist clean through the panel. 'You lot who were complaining about being homesick, are you happy now?' said a shellshocked Oscar. 'Well, you'll be home tomorrow.'[1]

Sócrates sat quietly in one corner of the room, but his outer calm hid what he called 'immense anguish' and he had no words to describe how he really felt. He had spent the previous month writing a daily diary for the sports magazine *Placar*, happily jotting down his notes on hotel stationery and handing them to editor Juca Kfouri. When Kfouri approached him to get his final entry, all he could muster were the words that adorned the magazine's cover: '*Que pena, Brasil*'. (What a shame, Brazil.) 'You write the last entry for me,' he told him . 'I don't have it in me.' He walked past the reporters waiting outside the dressing room and stopped only briefly to hug a friend before silently boarding the team bus.[2]

When they finally made it back to the hotel, an hour away in the hills of Catalonia, the 22 players and the entire staff got together for one last team meeting. Manager Telê Santana told them they had played the best football in the competition and could go home with their heads held high. CBF president

Giulite Coutinho thanked them for everything. Júnior tried to speak but could hardly finish a sentence without choking up. Juninho cried like a baby. Last of all, Sócrates got to his feet.

'People, we might have lost the game but let's not lose what we have here,' their captain and leader said in an inspiring speech about pride and friendship that none of the players has ever forgotten. 'This incredible unity we have is going to be ours for the rest of our lives. That's what matters.'[3]

His voice trailed off amid the sobs. There was hardly a dry eye in the house.

Brazil's golden generation were crushed by the loss. Zico, Toninho Cerezo, Leandro, Júnior, Serginho, they were more than team-mates, they were the best of friends and they dealt with the aftermath the only way they knew how. Still unable to digest the defeat and too wired to sleep, Sócrates led a bunch of players on an all-nighter. Months before, they had agreed to stop drinking and smoking to get in perfect shape for what they all knew was their best shot at a world title and now they were making up for lost time. They drank until 5 a.m., and when they got up a few hours later hitting the bar seemed like the only sensible option. July 6th was the hottest day of the year, with temperatures over 100 degrees, and as he sat by the hotel pool picking beers from a bucket packed with ice, Sócrates was no closer to explaining how they lost what he called the 'most exciting game I've ever played in'.

'It's hard for me to understand this defeat,' he said. 'If we'd made mistakes, then I'd understand. It would be easier to explain. But I didn't see any errors, I just didn't see them. I have never been as shaken as this while playing football. Even during the game, the rhythm was amazing. It was so even, every minute was hotly contested. We know we didn't play badly. I repeat, if we'd played poorly then we'd accept it. I don't think anybody should be questioned or criticised. There were no silly mistakes. Football is a game of mistakes. You're always fighting not to make a mistake. And there is just no reason to explain this defeat. That's what makes this elimination all the more shocking. We are always prepared to lose, especially in a sport such as football. But it's like the death of a loved one. You might know they are going to pass away but the shock is still the same.'[4]

The 1982 World Cup marked a summit of sorts for Sócrates. In the years to come, he would win more trophies and become an even bigger star both inside and outside the world of sport. But he would never again dedicate himself so completely to one footballing task.

Perhaps more importantly, it also marked a turning point for football. Brazil's defeat was a historic reverse for the purists, who saw it as nothing less than a victory of evil over good. Johan Cruyff called Brazil 'the moral champion', Zico said football died a death that sunny evening at the Sarrià, and Sócrates declared that Brazil would never again play with the same panache.

'The team's defeat on that fateful day in Barcelona against an Italian side who would go on to crown themselves champions was a crushing blow to the Brazilian style of play that side represented so well,' he wrote in his unpublished memoir 20 years later. 'From that moment on the emphasis changed to focus on results even more than was the case up until then. The business side of the game grew frighteningly quickly and money always goes to the winners, even if they are poor quality winners. From that point on Brazilian football would never be the same.'[5]

The defeat, however, was not the be-all and end-all for a man whose life was so much bigger than just football. Even as Brazil prepared to face Italy in the biggest game of his life, Sócrates was thinking about more important battles. He had already started what would become known as Corinthians Democracy, the most daring show of player power ever to rock a major soccer team. The Corinthians players were taking control of the club and demanding a say in its management. Sócrates wanted freedom and not just for himself. He wanted the whole of Brazil to follow suit, to unseat the military dictators and take back their country. He had power and personality and a nation of 130 million people were watching his every move. One dream had failed in Spain. He was not going to let the dream of democracy escape his grasp so easily.

Sócrates was always different.

One afternoon in the early 1970s, Botafogo Juniors were playing away in Batatais, a small town in Brazil's agricultural heartland. The summer showers had swept across the cotton fields and sugar cane plantations, and the rain was pouring down in big fat drops. Sócrates never liked playing in the rain but he was in the zone and had already scored twice when he got the ball in the middle of the park. He beat one man, dribbled round another and then loped forward through the mud. There were two defenders in front of him and he feinted to shoot, fooling one of them into a desperate lunge. He dipped his shoulder to ease past the second and darted into the box. He dribbled the ball round the flailing keeper and walked the ball towards the goal. He stopped on the goal line, turned around to face the other players and back-heeled his third and Botafogo's sixth into the empty net. It was a wonder goal made even more sensational by the awful conditions. But instead of punching the air or running the length of the field to celebrate, the gangly teenager just smiled. His team-mates jumped on top of him, screaming and ruffling his shaggy mane of black hair, but he trotted calmly back to the centre circle in that ungainly style of his, shaking a few hands and wiping himself down for the restart.[6]

The referee, a former Coritiba player named Leal, ran towards him and reached for his red card.

'What's wrong, ref?' asked Botafogo captain, Marinho.

'I'm sending Sócrates off,' the ref said. 'He's taking the mickey.'

Brazilian footballers have always loved the fancy stuff – the nutmegs, the keepy-uppy, the standing on the ball. But one team's dominance is another team's shame and those on the receiving end always hit back, scything down the man juggling the ball or whacking the guy holding out by the corner flag. To show off is to humiliate and humiliating the opposition is a major offence in South America.

'For the love of God,' Marinho cried, 'he's not taking the mickey. He's always like that – he just never shows much emotion.'

'He's humiliating them,' Leal said. 'He's off.'

Marinho knew the referee from previous games and stood in front of him, switching between the classic Latin American poses of hands behind the back, hands in the air, hands together in prayer.

'He's not that kind of player,' Marinho pleaded. 'Please, Leal, you have to believe me. He's just different.'

Leal took a step back and, grudgingly accepting the captain's appeals, he put the red card back in his pocket.

'That's all very hard to believe, Marinho,' he said. 'But I'll have my eye on him.'

When the match ended, Leal joined Marinho as they trudged through the mud towards the dressing room.

'He's one of a kind, that lad,' he said to Marinho, before shaking hands with both of them and heading for the showers, barely believing what he had seen.[7]

In a country where drama comes screaming and pouting from every street corner, television screen and relationship, Sócrates was the diametric opposite of his emotional compatriots. He never understood why his team-mates got so excited about football. It was great fun but it was only a game and, really, how important could it be if scoring goals like that was so easy?

He got that inner calm from his parents, two humble and hard-working people from the rough and tumble north of Brazil. The northern half of Brazil is the poor half, a region that starts on the gorgeous beaches of the Atlantic coast and sweeps westwards through the scalding scrublands towards the Amazon jungle. Life is hot and hard, and the people who live there have formed a culture that is vastly different from the more developed cities of the south. They have been moulded by the isolation, the heat and the poverty to bear their daily hardships with stoicism and good humour.

Sócrates' father, Raimundo Vieira de Oliveira, was one of them, born in Messejana, a small town on the outskirts of Fortaleza, the capital of Ceará state. Raimundo got a job 800 miles away, in the Amazonian town of Igarapé-Açu, and it was there that he met his future wife, Guiomar Sampaio de Souza. The town had a chaste dating ritual that involved the men form-ing a circle and walking in one direction, while the women formed another circle inside them going the opposite way. They eyed up their potential suitors as they passed by and it took only a second for the six-foot Raimundo and the diminutive Guiomar to realise they were made for one another. They exchanged knowing glances, made their introductions, and the rest is his-tory. 'We spoke a little bit and that was it,' said Guiomar. 'There was no holding us back.'[8]

Their first child was Sócrates Brasileiro Sampaio de Souza Vieira de Oliveira, born at 10.20 p.m. on 19 February 1954 at the Santa Casa de Misericordia hospital in Belém, a tropical city on the banks of the Amazon river. His father loved to read the classics and was deep into the Greek philosophers when his son made his debut appearance. He gave his boy two names, the first of them Sócrates and the second Brasileiro, making him Brazilian Sócrates, as if there were any chance of confusing the baby from Amazonia with his namesake from ancient Greece. Just 13 months later – while Raimundo was immersed in reading religious texts – his second son got similar treatment, and Sóstenes was named after a Corinthian mentioned in the First Epistle of St Paul the Apostle to the Corinthians. When his third son came along two years after that, he was reading *Oedipus Rex* and Sófocles was named in tribute to the Greek dramatist.[9]

Guiomar had had enough of the unpronounceable Greek names by the time their fourth son was born in September 1959, and so Raimundo Junior was rather prosaically named after his father. Next came Raimar, following the common practice in Brazil of joining part of both the father's and mother's name together, and Raí got his name in keeping with another Brazilian custom, that of naming children with the same letter or bunch of letters. The names were getting shorter and Guiomar joked it was just as well she stopped at six because the seventh would have to be called R.

Sócrates was a happy child and his earliest memories were of his dad's library. Outside their door was the Amazon rainforest, a seemingly endless expanse of land with no barriers other than trees and rivers, but Sócrates remembers being inside, out of the heat and the light, and surrounded by classics, textbooks and encyclopaedias. His father would devour every book he could get his hands on, often peering at the pages through flickering lamplight because there was no electricity at home, Sócrates sitting at his feet.

Seu Raimundo – everyone added the honorific *Seu* as a mark of respect – was obsessed with learning, and he read avidly both for pleasure and to get on. Like his three brothers and two sisters, he never finished primary school and was forced to go to work before he had even reached his teens. His brothers were manual labourers and semi-skilled workers, but Seu Raimundo sold hammocks on the beach and set up a small stand at the local street market selling *rapadura*, the blocks of unrefined cane sugar that were a staple in the impoverished north and northeast. They all worked to keep the family afloat, but Seu Raimundo understood the value of education better than any of them and he spent every free minute with his head in books. He perfected his reading and writing – an impressive feat in a nation where more than half the people were illiterate – and his hard work paid off when he got a job as a census taker with the government's statistics institute.[10]

Even after marrying and starting a family, Seu Raimundo would pick up his books as soon as his children were in bed and it wasn't long before he got his high school diploma. That was only the beginning, for he knew that the best way to advance was by passing the *concurso*, Brazil's public service entrance exam. Municipalities, states and the central government all held regular *concursos* for a vast array of jobs, ranging from lawyers to customs officials to university professors. Passing the exams required months and sometimes years of study, but the rewards made it worthwhile. Public sector employees got an excellent salary, could be fired only in the most extreme circumstances, and were allowed to retire in their fifties on a fat pension equal to their final wage.

Seu Raimundo set his sights on the most coveted of all civil service jobs, that of tax inspector. The inspectors were known as 'Brazilian princes' thanks to a salary that paid twice as much as the country's president and could be boosted through bonus payments for fines levied on tax dodgers. New openings were rare and when they did come up thousands of people applied. But his patience and hard work were rewarded and as the 1950s drew to a close, he became one of just 33 people – and the only one without a university degree – to pass the exam.

He was dealt another slice of luck soon after starting, when positions opened up in São Paulo state. A proud northeasterner, he was well aware that the move would take him almost 2,000 miles from an extended family he might never see again. But Seu Raimundo was keen to provide a better life for his children and the developed south was where the opportunities were. He was allowed to choose his new base and made reconnaissance trips to São Paulo, Campinas and Santos before opting to settle in Ribeirão Preto, a city of around 145,000 people 200 miles west of the state capital.

Ribeirão Preto was one of the richest cities in the state and a regional hub for the service industries and suppliers supporting the coffee, corn, cotton and cattle farmers who worked their land in the surrounding countryside. The city was growing, with a visible northeastern community attracted by the abundance of jobs and searing climate similar to their own. With a warm winter and a brutal summer in which temperatures frequently topped 100 degrees, locals joked there were only two seasons – 'summer and hell'. But that was not a problem for someone who had grown up near the equator and so, on the first day of January 1960, Seu Raimundo bundled his wife and four children on to a plane and made the move south.

Seu Raimundo loved sport, especially football, and just weeks after arriving in Ribeirão Preto he gave his eldest son a Santos shirt for his sixth birthday. Sócrates kicked a ball around every chance he got and tuned in to the Santos games on his dad's wireless, drawn to the exploits of Pelé, Coutinho and Pepe in what was one of the greatest club sides Brazil has ever seen.

He also loved the colour and noise of real matches and was fortunate that his father got a season ticket for the local side. The old man's gift for administration got him elected to Botafogo's board as a *conselheiro* (an elected adviser) and he took his son along every week, often balancing him on his lap or sitting him on nearby steps. One of his earliest footballing memories was seeing Pelé score a hat-trick in the 7-1 demolition of the home side in 1965 and it was a sign of how tall he was getting when, two years earlier at the age of nine, he inadvertently broke the light fitting when he jumped up and punched the air to celebrate a Santos goal against AC Milan in the Intercontinental Cup final.[11]

But although Sócrates loved watching football, he enjoyed playing the game even more. Seu Raimundo encouraged his sons to get involved in all kinds of sports, even opening an account at a local sporting goods store so that they wouldn't want for bats or balls or shoes. Sócrates tried his hand at judo and boxing, but it soon became apparent that his real talent lay with a ball at his feet. Where this talent came from was a mystery, and his brothers joked that their mum must have been a brilliant footballer because their dad certainly wasn't. His father unabashedly told people he played centre half at Ypiranga Futebol Clube back home in Igarapé-Açu, but the story was debunked when a relative visited and revealed that the old man – who was also the club president – played just once and only then because he picked the team after the regular coach failed to turn up.[12]

Sócrates' first proper team was Raio de Ouro, an amateur club that played their home games on one of the myriad pitches scattered around his home city. 'It was the first experience I had with a team outside my school,' he recalled of the run-out one Friday evening. 'I went to the trial, we went straight from school; it was the end of the afternoon and the sun was going down. The trainer was a guy called João and he said, "Did you bring your boots?", and I hadn't but I said, "I'll play in my bare feet!" And he asked me where I played and I said midfield and he said, "Midfield is all full but there's a place at right back if you want to play a bit." So I went to right back. And after a little while they invited me to play in a game the following Sunday.'

Sócrates was 11 years old and ready to play anywhere, although it didn't take long before the older lads realised he was good enough to take a more important role in midfield. He loved the shirt, 'plain white, like Santos, but with a gold stripe across the chest', as well as the sense of belonging that came with being part of an established team.[13]

His debut came in Bonfim Paulista, a small town about seven miles outside Ribeirão, and Sócrates travelled there with his new team-mates on the back of a flat-bed truck. The Raio de Ouro team featured players of all ages and backgrounds, and it was a huge eye-opener for the sheltered young lad from a solidly middle-class background. He would later win fame for his outspoken fight again the injustices that made Brazil one of the most unequal nations in the world, but this was his first taste of how tough things were outside his own little bubble. He came into contact with people he would otherwise never have met and Sócrates later said those early games were some of the most important in his life, for they introduced him to everyday realities he never knew existed, never mind saw up close.

'People ask what my most glorious moment in football was and I say, "Fuck, the glory for me was when I started with Raio de Ouro," because I was on the back of a truck with a load of guys, every one of them different,' Sócrates said. 'They each had a different life and different needs. Shit, I had eaten lunch, and some of them hadn't had anything, and we were on our way to play football! It was a learning experience that I never got at school; no one ever told me about these things at home. That was because my dad went through all that. I only discovered much later the difficulties he had. He never wanted us to know.'[14]

Sócrates took it all in his stride and, if his team-mates weren't fazed by the young man's innocence, they soon took notice of his football because he was blessed with a rare natural talent.

Sócrates could pass, shoot and control a ball with ease and he read the game like a veteran. They were skills he put down to the environment around his new home. After spending their first four years in Ribeirão Preto in a small house near the city centre, the Vieiras moved to a new place built by Seu Raimundo and his friends, which was large enough to accommodate the growing family. It came with a smaller annexe next door, where his youngest brothers Raí and Raimar would later live, and even boasted a patch of grass where they could play football.

The new neighbourhood wasn't quite rural, but it wasn't urban either. Built on the edge of the rapidly expanding city, it was surrounded by upwardly mobile neighbours and fields that doubled as glorious green playgrounds. The kids would cut the grass themselves using scythes and shears and then cobble together their own goalposts from tree trunks and bits of wood. Their childhoods were simple and, with no computers or cell phones or even television, they had little else to do except go to school and play. With almost no crime and a perfect climate, they were always outside on their bikes or kicking a ball around. Sócrates played wherever he could and if he and his friends didn't have a ball they would use the closest thing possible, often peeling the avocados that littered the ground to harvest the stone. Not everyone admired their initiative, though, and their youthful enthusiasm made them targets when they played in gardens or on private land – sometimes literally.[15]

One of their favourite places to play was just a few blocks from his new house, on a patch of grass alongside the Sacred Stigmata Seminary and Church. The brothers hated the young-sters running riot when they were studying or praying, and they could be less than charitable in their response. They first built a wall and sunk concrete posts into the grass, but when the kids insisted on kicking the ball outside their sanctuary they loaded their air rifles with salt pellets and fired them at their perceived tormentors. Sócrates complained that, as the biggest and most visible target, he would usually be the first one to get hit before they could scarper. But he would later look back and cite the attacks and the obstacles – both natural and man-made – as crucial in helping him develop his close control and his vision.

'The more difficulties you have when you start, the more interest you'll have in learning,' he said. 'If you play on a field full of holes, ant hills, with a tree in the middle and a ball that's as square as it is round then you develop skills that you wouldn't be obliged to learn in other situations. I got tired of playing football on pitches that had mango trees in the middle of them. The whole time you were looking at the tree because if you didn't then you'd run into it or the roots that were on the ground around about. So you are already starting to see the game differently.'[16]

By the end of the decade, having excelled for Raio de Ouro and helped the Colégio Marista win the Ribeirão Preto schools' cup two years in a row, scouts were beginning to take notice of the gangly young midfielder. Wherever he played, people could see he had real talent and word got around. By a stroke of good fortune, one of the teachers at the Marista also worked with youth teams at Botafogo and in 1970 he convinced Sócrates to try out with the club.

Botafogo was a typical small town team, where everyone knew each other and many of the players had fathers or uncles or big brothers who had played for or helped run the club. Founded in 1918, when the members of three teams in the Vila Tibério district of the city decided to pool their resources and form one superclub, the name was an amalgam of the words *bota* and *fogo*, which when put together literally mean 'to set fire'. The phrase, though, was also used more colloquially to mean to get things going, or, more earthily, to put a rocket up someone's backside. Some said the club's name was a tribute to the better-known Botafogo of Rio de Janeiro, but a more romantic legend had it that the players and officials who were organising the fusion took so long to decide what to call themselves that one man shouted: 'Let's come to a decision because if we don't then I am going to set fire to this place.'

Sócrates had already gone with a couple of pals to try out at Comercial, but Ribeirão's second club had left them standing around on the sidelines and they were none too happy at being ignored. So Sócrates, who preferred Botafogo anyway, was delighted when an opportunity arose on the other side of the city.[17]

He impressed in the trials and Botafogo officials were keen to sign him for their junior side, but the 16-year-old was already showing the streak of stubborn self-confidence that would make him famous. Football was fun but his dream was to become a doctor and his father had enrolled him in night classes to help him prepare for the university entrance exams. The courses took place at night, the same time the juniors trained, so Sócrates accepted Botafogo's invitation with one caveat: they could count on him to play in matches at the weekend, but his presence at the twice-weekly training sessions was not so certain.

The arrangement was perfect for Sócrates, for he loved to study and hated to train. He thought running laps of the pitch or doing star jumps was a waste of time and he couldn't be bothered with it. All he cared about was having the ball at his feet. He was also reluctant to spend too much time on what he insisted was only a hobby. Although he never knew why, Sócrates was determined to be a doctor and throughout his teens he acted as if football were a mere distraction from his primary goal of getting into university. Brazil was still poor and divided and football wasn't a serious profession for middle-class boys.

Sócrates dedicated himself to making that dream come true and, if he ever had doubts about what path to follow, his father never let him forget where his priorities lay.

The first sign that football was more important than he let on came when he was around 16 or 17 and about to finish high school. Mock exams for his prep course were scheduled for a Sunday morning, the same day that Botafogo were due to face Comercial in the final of a local youth tournament. Sócrates told his father about the clash and Seu Raimundo spent the whole week pestering his son about whether he preferred to take the exam or play in the final. Sócrates didn't want to let his father down and he assured him he would take the test and pass with flying colours.

Seu Raimundo dropped his son off at the exam hall early on Sunday morning, but Sócrates knew he'd made a big mistake. He walked into the classroom, took one look at the row of desks and decided this was not where he wanted to be. He turned around, rushed out the school gate and jogged across the city to the Estádio Santa Cruz. He was exhausted by the time he got there and worried sick about deceiving his dad, but he put those concerns aside and turned in a superb performance to delight the Botafogo fans who had turned up to see the youngsters.

When his father got home that night he asked his son how the mock exam had gone.

'It was cool, Dad, no bother,' Sócrates lied. 'I'm going to pass, you can relax.'

Sócrates didn't realise but some of the Botafogo fans who watched the juniors game also went to see the seniors that afternoon, and they were singing his praises. Seu Raimundo quickly discovered the deceit and went mad, more because of the lies than anything else, and there was hell to pay in the Vieira household when he got home. It was one of the very few times he ever hit his son, but Sócrates could at least claim that his disobedience was worthwhile, football-wise at least. He scored both Botafogo's goals in the 2-0 victory.

Such performances helped Botafogo Juniors win the City of Ribeirão Preto title three years in a row from 1970 to 1972. The club finished third in the state-wide competition, an impressive showing from a provincial squad that was up against big city teams like Corinthians and Palmeiras, and everyone could see that the lanky midfielder had the potential to step up to the professional ranks.

The first team pros at Botafogo knew a player when they saw one and they tried to convince Sócrates to join them. However, getting the young man to sign a deal was hard. Although attracted by the money, Sócrates didn't want the responsibility a pay packet implied; nor did he want to take up football full time and abandon his dream of becoming a physician. The club tried to pressure him into doing gym work to put some muscle on his skinny frame, but the plan backfired when he decided he'd rather not play football at all than have his visits to the ground ruined by barbells and weight machines.

He was lured back a few months later when the directors realised their mistake, and in 1973 he signed a preliminary deal that would tie him to the club and yet still allow him certain freedoms both inside and outside the dressing room. The agreement gave him his first salary and, while it wasn't much, it was more than the pocket money he got from his father. It was a welcome source of cash for a teenager whose interests were expanding to include music, girls and beer.[17]

Sócrates would later become famous as one of the sporting world's true rebels, a man who questioned not just authority figures inside and outside the game but also the rules that had long governed issues such as sleep, nutrition and training. He got his rebelliousness from his father, or rather he acquired it in battles with him. Both Guiomar and Raimundo were easy-going people who liked a quiet life, but by the time he reached his teens Sócrates had learned how to rub them the wrong way. He thrived on conflict, fighting constantly with his brothers, particularly Sóstenes one year his junior, and arguing with his father on a regular basis.

In a seminal work entitled *Roots of Brazil*, Brazilian sociologist Sérgio Buarque de Holanda famously described the Brazilian as 'the cordial man'. His version of cordiality, however, was not exactly that of good manners and civility, but was derived instead from the Latin *cor*, or heart. The cordial man was one led by emotion. Sócrates fitted the description perfectly. He spoke his mind and didn't really care what people thought. He loved being contradictory, if not outright confrontational, and the fearless pleasure he got from it was ideal training for taking on military generals, club presidents and millions of screaming fans.

His first major rebellion happened around the age of 16, when he was preparing for the famously competitive university entrance exams. The night classes his father had signed him up for took place a couple of evenings a week, from 9 till 11, but after two months of lessons Sócrates quietly dropped out. It was partly a reaction to his father's overbearing insistence and partly teenage insurrection. Sócrates left the house with his books in his bag but instead of sitting down to work he dedicated himself, as he euphemistically recalled, 'to discovering the world'. He went to the cinema, sat in bars and read books, and, most of all, partied with his friends. He pretended to be studying and his father, who had a full-time job and five other sons to keep his eye on, only found out he was bunking off after Sócrates flunked the exams he had supposedly been preparing for.[19]

Seu Raimundo read him the riot act and stressed just how important it was for him to get into university. Sócrates was savvy enough to realise that if he really wanted to be a doctor he had to study, and he soon buckled down. A year later, shortly before he turned 18, he sat the entrance exams for four universities and was accepted into them all with top marks. Thousands of people from all over Brazil took the exams, and Sócrates finished first on the list for the University of São Paulo in Ribeirão Preto (USP-RP) and near the top in the other three. He could have gone anywhere, but he loved his adopted home city and chose the USP-RP in order to stay close to his family and friends.

His adult life was about to begin and with it came new dilemmas, new responsibilities and new passions. Two of the things that would bring him most pleasure in the years to come were staking an increasing claim on his affections. But as he enrolled at university and joined the first team at Botafogo, beer and women were still secondary concerns. As the 1970s began, what really kept hm awake at night was the battle for his future. It was a debate that would bother him for the best part of a decade. It was football vs. medicine.

2

'Football gives you a contact with reality that other professions don't. Football is so democratic. I was always around people with different social situations from my own, with different levels of education. So you see reality up close.'

Sócrates

Sócrates made his first-team debut on 2 July 1972, when he replaced centre forward Hércules in a friendly against Nacional Futebol Clube away at Uberaba. The match ended 0-0 and was so unremarkable that even Sócrates didn't really remember it as his debut. When he was asked about his start at Botafogo, he recalled another match almost two years later, at home to América on 6 February 1974. By then Sócrates had already made 12 appearances for the club, mostly as a substitute and often in friendlies, and he was once again on the bench for a match they had to win to advance to the next stage of the São Paulo state championship. When midfield schemer Maritaca fell and dislocated his shoulder in the first half, Sócrates went on in his place and showed he was ready for the big leagues. His confident performance helped Botafogo to a 1-0 win. Fans raved at how he had taken control of the game and steered the team towards victory, and Sócrates remembered it as the match that changed his life.[1]

'I played fucking brilliantly,' he modestly recalled years later. 'I was so relaxed, I didn't think I was going to play but it all went right. And that was the moment I knew I wouldn't be out of the team again.'[2]

He was right, and it was the start of a dream season for the 20-year-old. Even when Maritaca regained full fitness a couple of months later, he couldn't dislodge Sócrates from the team that finished seventh in the Paulista first division. He made 49 appearances, scored 12 goals and walked away with the league's Young Player of the Year Award.

Sócrates played anywhere in midfield or up front, sometimes appearing on the left wing or even as a defensive midfielder. His main role was to lay on chances for the front players, and those early days of 1974 were memorable mostly for the killer partnership he formed with Geraldão, Botafogo's bustling target man. With Maritaca still in the team, Sócrates did not play the first eight games of the 1974 season and Geraldão never scored once. But with Sócrates as provider, Geraldão hit a rich vein of form, scoring 38 goals and winning the Golden Boot as the league's top goalscorer.[3]

Geraldão left for Corinthians in 1975 but was never quite as prolific, prompting some fans to joke that the club had signed the arrow but forgotten to bring the bow. His departure, however, allowed Sócrates to take on a more attacking role, although his exact position was never entirely clear. He wore the number 8 shirt in a 4-4-2 formation and was mostly employed as what Brazilians called a *ponta-de-lança*, a position between midfield and attack, usually on the right side of the pitch. Sometimes he would play *meia-armador*, slightly deeper, and he also did occasional stints as an out-and-out centre forward.

No matter where he played he wanted the ball at his feet, and it was when he had time and space that he did most damage. Everyone could see he was different and it wasn't just because of his peculiar, elongated body, with telescopic arms and curiously long legs that seemed even longer in the tight white shorts pulled up to his waist. Sócrates had an aura about him, an otherworldliness that people could discern but not define.

'What really caught my attention was not just the technique, the skill, the intelligence, the positioning, the versatility,' said Alberto Helena Jnr, a columnist with São Paulo's *Jornal da Tarde* newspaper who was one of the first people outside Ribeirão Preto to write about him. 'He gave me the clear sensation that he was operating on a different frequency from everyone else. He did the unexpected. He wasn't a player who had an extraordinary ability; he didn't have a great shot or a brilliant dribble. But he had this thing; he was on a different wavelength. He had his own way of doing things, different from everyone else, even different from the big *craques* [footballing superstars who have reached the very top of the game]. And that got me writing about him.'[4]

If Brazilian babies could recall what happened in the minutes after they left the womb, some of them would remember football teams before parents or midwives. Football is so important that fathers – sometimes even with the blessing of mothers – hang club flags in the delivery room so it is the first thing their newborn sees on arrival in the strange new world. They hear their first rendition of the club song just seconds after taking their first breath, as relatives sing the hymn to past glories as if it were a lullaby.

Most Brazilian footballers, if not most Brazilians, grew up kicking a ball and knew from an early age what they wanted to do in life. They lived and breathed the game and never thought of doing anything else, much less prepared for a future in which football was not the be-all and end-all.

Sócrates loved playing football but his passion was medicine. Brazil had won three of the previous four World Cups – more than any other country in the sport's history – and Brazilians had come to think of themselves as the true exponents of the game. Britain was football's home, but it was Brazilians who played it as it was meant to be played and football had firmly lodged itself in the national consciousness. However, it was still a game played by the lower classes and Sócrates' father was so insistent that his kids get a university education that his first-born son, even though he was now a regular at Botafogo, never considered football much more than a pastime, something to do when he didn't have his head in his books.

He enrolled at the USP-RP in February 1972 and his studies continued to take precedence over training. Even after renewing his contract at the start of 1974, he made it clear that football was still behind gynaecology, orthopaedics and neuroscience on his list of things to do. He told the club he would try to fit training sessions around his university schedule but do everything possible to be there for games. In truth, though, he made very little effort to attend the training sessions unless they were bounce games of attack against defence or first team vs. reserves. Sócrates hated any training that didn't involve an actual game of football.

The club were not overjoyed at the arrangement but they knew it was his way or no way and they didn't want to lose their star player. His professors, most of them football fans and some of them regulars at Botafogo, would occasionally help out by rearranging lectures or scheduling tests to fit around the

Botafogo fixture list. They knew the pressure he was under and they went easy on him. Friends and fellow students also played up to the star footballer, passing him their notes if he missed a class and helping him study.

During his first few years at university, lectures took place in the faculty wing of the Hospital das Clínicas, Ribeirão Preto's biggest public hospital. There were four lectures each day, two in the morning from 8 a.m. to noon, and then another two in the afternoon between 2 and 6 p.m. Sócrates sat at the back of the class, where it was easier to keep his head down and not get noticed, and he took notes in a scribble worthy of the most illegible doctor's prescription.

'There were some teachers who would pick on students, who'd push them to the limit, who'd swear at them, but that never happened with Sócrates,' recalled student friend Dr Said Miguel. 'The demands made on him were slightly different from those made on the other students.

'Sócrates was fantastically intelligent. He had the memory of an elephant, and he almost never studied. He managed to pass the course because he went to *repúblicas* [student flats]. There were a few of them, including mine, and he went there on the eve of the exams and listened to us studying, talking out loud, and he took it all in. The lecturers obviously loved him and they gave him a little bit of help and he passed, just managing to scrape through. He passed with scores of five or six, but he passed. And he finished the course, without failing any of the subjects.'[5]

Over at Botafogo, the week was split in two by games that were usually played on a Sunday afternoon and a Wednesday night. The players got the Monday off after a match, Tuesday morning was fitness training and Tuesday afternoon was a practice match. On the Tuesday nights before a match the players would stay at the *concentração*, where they would be kept in isolation before games. Thursday they had the day off, Friday and Saturdays were a repeat of Tuesday's schedule and on Saturday night they would be back at the *concentração*, in Botafogo's case a ranch fitted out as the team hotel, to rest before the next day's fixture.

Sócrates almost always missed the morning sessions due to lectures and he usually missed the afternoon sessions too. Sometimes he would come in at night for some solo work, but he rarely saw his team-mates except on match days and at the *concentração*, where he studied or played cards. When he did come in at night, he'd often run a lap in the darkness just so he could tell the manager he'd done something.

The other players soon got used to his unusual schedule and there was remarkably little grumbling about his privileged treatment. When they saw what he could do on the pitch – and picked up win bonuses thanks to his brilliance – any thoughts they had about demanding he do the same as them quickly disappeared.

'We knew he got special treatment but what mattered to us was what he did on the field,' said centre half Ney. 'There was a reason he got these privileges – he was the best player and he won games. Two or three players said something to manager Jorge Vieira and he told them Sócrates wins games. Better not training and winning games than training and not doing it on the pitch. Or he'd say, "You go study as well and you'll get the same advantages."'[6]

Sócrates' weight and lack of muscle mass were always an issue, which was exacerbated by his curious disregard for food. He liked a drink but he turned his nose up at proper meals, and he tipped the scales at around 81 kilos, positively skeletal for some-one who stood six-foot-four. At home or in bars, he would nibble at snacks or grab bite-size pieces from other people's plates. Friends' wives and mothers would cook meals and he'd pick at the plate, drinking the house dry but never eating the whole dish. His mother noticed he would throw back glass after glass of fruit juice but rarely eat the actual fruit, because, the family joked, he couldn't be bothered with the strenuous work of peeling and chewing.[7]

He was always thin – his father ironically called him 'Fatty' but all his friends knew him as Magrão (or Big Skinny) – but his reluctance to bulk up made him even more vulnerable to defenders and exhaustion. He lost so much weight during games that he would limp back to the dressing room seriously dehydrated. Even allowing for his reduced training regime, the day after a game was usually spent on the massage table, the physios trying to rub some life back into his puny and aching muscles. When he had his tonsils out and spent a week unable to eat much solid food, his weight fell to 68 kilos and he nearly collapsed in the games afterwards, such was his lack of resistance.

Sócrates estimated that his fitness levels were 30 to 40 per cent lower than other players and his team-mates knew they had to compensate for his lack of stamina, especially as the game wore on. He won a reputation as a first-half player, and he would frequently ask team-mates to cover back for him when he tired. But even though he flagged noticeably in the second half, he was rarely substituted because he could still decide the game with one of his perfectly weighted passes.

The club tried to get him into shape but he heroically resisted any form of weight training or physical slog. Even when the proposed measures didn't involve physical hardship, Sócrates would find a way to refuse, partly because he hated being told what to do and partly because the alternatives were always more attractive.

'Back then we'd inject players with Frutoplex, an intravenous vitamin supplement, so they could gain weight,' recalled the club's veteran masseur and trainer, João Sebinho. 'One week we didn't have a game. I lived near the stadium and he was supposed to drive over in his Opala every day at three, half three in the afternoon. He used to call my house when he was on his way, we never had cell phones back then, and I'd go downstairs and meet him. This one day I was slow in going downstairs and he kept beeping his horn. I said to my wife, "That's Sócrates arrived, he's not going to want to take his injection today." I went down and opened the door and he said, "No Frutoplex today." He had two bags filled with beer, salami, ham and mozzarella cheese. The two of us just sat there on the front steps until six o'clock, hanging out and drinking beer.'[8]

'In our passes, dribbles and flourishes with the ball there is something of dance and *capoeira* that rounds out and at times sweetens the game invented by the English. Our football, with its creativity and joy, is an expression of our social formation, our rebellion at excessive internal and external order, against excess of uniformity, of geometrisation, standardisation, and the totalitarianisms that do for individual variety or personal spontaneity.'[9]

Sócrates wrote those words in 2010, almost four decades after he first wowed Brazil with a move that summed up the country's love of individual variety and personal spontaneity. The back-heel made Sócrates famous and he developed it during the transition from indoor to outdoor football. Like many Brazilian youngsters, Sócrates honed his skills playing *futebol de salão*, a popular game played on cement or wood surfaces with a smaller and heavier ball. *Futebol de salão,* or *futsal* as it was better known, was more suitable for kids, especially in Ribeirão Preto, where it was played on a small indoor court out of the blinding glare of the sun.

The young Sócrates stood out thanks to his dribbling and

close control, but it didn't take him long to realise those skills were of limited use on a full-sized pitch against full-sized defenders. On grass, he had neither the speed nor the stamina to dribble very far. Defenders, even after he'd beat them, had the space in which to chase back and challenge him a second or even third time. Sócrates quickly ditched the close control for a one-touch game that made the ball do all the running.

Another reason was his small feet and lack of muscle mass. His size 8½ feet meant he had a small base on which to manoeuvre his long body and he found it hard to turn quickly. He learned that laying the ball off with one quick flick kept the move going and stopped him from getting clattered.

'When I arrived at the first team in Botafogo I was the antithesis of an athlete,' he said. 'The reality of my physical condition was very different from my rivals. I started playing against kids, then I moved on to play adults who were bigger and better prepared physically. My survival depended on me developing an alternative strategy, different from the ones that people were used to. I started to play one-touch football; as soon as I got it I laid it off because I couldn't stand the physical contact, I didn't have the muscle structure for that, I was very tall and thin.

'Whatever I could use with just one touch I would use – whether it was my backside, my knee, my elbow and my back-heel, which ended up being my signature move. It was pure sensibility, survival.

'That was my solution. I started to work on it. The sensation I had was that I couldn't fail with any pass because I had a physical inability to withstand contact.'[10]

He used the back-heel as often as he could, although calling it that was to diminish its complexity. It was more than just a straightforward striking of the ball with the back of the foot. Like no one before or since, Sócrates used every part of his foot to pass the ball. He used the back of his foot for volleys, to flick the ball sideways and to make defence-splitting 20-yard passes, and he would often put his foot on top of the ball and roll it to team-mates behind or in front of him.

The back-heel became his trademark and singled him out as one of the most original and exciting players of the era. Fans would roar with delight at what looked like showboating, but his flicks were rarely gratuitous. He was a pragmatic player who performed back-heels for a purpose, not for attention. Zico said it gave him a dimension that rivals didn't have and defenders didn't know how to defend. Pelé quipped he played better with his back to goal than most players did facing forward.

'We'd never really seen anyone play like that before and it used to befuddle defenders who were preparing to go one way and the ball was behind them before they knew it,' said Geraldão. 'Defenders didn't really know what to make of him.'[11]

Other colleagues said his unpredictability improved their game because they had to think more about the options available when they had possession.

'When he got the ball we didn't know what was going to happen,' said Walter Casagrande, a centre forward who became a close friend when they played together at Corinthians. 'If you just stood there and didn't accompany his thought process even a little bit you'd get lost and you'd end up looking like a fool because you'd be running the wrong way the whole time. In that sense it's easier to play with an ordinary player because you know exactly what to expect from them. In my head, I needed to be thinking of what might happen thanks to Sócrates' genius. I wasn't the genius or the player he was but I complemented him on the field and was an intelligent player. I went into space and when a team-mate had the ball I had already imagined three or four possibilities of what he could do with it.'[12]

*

Long after he had retired from football and was flitting from job to job and wife to wife, a friend once asked Sócrates what he wanted from life.

'I want to find happiness,' he said.

'What about other people's happiness?' his friend asked.

'I don't care about other people's happiness,' Sócrates replied. 'It's my duty to go after my own.'

Sócrates was just 16 when he first found happiness with Regina Cecilio, a student in the year below him at school and almost literally the girl next door. Regina's parents' house on Avenida Presidente Vargas backed on to Sócrates' home on the other side of the block and when he fell for the petite brunette he made no attempt to hide it. While most teenagers greeted love with an embarrassed awkwardness, Sócrates welcomed it with open arms. Even after he had left high school and was studying at night, every morning at seven he would be up and showered and waiting by Regina's door to walk her to school.[13]

Sócrates' younger brother Sóstenes first introduced the pair at a carnival dance in early 1970. They got on well and Sócrates made a lasting impression on the young girl by jumping up on stage, grabbing the microphone from the singer and belting out a song in one of the worst singing voices she had ever heard. Nothing came of that first meeting but, when they bumped into each other a few months later, Sócrates asked her out and a proper date confirmed their connection.

The couple were an item all through the early years of the 1970s and their relationship was formalised thanks to a night of rhythmic gymnastics in Sócrates' second-hand Volkswagen Beetle. It was hard enough getting his six-foot-four frame in the car to drive it, never mind have sex, but they managed and when Regina fell pregnant in September 1974 wedding bells soon followed. Three days after Christmas, Sócrates accompanied his bride down the aisle, resplendent in a tuxedo and bow tie, with a champions sash added for the photo session afterwards. Until then marriage had never been seriously discussed, but leaving his girlfriend to bring up their child on her own was not an option and the happy couple beamed as they started out on their new and unplanned life together.

They were both students and struggled to make ends meet on Sócrates' minimum wage at Botafogo, but they were helped along by their families, and particularly Regina's father, who had a good job as a bank manager. Fausi Cecilio knew half the city's finances and he used his insider knowledge to snap up properties when the owners required a quick sale. He lent one of those homes to Regina and Sócrates and they settled in together shortly before baby Rodrigo's arrival in June 1975.

Regina was in many ways the total opposite of her new husband. A mathematics student who grew up the only child in a well-to-do family, she was placid and traditional. While Sócrates spent every waking hour out and about, Regina was more content at home, living the quiet life with her family. She happily embraced her role as mother and wife and doted on the man she called 'Crateis'.

They might not have married had Regina not fallen pregnant, but their early life together was blissfully happy. They gave each other support and space and Regina was a lot like Sócrates' mother, quiet but determined, and content to fulfil a traditional role at home.

If the females in Sócrates' life were quiet, the males were less so. Sócrates' father was strong-willed and reserved, but he was one of those people who changed into hyperactive maniacs when the football kicked off. Seu Raimundo wasn't Botafogo's best-known fan but he was definitely one of those supporters who were euphemistically known as 'characters'. His screams of encouragement and abuse – much of it directed at his son – kept the people around him entertained as much as the game did. Sometimes more.[14]

In 1968, Botafogo moved from their original ground at Vila Tibério to a new stadium called the Estádio Santa Cruz. The stadium was built into a hillside on the south side of town and had open terraces on three sides, part of them newly laid concrete painted in the club colours of red, white and black, and part of them still just mounds of packed earth. Along the bottom edge of the hill sat an enormous grandstand with a roof that was more about keeping the sun off the season ticket holders than protecting them from the daily downpours of the rainy season. The big metal roof cast a shadow that crept slowly across the field each afternoon and Sócrates would gravitate to the shade like metal to a magnet. He never exerted himself if he could avoid it, and as the game went on he would spend more and more time in the refreshing confines near the touchline. Up in the stands, Sócrates' father watched with increasing fury.

'Get out the shade, number eight!' he shouted. 'Fatty! Get out the shade!'

Seu Raimundo watched his son play whenever he could and the old man would scream and gesticulate with as much energy and passion as the coach down below him. Seu Raimundo was a harsh critic and Sócrates didn't get any special treatment just because they were related. One Sunday, he gave his son so much abuse that a small posse of fans threatened to give him a beating. Sócrates was Botafogo's star player and the hard-core supporters didn't want him abandoning the club because of one over-enthusiastic boo-boy. They started towards him with menacing intent and it was only thanks to the timely intervention of nearby friends that he avoided a battering. 'But Sócrates is my son,' he told them plaintively as an incident was narrowly averted.[15]

Sócrates' fame grew throughout 1974 and into his first full season of 1975, but he remained an outsider whose peculiar ways perplexed his older team-mates. He only appeared on match days and sat quietly in the corner of the dressing room – sometimes with books or study notes – mostly keeping himself to himself. He looked weird; his face was scarred with pock marks from teenage acne, and he had an unruly mane of thick black hair. He sounded different, too, with university offering him a much wider vocabulary than most, and when he did get up the courage to speak he mumbled his words. He was contradictory, erudite and educated, but simple and down to earth, and his team-mates never really knew what to make of him.

Things were different on the field, however, and he seemed to grow in confidence the moment he left the dressing room. Sócrates' game improved slowly but surely as Botafogo established themselves in the Paulista first division and clubs from São Paulo and Rio de Janeiro were starting to sniff around. The *Folha de S.Paulo*, one of the country's biggest newspapers, wrote their first piece about him in October 1975 and Palmeiras made enquiries about signing him, only to be told that a move was out of the question until after he had graduated.

The attention was hardly a surprise to Sócrates, who had always stood out because of football. Whether he outplayed young lads like himself on the dirt pitches of Ribeirão Preto or labourers three times his age at sugar cane factories just outside the city, he knew people talked about him. At Botafogo Juniors and then as a professional, the attention increased as local newspapers and radio praised his performances and predicted a big future. The local media voted him Ribeirão Preto's footballer of the year in 1974, 1975, 1976 and 1977.

That spotlight presented both a problem and an opportunity for someone so shy. Sócrates had built up a well of self-assurance that came not just from football but also from school and university, where his performances won him constant praise. But while deep down he believed he deserved the acclaim, he was too modest and timid to show it. He didn't like talking about football because he knew that doing so would mean more responsibility and more demands. In a tactic he used throughout his life, he sought to downplay expectations to avoid the pressure of having to carry through and deliver.

The new attention, however, gave him more confidence and helped him face a world that was taking more and more of an interest in his life. But it wasn't the only thing that helped him come out of his shell. He had already found another infallible aid. At first he was reluctant to admit just how much he needed it, but as his confidence grew and his place at Botafogo became more established, he took a conscious decision to open up and acknowledge the truth: he loved a drink and he wasn't going to hide it any more.

3

'Our family are shy and introspective and Sócrates overcame that with beer. He was a different person when he drank. Drink to him was an anti-depressive and an anti-introspective. Beer was his medicine. It spiced up his life.'

Sócrates' brother Raimundo

Sócrates ambled into the Botafogo training ground just like any other day, his bag in his hand and his head in the clouds. There weren't many people in the building but director Hamilton Mortari immediately homed in on their star player. Mortari had been tipped off about Sócrates' escapades the night before, when a late session at a city bar had turned into an incident. As soon as he saw Sócrates he let rip.

'Hey, Sócrates, I want to talk to you,' Mortari shouted. 'In my office – now!'

Sócrates took one look at Mortari and responded with his characteristic composure.

'You don't have to talk to me in your office,' Sócrates said. 'I know what this is about and let me make one thing clear right now. I am a grown man. It's my life and I'll do what I want. I have made a commitment to Botafogo inside this stadium. What happens outside is my business. And you know why? Because if it was any other way, I'd quit.'[1]

Sócrates kept walking towards the changing room, leaving a dumbstruck director in his wake. He had made his position clear. He had no problems in taking direction when it came to football, but no one would tell him how to live his life.

Sócrates began drinking aged 13, and he drank for one main reason. Without alcohol in his system he was timid and reserved, a young man who would sit quietly on the edges of conversations, secretly longing to get involved. Alcohol oiled his voice box and when Sócrates had a drink in him, his chat – by turns witty, intelligent and sarcastic – was as memorable as his football.

It wasn't unusual for kids to drink at such a young age because in Ribeirão they downed beer like it was water. With summer temperatures topping 100 degrees in the shade and the mercury exceeding 80 even in winter, drinking was a guaranteed way to keep cool. The weak lagers were consumed straight from the freezer at sub-zero temperatures and Sócrates, like just about everyone else in the city, swore that drinking from morning till night was the one sure way to stay hydrated.

His home life was another significant factor. Seu Raimundo was well known in the city thanks to his senior position at the tax office, and migrants arriving from Pará and Ceará would stop by his house every weekend to pay homage. The old man was serious about many things, but he loved to socialise and like his number one son he loosened up when he'd had a drink. Weekends at the Vieira house were always busy and visitors to what jokingly became known as the Ceará Embassy never wanted for beer or company. The Vieira boys soon equated drinking with fun times and friendship.

The teenage Sócrates drank sheepishly at first but found camaraderie with his pals at Botafogo Juniors. Often they would drink until six or seven in the morning, run home to drink some milk and have a bit of breakfast, then take a shower and head out to play their game. He knew such behaviour was frowned upon in the professional ranks, but as he gained in confidence he didn't see why he should change. With an active social life at the university and regular nights out with his pals from the football, it wasn't long before he was famous for the huge amounts of beer he could put away.

Some of the more experienced players at the club were concerned his drinking might affect his game and they tried to talk to him. Maritaca gave him some fatherly advice but it went in one ear and out the other. The moralistic finger-wagging of people like Mortari was even less likely to have an effect.[2]

The footballing culture of the time also meant he felt free to indulge. Botafogo, like most other Brazilian clubs, had an environment in which players would drink after games and on their days off. The physical demands on players were much less than they are today and many of them could put away significant quantities of beer and *cachaça*, the potent sugar cane spirit that is Brazil's national drink.

Drinking was permitted as long as the players didn't go mad and embarrass the club. Many of them would go for a quick beer after training during the week, and the hardened drinkers would meet after the match on a Sunday or for an all-day barbecue and proper session on a Monday.

They were allowed to have a few beers on the coach coming back from away games if they'd got a result, but drinking was frowned upon if they lost. They would still do it if they managed to get hold of some beers before they left for home, hiding the 'ppssssshhh' of their cans opening by coughing loudly or pretending to sneeze.[3]

Sócrates and fellow medical student Zé Bernardes pushed their luck even further by buying beer on the way to the *concentração*, and in the 15 minutes it took them to drive there they'd put away as many cans as possible to get them through the boredom that was a night in an isolated hotel with nothing but television, cards and a ping-pong table to entertain them.

Sócrates never touched alcohol on the day of the game, but he hated being cooped up at weekends without a drink and he soon twigged that some of the older players in the squad had taken measures to ensure their Saturdays needn't be dry. The club's cook would prepare their evening meal and Sunday's breakfast before leaving at the end of the afternoon, and the hardened drinkers had convinced her to secretly prepare them some cocktails. Known as *batidinhas*, the drinks were made from *cachaça* or vodka, fruit juice concentrate and condensed milk, and they were usually drunk ice-cold. The cook made a big bottle or two ahead of time and then hid them at the back of the freezer under the plates of food.[4]

Sócrates would often turn up for training looking hungover, but he was still at an age where he could get away with it and his bohemian lifestyle – he smoked as well as drank – never affected his form. The directors and backroom staff were worried he would set a bad example to other players, but he was so decisive on the field and so single-minded off it that they ended up turning a blind eye. Over time, the club developed one rule for him and another for the rest of the squad.

That attitude was never clearer than the weekend manager Jorge Vieira asked João Sebinho to take a couple of players to represent the club at an important wedding. A local congressman was getting married and Sócrates went with Sebinho and defender Mario to the reception one Saturday night near the banks of the Pardo river.

They had only been there a few minutes when Sebinho turned around from his place at the bar, Coca-Cola in hand, to find Sócrates holding a bottle of whisky.

'Magrão, come on,' Sebinho said, in a vain attempt to appeal to his better nature.

'What's the problem, Sebinho?' Sócrates said.

'I'm supposed to keep an eye on you,' he replied, already fearing the worst. 'You're going to fuck me up.'

'Nooooo,' Sócrates told him. 'Just tell them what you saw.'

'Right then, go ahead and drink what you want,' a resigned Sebinho said.

The night wore on and Sócrates was having a great time, but the trainer wanted the players to get their rest. He eventually convinced them to leave shortly after 1 a.m. and when they got back to the *concentração* Vieira was sitting in the lobby waiting for them.

Sócrates arrived clearly the worse for wear and when he saw the manager he spread his arms out wide and sang out a happy welcome: 'Boooossssss!' he cried. 'Boooossssss!'

Vieira looked at Sebinho and asked, 'What happened?'

Sebinho shrugged his shoulders.

'I looked at him and said, "Seu Jorge, what is there to say?" And the next day Sócrates scored two goals and no one else ever mentioned it again.'[5]

Nobody was scoring very many goals for Botafogo at the start of 1976. They hit the net just eight times in their first 12 Paulista games – Sócrates getting three of them – before the tournament was halted in mid-May while Brazil played seven friendlies.

When it started up again a month later, Botafogo's first game was against Portuguesa Santista. Portuguesa were the second club in Santos but they were light years behind their better-known rivals and were on a poor run of form, having lost their last five games with a goal difference of minus 14. The match took place on a Sunday afternoon at the Estádio Santa Cruz and it turned out to be a landmark for Sócrates. He put Botafogo ahead after 17 minutes and added a second four minutes later, before providing the passes for João Marques and Zé Mário to score numbers three and four before half-time.

He came out for the second half totally inspired and, after Alfredo grabbed a fifth, Sócrates went on the rampage. He scored five more between the 63rd and 87th minutes to take the scoreline to 10-0. It was the biggest win in the Paulista all year and Sócrates' seven goals ranked behind only Pelé – who scored eight in an 11-0 win over Botafogo in 1964 – as the highest ever total in a Paulista state championship match.

Sócrates' ability to hit the target was not news to the coaches and fans in São Paulo, but the seven-goal spree helped spread his fame further afield. He got his first proper mention in the newspapers of Rio de Janeiro, while the big dailies in São Paulo gave their Ribeirão Preto correspondents space to write detailed profiles of the footballing doctor.

The performance also led to a new round of enquiries from more illustrious suitors. Corinthians, Palmeiras, Portuguesa, Santos and São Paulo had all been in touch to ask about his availability, and Internacional of Porto Alegre joined the hunt with an offer of 2.5 million cruzeiros (around $300,000). The clubs knew medicine remained his priority and some included special provisions in their deals. Santos offered to arrange for his transfer to a hospital in the port city, while Portuguesa said he could stay in Ribeirão Preto during the week and just come and go to São Paulo on match days.

Botafogo refused to even consider selling their star player and Sócrates never gave a moment's thought to leaving his home-town. He appreciated the attention but he was perfectly happy with the way things were. He was only 22, neither sophisticated nor worldly, and the thought of leaving the bosom of his family and his friends was not a prospect he relished. More importantly, he – and his father, whose influence over him remained powerful – still saw football as a pastime of secondary importance to medicine. Sócrates found it hard to imagine not becoming a doctor, much less gaining fulfilment from kicking a football about.

'Take a plane to São Paulo at the weekend and come back after games and go straight to the university? It's too much. I'd rather stay here, where I at least have time to have a beer after the game. Maybe after I graduate I'll think about earning some money and go to one of the big clubs in a state capital. But even then I don't know if it's worth it. Life here is calm and easy, there's no chaos. Ribeirão Preto is a city that is too good to leave without putting a lot of thought into it.

'Every day I go round to my house to see my parents, I always see my friends from the university and from school, and sometimes we get together at somebody's house. It would be very hard to leave that all behind to play at a big team. I am pretty content with what I have.'[6]

Such performances meant Sócrates was increasingly spoken of as a future Brazil player, but he was still treating professional football as a sideshow to the important business of university and medicine. Sócrates would rarely give football the respect it deserved, but even his newfound fame and the prospect of a real career as a sportsman did not force him to review his priorities.

A perfect example of his disregard for the professional game came one Wednesday night in 1976. It was a gloomy July evening at the Morumbi, a month and a day after he had hit the headlines with his seven goals against Portuguesa Santista. The match against São Paulo ended 1-1 and it was almost midnight when Zé Bernardes emerged from the dressing room to see a bunch of their university pals waiting for them by a VW camper van outside. The medical faculty had a team in the Intermed tournament, the competition held each year between the dozen or so universities of São Paulo state. Their pals had a game that night in Santos and they wanted Sócrates and Zé Bernardes to join them. 'Zé, we were supposed to play the Escola Paulista de Medicina in Santos earlier tonight but we've delayed the kick-off,' one of them said. 'We need to win to qualify for the next round. We need you and Sócrates to play. Will you come with us?'

Zé Bernardes had been on the bench and was desperate for a game, so sprinted back to find Sócrates.

'Magrão, the lads are out there and they want us to go down to Santos with them. Are you up for it?'

'Course I am,' said Sócrates. 'Let's go!'

'We better tell Tiri,' said Zé. 'The rest of the team are going back to Ribeirão tonight.'

Together they found coach Tiri and half-asked, half-told him they were going to Santos rather than heading home with the rest of the squad.

'No way,' said Tiri. 'We've a game on Sunday. I am going to need you both.'

'Fuck that,' said Sócrates, and he turned and ran to the car park gate. The van's engine was already running and Sócrates tossed his bag in the window and then jumped on board, Zé Bernardes piling in behind him.

They sped down the windy mountain road to Santos and an hour later the packed little arena went wild when Sócrates appeared courtside with a can of beer in his hand. The Intermed matches were held in municipal or university gymnasiums, and hundreds of students would turn up to boisterously cheer their friends. Everyone knew Sócrates and Zé Bernardes and they chanted Sócrates' name from the moment he walked in. The USP-RP won 4-0, sending the crowd into even greater raptures, and when the final whistle blew a bunch of them who had driven the five hours from Ribeirão Preto celebrated with an all-night session. They got a lift home as the sun came up over São Paulo, with Sócrates crashed out in the back seat and Zé Bernardes dozing in the front. When they arrived in Ribeirão, they took a shower, grabbed a bite to eat, and went straight to classes.

When Sócrates went to Botafogo to train later that day he was expecting to get a rocket, but he didn't really care. He firmly believed his football career would be over the day he graduated, and playing with his pals in front of their friends and classmates gave him much more pleasure than playing for a professional football club. To his surprise, the coach acted as though nothing had happened.

'Nobody said a word,' said Zé Bernardes. 'It was Sócrates.'[7]

April Fool's Day 1964 was no laughing matter. Overnight, motorised battalions of troops had moved on Rio to unseat left-wing president João Goulart and a feckless Congress soon capitulated, forcing Goulart into exile in Uruguay and marking the start of a nasty dictatorship that would last for 21 years and transform Brazil.

After a relatively bland beginning in which they sought to neuter their opponents rather than kill them, the military slowly but surely tightened their grip. They granted themselves decree powers and approved a draconian new constitution in 1966; and then two years later, shortly before Christmas 1968, they abandoned all pretence of legitimacy and closed Congress, started firing and retiring civil servants who didn't support their aims, and cracked down on defiant media. Most brutally of all, they began kidnapping, torturing and killing on a wider scale than ever before.[8]

The period between 1968 and 1974 was known as 'the lead

years' and it was a time that coincided with Sócrates' coming of age. Even though involvement in student politics was made illegal in 1969 and the country's main student union was banned two years later, the repressive campaign was no secret to those at the USP-RP. The university was not one of the focal points of opposition, but the small group of activists found ways to get their message across.[9]

Sócrates, however, could not have cared less. He knew some of the teachers and students who were arrested for speaking out against the tyranny, but their plight was not high on his list of priorities and he made a conscious decision to look the other way.

'We all knew about the repression, there was a lot of it,' said his doctor friend Said Miguel. 'There was a group of militants at the university. A lot of people from the medical faculty were arrested by the military for their activism. Several teachers and students were arrested because of it. But we couldn't do anything. The atmosphere was pretty heavy. There was a group that was more into politics but Sócrates tried to keep them at arm's length. He was all about enjoying life, playing football. Sócrates was totally and utterly uninterested in politics.'[10]

Just how uninterested became evident in July 1976 when he gave a long interview to the local *Diário da Manhã* newspaper, the first in which he spoke widely about non-footballing issues.

Sócrates was a voracious reader, but with his entire life revolving around university and football – and with a new wife and one-year-old baby at home – he clearly had little time to follow politics, let alone get to grips with what was happening in the world around him. He claimed to have read his more famous namesake and joked that he wanted to follow in his philosophical footsteps, but his opinions on matters outside the worlds of football, public health and the student faculty were those of an uninformed and largely indifferent young man who believed what the country's military rulers told him.

'I think censorship is necessary,' he told the wide-eyed reporters. 'There's been a transformation under way here since the 1964 revolution.

'If we can imagine that prior censorship didn't exist, or something like it, then things would get complicated for the government,' he said. 'Then it would be difficult to control the flow of facts and to protect the government's image in the eyes of the public. Personally, I find it very important for the government to retain a good image in the eyes of the public.'[11]

His use of the term 'revolution' was critical in understanding his worldview. Goulart's overthrow was in every way a military coup, but the junta tried to camouflage their actions by calling it a 'revolution' and Sócrates' acceptance of that fairy tale was a clear sign he had swallowed the generals' version of events.

There were several reasons for his deference. Schools at the time taught 'Moral and Civic Education' and 'Brazilian Social and Political Organisation', disciplines that were designed to indoctrinate young minds to nationalism and military rule. Children were taught to respect God and country above all else and were graded on how well they sang the national anthem. In addition to widespread censorship, the early 1970s marked the low point of the regime as decrees came into force that were intended to squelch any opposition once and for all.

Another key factor was the booming economy. The military invested heavily in infrastructure and Brazil grew exponentially as new factories opened, new roads were built and the middle class expanded. People who were once poor were now able to buy televisions, fridges and cars. Between 1968 and 1976 annual growth never dipped below 5 per cent and in some years went as high as 14 per cent.

His environment was also important. Ribeirão Preto was

conservative by nature, like most rural cities dominated by agriculture and surrounded by big landowners. It was growing quickly and was already home to more than a quarter of a million people, but it had only a handful of television channels, six radio stations and four newspapers, each of them censored to ensure favourable coverage of the regime. Sócrates paid little attention to any of them but, when he did, the message he received was filtered to present the military in the best possible light.[12]

The simplest explanation, though, was that he was still immature. When he wasn't playing football or studying, he was chasing skirt or drinking beer, or both. He was acutely aware of Brazil's shocking inequality and offended by it, but he was still conservative when it came to social issues. He opposed birth control, was 'totally against' politics mixing with sport, and dismissive of any notion that his privileged upbringing or higher education marked him out as a leader at Botafogo.

'I've never been one to support a party or to be a leader in anything,' he told his interviewers. 'I don't like to express my opinion to anyone except to my circle of friends I trust. I am quite a retiring kind of guy, so I look to keep my opinions to myself. I really don't pay much attention to politics; I like to read about the problems that appear but I don't like to debate politics. I am just not into it.'

When asked what would become of society if no one ever gave their opinions, he giggled: 'One thing is for sure, there might not be any progress but there also wouldn't be any war.'[13]

The only progress that concerned Sócrates in the middle of 1976 was in the Campeonato Paulista. Botafogo fell back to earth after thrashing Portuguesa Santista and it was only thanks to their superior goal difference that they qualified for the next stage of the tournament.

They began that second stage with a new coach as Jorge Vieira returned to the club after a spell with Coritiba. The son of a successful Carioca industrialist, who never made the grade as a professional, Vieira began coaching in his early twenties and won his first title at the age of 26 when he took América to the Campeonato Carioca in Rio de Janeiro. After leaving América, he spent the decade shuttling between Brazil and Portugal, invariably instilling his teams with the guile and belief that enabled them to punch above their weight. He took the unheralded Galicia to their first Bahian title in 25 years, helped Bahia and Coritiba to state trophies, and in 1974 he lifted América-MG to their highest ever league position in the Brazilian first division. He spent the second half of 1975 at Botafogo and was lured back a year later with the promise of a shot at the national title.

Sócrates knew he had lots to learn and that experienced coaches like Vieira were vital if he wanted to mature as a player. But Vieira's authoritarian approach was exactly the kind of attitude that made him question whether football was really worth it.

Vieira famously said that many players need to be treated like children and he got the squad together on his first day to remind them that his word was final. No one would be given special treatment, Vieira told them, as he sketched out his plans to build a squad that could compete in the Brasileiro. Sócrates, believing the message was aimed directly at him and his student privileges, deliberately turned around and started to walk away.

Vieira dragged him back and threw an arm around him. He was a disciplinarian but he wasn't daft. He knew he couldn't do without the team's best player and he was aware the fans would lynch him if he hounded out their star. He smoothed Sócrates' ruffled feathers and assured him his part-time arrangement would not be altered.

They were never close friends but Sócrates formed a great respect for Vieira's motivational skills, on more than one occasion declaring him 'the only coach who was capable of changing a game at half-time'. But he was not impressed when Vieira insisted on pushing him further forward into a more out-and-out striker role. Sócrates scored three times in the four games that followed the hammering of Portuguesa Santista, but he didn't adjust to Vieira's new tactics and went nine matches without finding the net. (His brother Sóstenes did better, scoring against Jardinópolis in what was the first game of a short-lived professional career.)

Sócrates missed a hatful of opportunities to break his drought in the 0–0 draw at home to América on 8 August and he was clearly struggling to play with his back to goal. His physique – those small feet again – made it difficult to turn quickly and, when he did manage to free himself from his marker, there always seemed to be another defender on hand to thwart him.

His drought meant that he went into the last match of the campaign needing to score to take the Golden Boot trophy and he succeeded in doing just that, sitting deeper and getting both Botafogo's goals in the 2–0 win over São Bento. The victory meant Botafogo finished the season in fourth place in the final Paulista table, a creditable return for a team in the making. The omens were good for the campaign to come, their first ever shot at a national title. That would be a test for a small provincial side and it wasn't a tournament they thought they could win. The Paulista, however, was a different matter. They were ready to make history.

That fourth-place finish was indicative of a broader change taking place in Brazilian football. Ever since Charles Miller brought the first football and rule book across the Atlantic in

1894, the big city clubs had dominated the game. That dominance started to wane in the 1970s and nowhere was the change more evident than in São Paulo, Brazil's richest and most populous state and where Miller made his home. A burgeoning agricultural sector and an influx of immigrants from other parts of Brazil boosted the provincial cities, and their clubs used the newfound power to invest in bigger stadiums and keep their best young players. Botafogo refused to sell Sócrates and winger Zé Mário; Ponte Preta held on to future internationalists Carlos, Juninho and Oscar; and classy centre back Amaral was still at Guarani.

They were also helped by new rules and new rule-makers. A 1969 law that abolished relegation allowed them to play without fear of going down and the election of São Bento's Alfredo Metidieri as head of the Paulista Football Federation – the first time a president of a smaller club had led the league – gave them greater influence.

The effects soon became clear. América of São José do Rio Preto finished fourth in the Campeonato Paulista in 1975, ahead of both Corinthians and Palmeiras. XV de Piracicaba were runners-up in 1976 and Ponte Preta, who were establishing themselves as a real force to be reckoned with, would finish second in 1977. Guarani, who reached the semi-final stage three times between 1976 and 1979, were strong enough to excel on the national stage, winning the Brazilian championship in 1978 – a feat no other provincial team has ever equalled.

Botafogo were desperate to join that new elite and the club's president, Atílio Benedini, backed by a group of rich directors dubbed 'the men of gold', spent big to make it happen. Six new players were signed before the 1976 Brasileiro started on 4 September and the new boys gelled quickly, losing just two of their first eight games – a run that included a 0-0 draw at Copa Libertadores champions Cruzeiro – to finish top of their group and progress into the next round. They were equally impressive in the second phase, losing only one game in five and holding a Fluminense side that featured Rivellino and Carlos Alberto Torres to a 1-1 draw in front of a record 44,292 crowd at the Estádio Santa Cruz.

The third stage was, according to Sócrates, like taking the university entrance exam after studying through two preparatory courses. But if that were the case then Botafogo failed to make the grade. They lost their first two games to Ponte Preta and eventual champions Internacional and, although they recovered slightly to record three wins in their final six matches, an exhausted Sócrates failed to score in any of them and the season petered out.

Nevertheless, finishing 13th out of 54 teams was a highly creditable result in their first ever national competition and was all the more impressive for Sócrates given his increasingly brutal workload at university. The fifth year was when students started seeing patients for the first time, and at the start of 1976 he began accompanying doctors on rounds and assisting with minor surgeries. That meant overnight shifts starting around 7 p.m. and continuing until 7 a.m. the next day.

His fellow students helped him juggle his schedule so that he was available for matches, and he would spend half his holidays filling in for the colleagues who had helped him out the previous term. But although he never missed a match, it was sometimes a close-run thing.

One of the most famous incidents occurred when Botafogo played Corinthians in São Paulo. It was an evening kick-off and Sócrates had classes until late in the afternoon, so a club car picked him up at the university and hurtled along the motorway to the state capital. The journey took more than four hours and he arrived at the Pacaembu stadium just minutes before the game was supposed to get under way.[14]

'Do you know where the dressing rooms are?' Sócrates asked the driver as the car edged its way through traffic towards the stadium's magnificent art–deco entrance.

'I've no idea,' he said.

'Shit, me neither,' said Sócrates. 'Just drop me out front and I'll get inside and work it out from there.'

Sócrates jumped out of the car and fought his way through the crowds towards the turnstiles. He bought a ticket for the game and, once inside, accosted the first official-looking person he could find.

'Where are the dressing rooms?' he asked.

'Away at the far end,' the man replied.

Sócrates stuck his bag under his arm and sprinted round the terracing as fast as he could. At the other end, a portly security guard was sitting on a chair minding the metal gate.

'Can you let me through?' he said between gasps. 'I'm playing for Botafogo.'

The man looked at the youngster in front of him. He was thin, out of breath from running around the ground and his hair was sticking out in every direction. He was dressed in a white coat and he carried a medical bag in his hand. He looked like he had just escaped from a mental asylum. The guard laughed in his face.

Sócrates appealed and cajoled and begged and eventually convinced him to send a message to the Botafogo dressing room. A few moments later Tiri appeared and Sócrates was hustled through the gate. The Botafogo players were already waiting in the tunnel and he threw on his strip as fast as he could and ran out on to the pitch with just seconds to spare.[15]

That example was extreme but similar situations were not unusual. The club did everything possible to facilitate his movements, including providing a car and driver. Their support was particularly important over his last two years at the club, when rural internships, exams and long shifts at hospital meant he could not always travel with the rest of the squad. His star value had risen so much that small clubs across Brazil would pay Botafogo to come and play friendlies on the condition that Sócrates appeared. If he wasn't on the pitch for kick-off the fee was halved and so the club moved heaven and earth to get him there on time. Benedini suspected that Sócrates would sometimes abuse that privilege to catch up on sleep, but he turned a blind eye because the club wanted him rested and needed him playing.

'When he didn't appear we sent a car to look for him at his house and we got him there on a plane,' said Benedini. 'I had a small plane, just a one-engine prop. It would be him and the pilot and sometimes I'd go with them. Sometimes we would hire a plane. One of the directors had a plane and we used that, and sometimes we even asked big Botafogo fans who had planes if we could borrow theirs. They weren't long trips, maybe an hour to Uberaba, Campinas. It happened quite a lot. We had to get him there because if we didn't, we wouldn't get paid the same. But it paid off. He had so much more quality.'[16]

As if that wasn't convoluted enough, 1977 was his final year at university and his life got even more complicated due to the obligatory rural internships that took him far from Ribeirão Preto. Small towns and cities all over Brazil lacked doctors and so final-year medical students were sent in pairs to run health clinics in the countryside. The clinics were basic, with little more than a trolley, a half-stocked medicine cabinet and elementary equipment for measuring heartbeat and blood pressure.

In March, Sócrates spent a fortnight in São Joaquim da Barra, around 45 miles north of Ribeirão Preto, and then in October he went to Cássia dos Coqueiros, 50 miles east of the city. He was accompanied during that second spell by Said Miguel and the pair lived in the clinic's annexe where a cook provided them with food and basic necessities. Sócrates' arrival as the local doctor was the biggest thing ever to happen to the town, and Miguel suspected that patients would turn up with imaginary ailments just to meet the football player and get his autograph on a prescription.

Sócrates revelled in the role, taking part in local events and making friends with a couple of country singers, whom he would visit several nights a week to strum his guitar and sing with. He enjoyed being in such close contact with poor Brazilians and even turned out for the Cássia dos Coqueiros' five-a-side team in their annual grudge match with local rivals Cajuru.[17]

But the distance made training almost impossible and, although Miguel would cover for him on match days, the comings and goings were tiring, particularly in the second half of the year. He also had the stress of final exams, as well as a wife and family to look after, and the massive workload had an effect on his performance as the season wore on. He was exhausted and everyone could see it.

Before that, however, came the halcyon days of early 1977. Sócrates and Vieira had overcome their initial differences, with the manager understanding just how important he was to the team and learning that when it came to Sócrates the carrot was more effective than the stick. Vieira nagged at him to stop smoking and when those pleas fell on deaf ears he bought him off with toffee, correctly believing that he'd smoke less if he had his mouth full.

Sócrates shared top billing with the mercurial young winger Zé Mário and Vieira was savvy enough to back them up with a host of experienced signings who had something to prove. Among those brought in during the second half of 1976 were Raimundo Aguillera, a Paraguayan keeper who'd been sidelined with dodgy knees; Lorico, a 37-year-old midfielder who had played with Pelé on the Brazilian army team; and Arlindo, an old-fashioned centre forward with a nose for goal. They had by now settled in and were ready for a real shot at the Paulista title.

They played a versatile formation that morphed between 4-4-2 and 4-3-3 depending on whether Sócrates played in midfield or as a more orthodox striker. They conceded very few goals and their pace on the flanks, combined with Sócrates' goals and inch-perfect deliveries from midfield, meant they were lethal on the counterattack.

Vieira was confident his side could go far and they began the season at a whirlwind pace, winning five of their first seven games and drawing the other two. Those first six months of the year were among the most memorable of Sócrates' career. He turned on the style at Santos in March, scoring two goals in Botafogo's victory over the home side after coming from behind. His performance in a rare televised match, including a goal in which he ran from the centre circle and then scored with the sole of his boot, was brilliant enough for Pelé to talk him up afterwards. A few games later, one fan hung a banner at the Morumbi declaring: 'Sócrates is the new Pelé'.[18]

His goals helped Botafogo to the top of the table at the half-way stage and straight into the play-off to decide the winner of the City of São Paulo Cup, the trophy given to the best team during the *Primeiro Turno*, or the first half of the season. Botafogo boasted the second best attack and the best defence, and a 0-0 draw with Guarani took them into a final showdown with São Paulo.

It was the biggest game in the club's history and, even though the final took place at São Paulo's home ground, Botafogo were unawed. A crowd of more than 56,000 – including 15,000 from Ribeirão Preto – saw them start nervously, but they soon composed themselves and got the better of their opponents. Sócrates had the ball in the net after winning a challenge in midfield and then slotting it home from just outside the box, but the referee adjudged him to have gone in with a foot up and pulled play back. It was 0–0 after 90 minutes and there was little action of note until the dying seconds of extra time, when Waldir Peres just managed to stop a shot from Motoca squirming over the line.

The final whistle went seconds later and an exhausted Sócrates lifted both hands in the air and skipped towards the centre circle. It wasn't a victory but it was still a triumph. Botafogo were champions of the *Primeiro Turno*, the first team from the provinces ever to take the title in its 75-year history.

'A manager who wins titles with big teams, who are used to getting to finals, is just doing his job,' an overjoyed Sócrates said afterwards. 'At Botafogo, a small club from the provinces, it's different. I can tell you right now that this is one of the happiest days of my professional life.'

The terms *técnica* and *tradição* are key words in Brazilian football dictionaries and they set players and nations apart. A player with *técnica* is a player with great technique or skill, someone who has worked to develop his talent into something more comprehensive and potent. Teams with *tradição*, meanwhile, are those with a track record that Brazil respects. Italy, Argentina and Germany all have *tradição*; Scotland, Colombia and Sweden don't.

Long after he had hung up his boots, Sócrates was asked at what point in his career he thought he played his best football. The answer, he said to some surprise, was at Botafogo. At Botafogo, *técnica* was all he had to go on. He was skinny, weak and not always as committed as he should have been. But he could still control a game of football using skill alone, and that was enough to put both him and Botafogo on the map.

'I was at a small team, I didn't train,' he said. 'Skill was all I had. I had to play well. Obviously, I wasn't the most consistent of players but, fuck, I had to be technically brilliant, I had to work miracles. It was there that I learned to play.'[19]

Sócrates had frequently voiced his desire to play for Brazil, and he hoped that the men who ran the CBD would recognise that brilliance and give him a chance to wear the famous yellow jersey. The problem was that few people outside Ribeirão Preto, and almost no one outside São Paulo, saw him perform those heroics on a regular basis. Away from his home city he was still seen as either a freak or a flash-in-the-pan, or both. He had his fans, but there were still directors, coaches and even players who viewed him with suspicion. To those who didn't know him, his dedication to medicine, the unapologetic importance he gave to beer and cigarettes, and his reluctance to train, celebrate goals or repeat the same set phrases, looked not just like a lack of professionalism but a lack of interest.

That was particularly clear at international level. The national side was overseen by the military, and the officials and coaches in charge were used to hierarchy. Even reasonably sophisticated men like Claudio Coutinho and Carlos Alberto Parreira liked players who could follow orders, and they were afraid that Sócrates, who did things his own way, would set a dangerous example to others. He was a rebel and the men who ran football never took kindly to rebels.

The media were more open-minded, however, and many in the Paulista press were convinced he would be called up for Brazil's tour to the United States in May 1976. Coach Osvaldo Brandão ignored him on that occasion, and being chosen to play for a Paulista state selection against Brazil in January 1977 was for him scant compensation. But if he thought a decent performance in that match might open doors, he was sadly mistaken.

He was overlooked for four World Cup qualifiers in February and March, and passed over once again later that year when the national side played eight friendly games in preparation for the next round of qualifiers. When Zé Mário became the first Botafogo player ever to be called up to the national side for those games it was not a shock, but Sócrates' omission was surprising enough for one big paper to run the headline: 'Zé Mário Is Called Up, Sócrates Isn't'.[20]

Sócrates' outstanding performances in Botafogo's title triumph convinced many fans he was ready to go to Argentina, but his hopes of making a late breakthrough faded as his form dipped at the start of 1978. Coutinho had already hinted at his intentions the previous year, when he said Sócrates wasn't a true professional because he was still a student. Sócrates quite rightly pointed out that he had finished top goalscorer in the country's toughest state league, even while training part time and completing weekend and overnight shifts.

That argument, however, held little sway with the men who ran the game and, after CBD president Heleno Nunes saw Sócrates' attacking threat snuffed out in the 1-1 draw with Comercial on 23 April, he publicly declared him to be 'a star on the wane'. They left their options open by naming him on the 40-man long list for Argentina but it was no more than them hedging their bets and when Coutinho cut his list to 22 on the eve of their departure Sócrates was not on it. His dream of playing for Brazil at the World Cup would have to wait.

The solution, he realised, was to sign for a bigger club. So he did.

4

'To play for Corinthians is to respect a culture, a people, a nation. To play for Corinthians is like being called up for an irrational war and never doubting that it's the most important that ever existed. It is like being asked to think like Marx, fight like Napoleon, pray like the Dalai Lama, give your life to a cause like Mandela, and cry like a baby.'

Sócrates

In December 1977 Alberto Helena Jnr got a letter inviting him to Sócrates' graduation ceremony and cocktails at the Exhibition Centre in Ribeirão Preto. Handwritten on the back was the message: 'Thanks largely to you I have decided to hang up my diploma and put on my football boots.'[1]

The note was a kind acknowledgement of Helena Jnr's early and incisive reporting that was crucial in bringing Sócrates to the wider attention of the São Paulo press. But it didn't tell the story of how close he came to choosing a stethoscope over football. Throughout the hot summer months of December and January, Sócrates sweated over what course to take, going as far as registering for a resident's position only to back out at the last minute when he signed a new contract with Botafogo.

The main factor in his decision was the most obvious one, as his father constantly reminded him: he could practise medicine after playing football, but he couldn't play football after practising medicine. Money was also a factor. Even in an era when the gap in pay between footballers and other workers was not nearly as pronounced, Sócrates was guaranteed to earn at least 10 times more as a footballer than a young doctor and he would not have to put in overnight shifts every month to make ends meet.

His closest friends knew how much turmoil the decision was causing him, but they did not sit on the fence: they, and sometimes it seemed the whole city, from team-mates to newspaper columnists to neighbours, chipped in and implored him not to squander his talent.

Sócrates had promised Helena Jnr that he was going to play football but he still wasn't 100 per cent sure. Just days before the 1 February deadline to start his residency, Botafogo's two medical students sat in the cramped rooms of their *concentração* hotel and debated Sócrates' dilemma.

'You haven't told me what you think. Do I give up or do I keep playing?' Sócrates asked Zé Bernardes, who was three years below him at the USP-RP.

'I think you have to keep playing,' the centre forward said.

'Fuck,' said Sócrates. 'Why?'

'Because I've known you since you were a kid,' Bernardes replied. 'And if you stop playing now Brazil won't see you do what I've seen you do and it would be a huge loss. You have to keep going.'

Sócrates threw a pillow at his pal and flopped back on the bed. Within days he was a full-time footballer.[2]

Having finally made the toughest decision of his life, Sócrates knew he had to up his game if he wanted to make it big. The early months of 1978 marked the first time in his life that he had trained every day and the increased workload should have translated into more robust performances. However, the year began disappointingly, as he turned in a series of inconsistent showings that highlighted just how difficult he found the demands of full-time football.

Botafogo lost several of the regulars who had made them such a tough side to beat the year before, with Aguillera and Mineiro gone from the defence and Zé Mário tragically succumbing to leukaemia at the age of just 21. They performed decently enough in the 1978 Brasileiro that kicked off in March, just three weeks after the 1977 title had been decided. They sailed through the first two rounds but could only finish third in the next stage, and with only two teams progressing to the quarter-finals their old habit of running out of steam once again cost them dear. Their final place – 13th out of 62 teams – appeared to confirm that this was as good as it gets.

In spite of his troubles, Sócrates was still more than good enough to secure the move he so coveted and the favourites to sign him were São Paulo. São Paulo were, along with Corinthians, Palmeiras, Portuguesa and Santos, one of the five big clubs in the state, and they were considered one of the most prudent and best run. São Paulo's president shook hands with his Botafogo counterpart Atílio Benedini at the end of 1977 and they agreed that São Paulo would have first refusal when Sócrates was ready to leave. São Paulo wanted a package deal that also included centre half Ney, and the two clubs decided that when the time was right they would hand over 7 million cruzeiros ($400,000) to bring the pair along the Bandeirantes highway to the state capital.[3]

Sócrates signed a new contract in February on the condition that Botafogo would let him go when the first big club came in for him. He was vaguely aware of a gentleman's agreement with

São Paulo but he waited patiently – and in vain – for a club to make their move.

Brazil spent the first half of 1978 focused on the upcoming World Cup finals in Argentina, and when the tournament ended attention turned to the decisive games of the first division race, in which Guarani beat Palmeiras to become the first team from outside a state capital to become Brazilian champions. Palmeiras' good showing meant they were not interested in new signings and Corinthians, who had splashed out fortunes on a handful on new players over the previous two years, were never really considered a contender. The way was open for São Paulo to seal the deal.

However, the capital club had to sell before they could buy, and they expected to get the money from the most talked about transfer of the year, the sale of Chicão to Corinthians. Corinthians had been after the rugged midfielder for months and, at the start of August, it finally looked like they were going to get their man. The 29-year-old international knew this might be his last chance at a big-money transfer and he wanted a decent payday – he would get 15 per cent of any transfer fee – as well as an opportunity to shine at a club that finally looked like it was going places. Moreover, his style, that of a tireless midfield enforcer, would go down a storm with fans who loved a fighter.

São Paulo president Toninho Galvão spoke with Corinthians president Vicente Matheus in early August to try to finalise the deal and the two men arranged to have lunch at the Jockey Club, a ninth-floor restaurant that had spectacular views over the ever expanding northern half of the city. Matheus was a showman famous for his homespun philosophy and hilarious quips, and his version of what happened has long gone down in footballing folklore.

After Galvão had agreed to sell Chicão to their rivals, Matheus said he left the restaurant and delegated his brother Isidoro to iron out the final details. However, the old man claimed he was laying a trap. While his brother played for time, Matheus jumped into his car and raced to Ribeirão Preto. Matheus had wanted Sócrates all along and had used Chicão as a smokescreen. By the time São Paulo realised what was going on, it was too late. Matheus and Benedini had done a deal to make Sócrates a Corinthians player.

The yarn is a good one but the true story is more prosaic. Corinthians' coach at the time said he was against signing Chicão because it would have gifted São Paulo the money to secure the services of both Sócrates and Ney, two players who would have strengthened his rivals. José Teixeira had taken over less than a month before and he told Matheus to forget signing Chicão, who he considered injury prone, and go after Sócrates instead. He drove Matheus to the Jockey Club and waited in the car while Matheus informed Galvão that the Chicão deal was off. The next morning, at Teixeira's insistence, Matheus drove to Ribeirão Preto and signed Sócrates.[4]

Botafogo's then vice president told a similar story. Hamilton Mortari said that when the Chicão deal fell through, the president of São Paulo called him to say they would take longer than planned to raise Sócrates' transfer fee. Botafogo, who were in desperate need of cash, called Corinthians to see if they wanted to step in and by noon the next day Matheus was at Mortari's ranch haggling over the details.[5]

However Matheus overtook Galvão on the way to Ribeirão Preto, he didn't waste any time once he got there. He quickly closed the deal for a transfer fee of 5.68 million cruzeiros ($300,000) and at the end of the afternoon Matheus called Sócrates and his father to discuss – or rather dictate – personal terms for the two-year deal. Sócrates had asked for a transfer and was prepared to go anywhere at any price. He got a 1.1 million cruzeiro ($61,000) signing-on bonus, but he naively accepted Matheus' first salary offer of 30,000 cruzeiros ($1,667) a month for the first year and 45,000 cruzeiros ($2,500) a month for the second.

It was a beginner's mistake and one that would cost him dearly. The salary was just 2,500 cruzeiros ($140) more than he was on at Botafogo. He not only failed to take into account the higher cost of living in the state capital, but he also forgot he had been living rent free in a house owned by his in-laws and that they were helping foot his bills.

The lack of cash would cause him and Corinthians all sorts of problems in the months and years to come and jeopardise Sócrates' continued presence at the club.

August 4th was a sunny afternoon and Corinthians fans eager to see their new star had gathered at the entrance to the Parque São Jorge (St George's Park), the club's headquarters and training centre. Corinthians had a long-standing tradition of sounding a siren when a new signing arrived and when Sócrates drove through the gate in a white Mercedes the deafening wail was accompanied by the crack and bang of celebratory fireworks.

His capture was a coup and supporters had high hopes for a player they had watched develop slowly but surely into one of the country's hottest prospects. Sócrates' love affair with Corinthians, however, began with indifference. Corinthians had shown little interest in him and he had shown little interest in Corinthians, but like the ugly kid in the class who finally gets asked to dance, when the offer arrived Sócrates didn't look too closely at his suitor.

To Sócrates, this was a business transaction pure and simple and Corinthians was an employer like any other. He needed to be at a big club to realise his ambition of playing for Brazil and the name of that big club was of little importance. When asked if he was a Corinthians fan, his response was as shocking as it was sincere:

'I've never been a Corinthians supporter,' he told reporters who gathered around him for his first interview. 'Quite the contrary, I was a very big Santos fan.'[6]

Such candour was unheard of and quickly singled the new man out as suspect. Sócrates knew his words might cause a furore but he couldn't stop himself from giving an honest answer. The reporters' reaction prompted him to quickly stress that his loyalties were now with Corinthians, and he assured them that his love for Santos was in the past and that he was looking forward to giving his all for his new club.

'Now I am a football player,' he said. 'Medicine is now limited to studies when I am not playing. But I am not making promises. What I will say is that I am here to collaborate, to help the team, and hold the champions' flag aloft. And, of course, take advantage of this opportunity to project myself in Brazilian football and finally reach the national side ... As from today, I support Corinthians. I am absolutely delighted to come and play here.'[7]

The deal, meanwhile, was nothing short of disastrous for Botafogo. One director resigned when he heard of the sale and the fans were understandably upset. President Benedini explained that the club needed cash to finish building their stand and said selling Sócrates was the only way they could raise the money.

He appealed to fans to give him a year to finish the stadium and promised he would then start buying players again. Club treasurer Benedito Sciência, meanwhile, had come to São Paulo with the player and was beside himself. 'We didn't want to sell Sócrates. But Matheus really insisted. At one point we offered him 500,000 cruzeiros [\$28,000] just to go back to São Paulo and forget about Sócrates,' he claimed. 'Now I am here I'm thinking of offering a million just to give us the player back.'[8]

Whether that was true or just words designed to placate angry fans, only Sciência knows. But he was right in understanding just how big a loss Sócrates would be to the provincial club. In the short term, they didn't win any of their next nine games without him and they failed to score in six of them. It was another 23 years before they challenged for the Paulista title again.

Corinthians were one of the biggest clubs in Brazil but they had failed to live up to that billing for the longest time. Named after the Corinthian Casuals, the English amateurs whose tour to Brazil inspired their formation by factory workers in 1910, the club was forever identified with São Paulo's working-class populations and the immigrants and Afro-Brazilians who streamed into the city from the impoverished northeast. They won 15 Paulista state championships between their formation and 1954, and then went more than two decades without touching another piece of silverware. They finally ended that torturous drought in October 1977, when João Roberto Basílio got the winning goal in the decisive best-of-three contest over Ponte Preta. The relief was not just enormous for the fans; it was hugely serendipitous for Sócrates, who arrived at a club that had exorcised the demons that had been stalking it for more than 20 years. The atmosphere at the Parque São Jorge was lighter and less demanding than at any time since the 1950s.

Matheus got rid of half that winning team just a few months after the victory, much to the dismay of both players and fans. But he nipped any revolt in the bud with a spending spree that saw Goiás' right winger Piter, Guarani's classy defender Amaral, and Uruguayan midfielder Martín Taborda all sign for the club.

Sócrates' arrival was the most curious of them all, in part because it was so sudden. Some of his Corinthians team-mates knew him from select games and league clashes, but they didn't quite know what to expect from a player who was so obviously different.

'He was a weird signing,' said Zé Maria, the team's inspirational captain at the time. 'Corinthians wanted Chicão. We knew who Sócrates was but it wasn't him we were expecting. We were expecting someone more efficient, but when Magrão arrived he soon showed he was skilled and intelligent and that he had answers to some of our problems.

'Players usually take time to adapt but that wasn't the case with him; he fitted right in and hit the ground running. We knew that when players come to a big team they change and Magrão changed. We knew that he was a doctor and that he didn't come to the *concentração*. And we knew that he loved the nightlife, like all students do. But we also knew he was coming to play football not study, so we expected him to change.'[9]

After two weeks of medicals and coming and going from Ribeirão Preto, Sócrates made his debut against Santos on 20 August, the opening day of the 1978 Campeonato Paulista. More than 117,000 people packed the Morumbi to see him turn on the style with shimmies and back-heeled volleys from an unfamiliar role in left midfield. He almost capped what would have been a perfect start but was brought down in the final minute as he rounded the Santos keeper on the edge of the box. He put the resulting free kick narrowly wide and the match ended 1-1, but it was a fine debut.

A week later he went one better, scoring the opening goal and turning in a man-of-the-match performance in the 2-0 win over Ferroviária. Corinthians racked up the points as they went unbeaten in their first seven games, but Sócrates found goals hard to come by and it was another nine matches before he hit the net again. The lack of a holding midfielder – Taborda had been signed but would not make his debut until October – forced manager José Teixeira to employ Sócrates in a deep midfield role far from goal. Two other youngsters made their debuts on the same day he did and several players were being played out of position. When injuries kept striker Palhinha out for parts of September and October, Teixeira forced Sócrates to play as an orthodox number 9, another role that didn't suit him. The side was unbalanced and inexperienced, and Sócrates was one of those suffering in what was still a work in progress.

The injury to his new partner Palhinha was a major setback. Sócrates had linked up well with the former Cruzeiro forward in those first few games and the press were purring over their potential to do damage. Teixeira said they 'looked like they had been working together for years' and there were more than a few overenthusiastic comparisons with Pelé and Coutinho, the Santos duo known for their almost telepathic understanding a decade before.

Fast, cunning and with an eye for goal, Palhinha had been a key member of the Cruzeiro side that won them their first Copa Libertadores in 1976, and he was Corinthians' biggest ever signing when he joined them the following year. His record of a goal in every three games for the club made him a fans' favourite and he was one of the stars of the 1977 Paulista-winning side. He liked to run and Sócrates liked to pass and their early performances suggested they would hit it off.

Palhinha was also Sócrates' most important partner off the pitch. Four years his senior and with a year's experience in São Paulo, Palhinha knew what it was like to come from a sleepy city to a bustling metropolis and he took Sócrates under his wing. He found him a flat in the same building where he lived and the pair drove to and from training together. They both had two children and their wives – coincidentally both called Regina – also became friends and before long the families were inseparable.

'From the start I tried to help him because I could see he was finding it hard in São Paulo,' Palhinha recalled. 'When you leave a small city such as Belo Horizonte or Ribeirão Preto to visit São Paulo, well that's one thing. But when you go to live there . . .

'There are people who live in São Paulo for years and don't know São Paulo. So it is very difficult to adapt when you get there. It takes time. I said to him, "Sócrates, you're arriving here and if you need a hand there's a flat free in my building for rent. Let's go see it." And he liked it. I had been there a year so I gave him some help. We learned together. He had a really great memory. He would learn a way to drive to the club and teach me and I'd learn something and teach him.

'When he was your friend he was really your friend and we got on, both in the family aspect and as footballers. I played with a lot of centre forwards and the way I related to Sócrates was almost perfect. That had a big effect on us. It was the best moment of my career. We were going through a fantastic period.'[10]

Footballers love nothing more than playing alongside intelligent team-mates and the men who lined up with Sócrates were no exception. But when the whistle went and they returned to the dressing room, things got a bit more complicated. Sócrates was glaringly different from most of the other players in the squad and his arrival changed the dynamic.

It wasn't just that he looked different. It wasn't even that he sat in the corner and read books. The manager didn't quite know what to make of him and, confused by his erudite presence, addressed him in formal Portuguese before turning to the others and speaking a more earthy slang. His new team-mates found him reserved and even distant, and they were baffled by his total disregard for his appearance. Sócrates mostly wore shorts and flip-flops in Ribeirão's repressive heat and was gloriously uninterested not just in fashion but in clothes. He maintained that laid-back style in São Paulo and would turn up for training in T-shirts and shorts that were torn or unironed, and wearing old shoes with soles that flapped as he walked. As part of the usual dressing-room banter, his team-mates threw his shoes in the toilet and burnt his underpants because they were so disgustingly old. 'He didn't care,' said goalkeeper Jairo. 'He just asked Paulo, the kit man, to find him an old pair of flip-flops. And off he went in his flip-flops.'[11]

He was also not afraid to be himself and he continued with a strategy perfected at Botafogo to avoid training the morning after a heavy night before. Sócrates would invariably go out with friends after a match or invite people round to his place where they would drink into the wee hours. The next morning, his body was sore from the exertions of the game and his head was fuzzy from the post-match libations. He would often invent niggles and injuries and spend the morning on the massage table or in the sauna.

'He didn't train when he was hungover,' recalled veteran midfielder Basílio. 'And that happened all the time, it was very common. So eventually we knew that on the Monday or the Thursday he wouldn't want to train. We just needed to look at his face and we could tell. He arrived with his bag and when he was wired we could tell, Magrão's in good shape. But when he arrived hungover we all could tell, he's only going to train this afternoon. So it became a routine and we got used to it as we got to know him better. And it paid off. That was his way, there was no changing him.'[12]

Another characteristic that baffled – and often angered – his team-mates was his honesty. In one of his earliest games for Botafogo, Sócrates was awarded a penalty and then surprised reporters after the match by announcing that the ref had got it wrong. His team-mates weren't happy and his dad told him he ran the risk of never getting another penalty in his life. His sincerity, however, served him well. He never argued with officials because he knew it was pointless and he was never shown a red card in his entire career. Officials learned to ask his opinion about borderline decisions because they knew he would tell them the truth. It could lead to spats in the dressing room but he refused to compromise.

'Sometimes the referee would give a penalty and he'd say, "That wasn't a penalty,"' Basílio recalled. 'The same with off-side. Sometimes we didn't say anything at the time but later we'd say, "For fuck's sake, Magrão, come on!" And he'd say, "But it wasn't!" And we'd go, "Whose side are you on?" And he'd reply, "That's not important. What's important is that he asked my opinion and I gave him it."

'He lived within the truth. And we had to respect that. He was a football player but wasn't a *malandro* [a hustler who uses charm and cunning to get what he wants, often unlawfully]. He was always correct, always clean, always had the right attitude. Magrão didn't use that cunning; he didn't dive to get fouls or try to fool the referee. He simply thought that you had to play football. We couldn't complain. He was who he was.'

Sócrates might not have been a *malandro* when it came to football, but few people were slicker when it came to women. His roving eye and roguish charm guaranteed him his fair share of flings, but his success with the ladies was down more to his fame and charisma than any physical or sartorial attributes. He was gangly and unkempt, if not downright ugly, but the unflattering nicknames given him by team-mates didn't bother him in the slightest. His most charitable friends at Botafogo called him 'Magrão', while the less complimentary names ranged from 'Caveira' (Skull) to 'Ducha' (Shower), because his heavily pock-marked face reminded them of a shower head. His team-mates in the 1982 Brazilian team christened him 'Monster'. When he later had an affair with a *Playboy* model, his friends wasted no time in dubbing them Beauty and the Beast.

Sócrates simply laughed off the insults, smug in the knowledge that he didn't need good looks to score. He had an aura and sincerity about him that most other players simply didn't possess. Older women saw it as vulnerability and tried to mother him, while younger ones were seduced by his honesty and carefree attitude to life.

'It was impressive,' said Zé Bernardes. 'I'd go out with him and you had to see the girls. He was ugly as sin but the girls couldn't take their eyes off him.'

Like many Latin American men his age, Sócrates lost his virginity to a prostitute in one of the red-light districts located in and around Brazil's big cities. Minors were forbidden from entering the bars and brothels located there and police zealously patrolled the area on horseback and in squad cars. Sócrates was still only 14 or 15 and his first sexual encounter was fraught and quick. 'It wasn't one of the best experiences,' he told *Playboy* in a 1979 interview. 'It was filled with tension, with police cars nearby. There were always police cars doing the rounds. You can imagine my emotional state. Just a kid. The first time . . .'[13]

The experience left its scars but they were superficial and Sócrates admitted that the appeal of working girls was strong enough for him to seek out their company on a regular basis and not just for sex. 'I like that atmosphere, I like debauchery, the fucking around,' he later confessed. 'I like whores, I really do. They are very interesting people and I always liked to talk and all that kind of thing. I always got involved in some way or another.'[14]

He wasn't the only one, and the lads from Botafogo often hung out at the same bars where he had lost his virginity a few years previously. Several of the Botafogo players were well known to the girls – many of whom were students out to make some cash to pay for their tuition. They were such good customers that when the girls realised their clients were football players they became fans, even turning up at training sessions to watch the boys being put through their paces. When the sessions ended they would hang around the players' entrance, hoping to sneak off for either a drink or a quickie. When their presence became too glaring and the liaisons too scandalous, the Botafogo directors nipped it in the bud with a quiet word in the girls' ears.

Sócrates was particularly keen on one prostitute, one drunken night even climbing the brothel wall and screaming her name, only to be sent packing by the madam who gave him a dressing-down and informed him she was with another client. He had other dalliances with students and girls he met in bars – almost always blondes or brunettes – but he managed to keep them quiet. Those in the football world knew he enjoyed playing away from home but the affairs never got reported because there was a different code in play. Many hacks were friends with players and it was in no one's interest to write about their extra-curricular activities. Sócrates, moreover, was in his own way gallant, never boasting about his conquests, even when they were over.

'He wasn't the kind of guy who talked about women,' said Helena Jnr, who witnessed the goings-on and knew the players and managers of the 1970s better than almost anyone else. 'Deep down he was idealistic and very romantic, in the full sense of the word, in the way he saw the world, in his friendships, in politics. He wasn't the kind who wanted to show off, "I'm with this woman and I'm with that woman, I screwed that one, and I am now after this one." He spoke a lot about politics, music, books, football, but he didn't say much about women.'[15]

The carousing had surprisingly little effect on his personal or his professional life. The infidelities continued after he moved to São Paulo, but his wife either didn't know or turned a blind eye to them, and he was still young enough to be able to drink into the small hours and get up early for training.

'I was single at the time and he'd say, "Let's go out", and so we'd go have a few beers,' recalled Arlindo, his striking partner on the pitch and wingman off it. 'Sometimes his wife Regina would come and there'd be a time in the night when she'd had enough and said, "Arlindo, take me home. I know he's going to be here a lot longer." So she'd go home and we'd be there till one, one-thirty and I'd say, "Magrão, man, let's go, we have to train tomorrow." And he'd look at me and go, "Nah, don't worry about it. We'll put on flip-flops and we'll go to the treatment room." And I'd say, "You can do that, but I can't." I came from a big team and I didn't have the privileges that he had. If I missed a chance, the fans would get on my back. He could miss chances and get away with it. He'd make one mistake and for every mistake he'd do five great things. You can't boo a player like that.'[16]

Sócrates got away with such shenanigans because, as Arlindo and everyone else knew, he did the business on the field. That didn't change at Corinthians and he made the step up with consummate ease. He finished his first season with 25 goals in 52 games and confirmed the early promise. The next task was to push on and do the same at international level. He wouldn't have long to wait. His first footballing dream was about to come true.

5

'Corinthians scared me. It was all so aggressive. I moved
and suffered like I'd never suffered before; it's like a truck
driving over you again and again. Every day. But you go
on and slowly you create relationships, friends . . .'

Sócrates

When Corinthians played Flamengo, Zico would wind up
Sócrates by calling him Frankenstein. Sócrates responded with
insults of 'Shorty'. The five-foot-eight Zico snapped back, 'Size
doesn't matter.'[1]

It was trash talk, but it was friendly trash talk and the stars
of Brazil's two biggest clubs would form a friendship that
went beyond the football pitch. They first crossed paths in
June 1977 when Brazil took on a Paulista selection at the
Morumbi. Zico already had 13 caps and was the man that
Brazil would build their side around for the best part of a
decade. The Flamengo star was eager to meet this strange-
looking hotshot who was making headlines at Botafogo and
they felt an immediate affinity when they chatted before and
after the 1-1 draw.

A real rapport, however, only developed in 1979 when manager Claudio Coutinho began to rebuild the seleção after an unhappy World Cup in Argentina. The hosts won a tournament tainted forever by allegations of match-fixing and, as the only team to go unbeaten, Brazil were not ashamed to declare themselves 'moral victors'.

Brazil, though, still didn't have a full-time coach and Coutinho devoted himself to his club Flamengo as the national side took an 11-month break from action after finishing third in Argentina. When they returned for a series of three friendlies in May 1979, he called up Sócrates, Flamengo's attacking full back Júnior, and 21-year-old left winger Éder, who was banging in the goals for Grêmio.

Sócrates would later say that Coutinho was one of the best managers he ever had. But the two men appeared to have little in common. Coutinho was an army captain who never played professional football. He got his break because of his military connections – his father was a general – and he seized it with both hands. He went to the 1970 World Cup in Mexico as a trainer and, along with Carlos Alberto Parreira who was also a military man, he fine-tuned the team to play at high altitude and in great heat.

Coutinho followed that with a stint on the backroom staff with Peru, then returned to Brazil to back up Mário Zagallo at the 1974 World Cup. After a short spell in France with Olympique de Marseille, he was invited to coach the Brazil team at the 1976 Olympics. Although he had never managed a team before, Coutinho led them to the semi-finals, their best performance ever, where they were beaten by a Polish team of alleged amateurs containing all-time greats such as Jan Tomaszewski, Grzegorz Lato and Kazimierz Deyna. He was appointed at Flamengo soon after and was a surprise pick to replace Osvaldo Brandão as Brazil manager in 1977.

Like many football fans of the time, Coutinho was enraptured by the Netherlands' total football, and he wanted his team to play a tropical version he called 'the floating lozenge'. The formation comprised a revolving diamond in midfield and he wanted a Zico–Sócrates partnership to be an integral part of it. He talked them both up during the early months of 1979, and even compared Sócrates to Tostão, a player he said could come and go from the penalty box, swapping positions with Zico like Tostão did with Pelé.

That possibility delighted both Zico and Sócrates and their mutual respect was sealed when the weekly sports magazine *Placar* got them together just before the friendlies and asked them what they would bring to the new-look national side.

Sócrates predicted they would form 'a great double' of 'rotating creativity'.

'Your quick dribbles and long passes really go with my style of short one-twos and quick bursts into space,' he said. 'We will form an attack that is mobile and exciting. When we kick off you'll start in the middle of the park and I'll go more to the wings and during the game we'll move around. We'll make up a seleção that is free, open, relaxed, that gives the fans back their joy and confidence.'[2]

Zico agreed, saying their football 'is similar and complements each other'.

'Three things about him surprise me,' Zico said of his future partner. 'The intelligence with which he plays football, the fact that he is tall and at the same time quick, and finally, his mobility. He appears all over the pitch, always creating.'[3]

'We're going to score a lot of goals,' he added confidently. 'The hard part will be getting up there to congratulate you.'[4]

The series of friendlies were warm-up games for the Copa América and Sócrates finally had the chance he had craved for so long. He was confident he had the talent to succeed on the international stage and it took him just five minutes to show what he could do when he drifted past the Paraguayan full back and crossed for Éder to score. Zico added a second from the penalty spot and then Sócrates turned provider again, splitting the defence for Nilton Batata to deftly chip the goalkeeper. Brazil won 6-0, but it could have been double figures and Sócrates was rightly fêted as one of the best players on the field.

He would not have long to wait for his next opportunity, with Brazil facing an inexperienced Uruguay side at the Maracanã just two weeks later. Sócrates was again in the starting line-up and he scored two goals in the 5-0 victory, the first a lovely side-footed finish after chesting down a Zico pass, and the second a header from close in. Uruguay coach Raúl Bentancor singled out Sócrates and Falcão as the best players on the pitch and had warm praise for both.

The most interesting match, however, was his third, for it pitted him against European rivals for the first time. Brazil had arranged to play Poland but the Poles pulled out and so a game against Ajax, who were in the middle of a short tour of Argentina, was hastily arranged to fill the gap. Brazilian players only ever saw European teams at the World Cup or in rare friendlies, so matches against such exotic opposition were eagerly anticipated.

Ajax were holders of the Dutch league and cup double, but they were not the team they had been a few years earlier and Brazil eased past them 5-0. Once again Sócrates excelled, scoring twice and running the midfield before going off with an ankle knock after 62 minutes.

His first goal was particularly memorable because it had almost everything – grace, vision and accuracy. With the game less than nine minutes old, Falcão got the ball just inside the

Dutch half and sent a long, cross-field pass to Sócrates, who was 30 yards from goal and sandwiched between two defenders. On the left of the field and running towards goal, he brought the ball down on his chest and let it bounce once before chipping it over the outstretched leg of one defender with his left foot. He feinted to shoot, fooling the second defender into committing himself, and instead dragged the ball over to his right. From the edge of the box, and with another defender approaching to close him down, he fired the ball low to the keeper's left, just inches inside the post.

It was a lovely goal that capped a great performance and was all the more surprising to the Dutch because they had never even heard of him. 'I didn't expect the number nine to be so good,' Ajax manager Cor Brom said after the game. 'He looks clumsy because he is so tall. But the truth is he is a very useful player for his side, he lays the ball off well and moves around the pitch perfectly.'[5]

The game was also memorable for highlighting the petty rivalries that dogged Brazilian football at the time. Brazil has long revolved around the Rio de Janeiro–São Paulo axis and the two cities are constant competitors and antagonists.

Cariocas, as people from Rio are known, think Paulistanos are dull, uptight and materialistic, while Paulistanos think Cariocas are sly, lazy and irresponsible. The football field was a place where the rivalry was most evident, and the press in each city would big up their local lads with undisguised bias.

The state championships were still more important than Brazil's national league and television coverage was regional so viewers rarely saw games from outside their own states. That meant fans only knew their local players and many were reluctant to believe that 'outsiders' were all they were cracked up to be. Many in the São Paulo press, for example, thought Zico was overrated, that he shirked tough tackles and that he only turned it on at the Maracanã. Zico scored the last two goals in the 5-0 rout of Ajax. But the scoreboard operator at São Paulo's Morumbi stadium acted like they hadn't happened.

'The score was 3-0 to us,' Zico recalled. 'I scored a goal and the scoreboard didn't change. I scored another and the scoreboard continued to ignore my presence. Right till the end, the scoreboard still had that smart-ass 3-0. I don't know why those responsible for the stadium didn't have the brilliant idea of counting my goals for Ajax.'[6]

The press in both states began to whip up a debate – and, they hoped, a rivalry – over the merits of the two stars. They were the most exciting young players to hit the scene since Brazil won the World Cup in Mexico and although they looked completely different – the languid and gangly Sócrates alongside the compact and buzzing Zico – the roles they fulfilled were not dissimilar.

Both were modern-day forwards who offered an enticing alternative to the burly and static target men who were still in fashion. They could be clinical inside the box but they did much of their most dangerous work outside it, threading passes to forwards, striking free kicks from all angles and coming deep to link up play between midfield and attack.

In 1979 there was little doubt that Zico was the more accomplished of the two, as Sócrates himself repeatedly stressed in a bid to prevent a rivalry developing. Although he was only 11 months older, the 26-year-old Zico had already played in a World Cup and was considered the first name on Coutinho's team sheet. *Placar* rated his transfer fee at $2.4 million, more than twice the value they put on Sócrates.[7]

But Sócrates' performances for the national side had brought him to the attention of football fans all over Brazil and they were enchanted by his style both on and off the field. A poll taken in five of Brazil's biggest cities was almost evenly split over who was the better of the two. Sócrates won in the northeastern cities of Recife and Salvador, but in the south, in Belo Horizonte, Curitiba and Porto Alegre, Zico came out on top. On average, 54 per cent of fans thought Zico was the more complete player.[8]

A week later, another poll in the same magazine asked more than 2,000 fans of 17 top clubs which of the two they'd most like to see on their team. Nine preferred Sócrates and eight plumped for Zico.

Unlike many players who donned the famous yellow jersey for the first time, Sócrates showed no fear and his assured performances boosted his confidence. A more assertive player returned to the Parque São Jorge after the break and his team-mates at Corinthians noticed the change. The series of caps was a transformative moment for him, as he realised he was more than good enough to play alongside those who had represented their country dozens of times.[9]

Sócrates missed Brazil's next two matches after pulling a muscle with Corinthians in July, but he was back for key Copa América encounters in August. Unlike today, when the Copa América is a small-scale version of the European Championships or the World Cup, the tournament back then was played home and away in the five months between July and December.

Brazil were drawn in a group with Bolivia and Argentina and lost their first match 2-1 in La Paz, before beating Argentina by the same scoreline at the Maracanã in early August. Sócrates returned from injury to play in the 2-0 win over Bolivia at the Morumbi on 16 August, but it was the game against Argentina at the Monumental five days later that really stuck in his mind.

He had never played outside Brazil before and it was a

frightening experience, both on and off the pitch. Argentina was in the grip of a brutal right-wing dictatorship and the military-backed thugs thought nothing of bundling opponents into cars in broad daylight, torturing them in underground cells and then loading them on to helicopters to be thrown alive into the icy waters of the South Atlantic. Official figures would eventually document 8,961 people murdered or disappeared, although the real number could have been as high as 30,000. It was in this atmosphere that Brazil turned up on a cold and windy night in the Argentine capital, needing a draw to qualify for the semi-finals.

Sócrates was freaked out by the police who patrolled in and around the stadium, and the deafening chorus of boos and whistles that greeted the Brazil side as they walked on to the pitch did nothing to put his mind at ease. But when the game kicked off he quickly confirmed he was a man who could handle pressure. He stooped to head home the opening goal after 17 minutes and then effortlessly assumed a leadership role when Zico was sent off for fighting with Américo Gallego 10 minutes later.

Daniel Passarella equalised for the home side shortly before half-time, but Sócrates kept plugging away, and when Brazil were awarded a penalty Coutinho sent word from the bench that he was to take it. The decision was a complete surprise because no one had drawn up a plan B for when Zico was absent, but Sócrates was unfazed and slotted home the kick with consummate ease, not just once, but twice, after the referee made him retake it for encroachment. Rubén Díaz made it 2-2 with 19 minutes left, but a point was enough and both Brazil and Sócrates had passed another test.

'I had been in stressful situations like this before but never in moments as big as this,' Sócrates said of the penalty award. 'But there was no way out. It was all or nothing. I picked up the ball, placed it under my arm and slowly walked towards the enemy's penalty area. The crowd were booing, shouting abuse and doing everything else possible to unnerve me. When I heard the crowd go silent and saw the ball in the back of the net I knew that I would not want for excitement in my chosen profession.'[10]

In September 1979, General João Batista Figueiredo made a guest appearance at Corinthians and was greeted with rapturous applause. Just days before, the new president had signed an amnesty decree that would allow the first political prisoners to be freed. Exiles who had fled the bloody crackdown were also given permission to finally return home without fear of arrest. Figueiredo was invited to the Parque São Jorge to celebrate the club's 69th birthday and almost 2,000 people gave him a standing ovation when he arrived for a late lunch of Waldorf salad and chicken supreme.[11]

He told the delighted crowd he had been a Corinthians fan all his life, helped Vicente Matheus blow out the 69 candles, and then shook hands with the player he had most wanted to meet. Figueiredo had specifically requested a signed shirt from Sócrates and the player, who in an interview a few days earlier gave the former secret service chief 10 out of 10 for his performance at the head of the dictatorship, was happy to oblige.[12]

Football had always been used by the regime, especially after 1970, when it touted the World Cup triumph as a victory for their 'new' Brazil. The first national league was set up by the military-run CBD the following year as a nationalist gesture designed to unite the country. It grew from 20 teams the first year to 94 teams eight years later, largely because the dictators thought that adding lesser-known clubs would win them support from fans. (A slogan popular at the time made reference to this policy by the ruling ARENA party: *Onde a ARENA vai mal, um time no Nacional* (Where the ARENA isn't doing well, a team in the national league). When they added even more teams as the 1970s went on, the slogan was expanded to read: *Onde a ARENA vai mal, um time no Nacional; onde vai bem, um time tambem* (Where the ARENA isn't doing well, a team in the national league; where it is, a team in the national league anyway).)

However, although the average football supporter was solidly working class, most of the people who went to grounds were as uninterested in politics as the players were, and it wasn't until 1979 – not long after São Paulo metalworkers launched the first mass strikes against the regime – that sport and politics finally came together on the terraces. Figueiredo had recently revoked one of the military's harshest decrees and Corinthians fans felt emboldened. One February night at the Morumbi, a small group of supporters unfurled a banner they had smuggled into the match against Santos. The banner read: *'Anistia, Ampla, Geral e Irrestrita'* (Amnesty, Wide-ranging, General and Unrestricted) and it was the first sign that football fans were willing to take a position against the regime.

Sócrates did not comment on the banner after scoring in the 2-1 win in front of 109,000 people. But Figueiredo could not have missed it and the presence of such a daring and public protest doubtlessly played a part in his decision to grant the amnesty just a few months later. The general took power in March and vowed some sort of military-sponsored elections as the first step in what was officially described as the 'slow, gradual and safe' return to democratic rule. He gave no timeframe and his promises were met with scepticism, but the hard line was definitely softening. Brazil's economy was slowing and the effects of the global oil crisis were becoming more and more evident. The currency, the cruzeiro, was devalued five times against the dollar in the first three months of 1979, and inflation was running at almost 50 per cent and gathering speed. Oil shortages meant that petrol stations were open only part time, and strikes by workers looking for the wage rises that would help them keep up with inflation were increasingly common. The generals realised things were going to get worse and they were looking for an out.

Like many people at the time, Sócrates was still doing his best not to get involved in politics. He was still politically naive – not to mention uninterested – but there was one issue that he could not ignore. Brazilian footballers were effectively slaves whose careers were controlled by the clubs that owned them and Sócrates couldn't understand why his team-mates let coaches and directors take advantage of them.

The issue first arose for Sócrates in 1976 when a journeyman midfielder named Lorico arrived at Botafogo. Lorico was 37 and had played alongside some of the country's all-time greats, men such as Pelé and Bellini, the man who captained Brazil to the 1958 World Cup. Sócrates was only 22 but he was shocked at how they treated Lorico 'like a big kid' and how Lorico didn't seem to mind. Sócrates got better treatment than most because not only was he middle class and educated, his father was a *conselheiro* at the club and held some sway in the local community. Few of his team-mates had those advantages, and they knew that if they spoke out against the system they risked their careers. Botafogo could simply ship them out to a club of their choosing or, even worse, refuse to sell them and leave them to waste away on the sidelines.

Sócrates thought such treatment was deliberate, designed to keep players in line. 'I realised it was a way of disrespecting them, putting them in an inferior position,' he said. 'From the very start I always thought that the treatment given to players was to reduce the sensation of power that they could have in terms of communication.'[13]

Sócrates identified the lack of free agency as the biggest issue facing footballers and he would try for years to get his colleagues interested in changing it. He didn't care about politics but he was interested in personal freedom, and he passionately wanted his team-mates to be more independent. At Botafogo he tried to start conversations about current affairs and economics, but he got nowhere and so he tried another tack. Each weekend at the *concentração* he would turn up with a newspaper. He'd remove the sports section and leave the rest on the table as an invitation for his team-mates to educate themselves.

'No one picked it up,' he recalled. 'Ever. I said to them, "Fuck, you need to learn, keep up with things, grow as people."'[14]

Sócrates' lack of interest in formal politics had so far been a blessing in disguise. In 1976, when he gave the interview to the *Diário da Manhã* backing the military, he was still just a talented young gun from the provinces, yet to prove he had what it takes to play for a major club. People inside the game viewed him with suspicion because of his education and his unapologetically bohemian lifestyle. Had they known he was also a progressive radical, his career might have been over before it began.

There was good reason to believe that a liberal and articulate worldview could be fatal to a footballer's career. A creative midfielder with the other Botafogo had been marginalised just years before after taking a very public stance on players' rights. In 1970, Afonsinho fought with Botafogo manager Mário Zagallo and was loaned out to little Olaria as punishment. When he returned six months later with long hair and a bushy beard, Zagallo said he looked more like a hippy than a football player and ordered him to cut it off. Afonsinho refused and was further ostracised. The club would neither play him nor sell him, so he took them to court in a case that presaged that of Jean-Marc Bosman in Europe a quarter of a century later. In

1971, he won the right to free agency and while the ruling did not extend to all players he set such an example for his peers that Pelé famously dubbed him the 'only free man in the country'. Documentaries were made about his case, books were written, and Gilberto Gil even penned him a song entitled '*Meio de Campo*' (Midfield).[15]

Corinthians' famously authoritarian president Vicente Matheus brooked no such nonsense, and he'd have thought twice about signing Sócrates if he'd known the challenges he would present. An immigrant from Spain who never finished primary school but whose business acumen helped expand his family's small stonemason's into a major firm that made asphalt and paved roads, Matheus was Corinthians mad and served as club president first from 1959 to 1961 and then again when he took over in 1972. He was dictatorial enough that his critics dubbed him 'Idi Amin', and was famously frugal when it came to contract negotiations.[16]

Sócrates had a great respect for Matheus' intelligence and street savvy, but he was on one of the lowest salaries at the club, earning, by his reckoning, less than a fifth of what the older players were getting. His desperation to join a big club had led him to accept a basic salary of just 30,000 cruzeiros ($1,667) a month, and although he almost doubled that in bonuses each month, around half of his take-home pay was set aside for rent with the rest going on the children's nanny and other essentials such as food and clothing.

He had invested his signing-on bonus in a one-year bond and he only managed to scrape by thanks to sponsorship deals he had with Topper, whose clothes and boots he wore, and Arapuã, a chain of shops that sold electrical appliances. Times were so tight that his father-in-law would fill his car with groceries each week and drive the 200 miles from Ribeirão Preto to São Paulo to help them out.

Sócrates was riding high after his starring performances for Brazil and he felt the time was right to ask for a pay rise, so in July 1979 he went to Matheus with a proposal he thought was good for both of them. His current contract still had a year to run and he was about to get an increase to 45,000 cruzeiros ($2,500) a month. That was still low and so Sócrates proposed renegotiating the current deal to extend it for a further one or two years. He would get an immediate salary increase to 125,000 cruzeiros a month and in return Corinthians could secure him on a longer contract. Matheus turned him down flat and Sócrates slunk out of his office, angry but resolute and with a plan.

Under Brazilian legislation at the time, a player's income during the final year of his contract was used to calculate the value of his *passe*, or contract. The more he pocketed in salary and bonuses, the higher his transfer fee would be. Sócrates was so angry at Matheus' refusal to negotiate that he decided to stop taking any bonuses and therefore force down his market value. The club did not want to see him go for a song and so they deposited thousands of cruzeiros into his account every month. Every month Sócrates returned the money.

'It was war,' he wrote in his unpublished memoir. 'And it was like that through much of the second year of my contract. As a result of my simply exercising a right – something unusual in this country, especially in the world of sport – I became a threat to the institutions, such was the reaction it caused. But the most important thing at that moment was that I had a high degree of value to the system and a relatively small value on the transfer market and that allowed me think of ways in which I could free myself using my own resources. In addition to which, I sent a clear and direct message to all my professional colleagues: they should pay more attention to the rights explicitly afforded them under the law at the time, which weren't many.

'The end of this conflict with Corinthians' directors came a year after the confrontation began and I signed a new contract with the team for a sum that was exceptionally higher than what I was on up until then: I went from getting 26,000 cruzeiros a month to 1,250,000 [$22,300] a month. Which was more than 10 times what I had asked for a year previously. Putting the squeeze on them was worth it.'[17]

The clash annoyed Sócrates deeply and he would later cite it as a defining moment in his career, the point at which he realised he would need to 'fight the system' if he wanted to live life his own way.

Until he arrived in São Paulo, Sócrates had always been in charge of his own destiny, but that changed at Corinthians and it made his first year a fraught one. He faced far greater demands, both physically and mentally, and with the attention from fans and the media much more intense than he had anticipated, he felt adrift and even afraid. His shyness prevented him from doing more and he admitted to breaking out in cold sweats at the mere thought of going to the bank or post office.

One of the biggest shocks was having to adapt to new rules. He was forced to train every day and spend several nights a week at the *concentração*. He was no longer free to come and go as he pleased and the interminable hours spent with people he barely knew was a shock to the system. He missed the support of his family and friends back in Ribeirão – not to mention the weekend barbecues and warm nights drinking beer – and he made little effort to integrate himself with his new team-mates. It was, he said, the one time in his career when he didn't even try to fit in, and his principled stance against Matheus made him stand out even more. No one had refused to accept a win bonus before and Sócrates' position caused a stir. Some fans thought he was fighting the club rather than the situation and they began to question his commitment to the cause.

He was also struggling to adapt to the manic pace of life in his new home. São Paulo was a far cry from Ribeirão Preto, a seething conurbation of two dozen municipalities housing close to 15 million people. Compared to Ribeirão it was scarily schizophrenic, going from luxurious modernity to rural poverty within a couple of miles, and grim monochrome to glorious technicolor in a matter of blocks. It was built up and impersonal, sometimes hot and dry, other times cold and wet; and the few parks dotted among the brutal panorama of concrete could not compensate for the depressing lack of space or greenery.

Sócrates was by now one of the most famous faces in the country, as both critics and fans fell in love with his football and his refreshingly honest personality. In September, weekly sports magazine *Placar* published a special edition telling his life story, and he was also the interview of the month in *Playboy*, a rare honour given only to the country's most interesting people. The downside was that he couldn't take his kids to the park because they would get mobbed. He restricted his visits to the cinema and theatre for the same reason, and he even moved to a house without a telephone because his number leaked and random people were calling to have a chat. The pressure was greater than anything he had felt before and, like many workers who arrived in São Paulo from the provinces, the walls sometimes felt as though they were closing in. In September it all got too much for him and he threatened to quit.

'I've thought about that hypothesis a lot recently,' he said in an interview with *Placar*. 'In less than a year my life has undergone a radical transformation that has left me very confused. Football has become a weight around my neck. At Botafogo I played for the joy of it, it was a pleasure. Today that's all changed. Corinthians is a huge club and it demands a huge investment. I feel the professional side of things more and more and that scares me. I take the field and the sense of obligation that I feel is stronger than the sense of pleasure. It's not that I have a problem with the training, the *concentração*, the games one after another. The problem is that there is such huge pressure, the commitment is so great that it is hard to play and enjoy it.'[18]

'It's a difficult process because I want to live my life, give my family attention, and do the things that I like to do and that's impossible. I no longer have any right to privacy. I no longer have any right to myself. I am trying to organise myself to face up to this new situation. It's difficult, but I want everything in its right and proper place. One thing is certain. If I had to choose between living my life with my family and playing football I'd have no doubts. I'll stop playing football. And I won't even wait until after the World Cup.'[19]

The threat was genuine – at the time he made it, he couldn't see a way of enjoying his glamorous new life without losing the benefits of his comfortable old one. But it was also typical Sócrates. He said what was on his mind at the time. The chances of him giving up football before the World Cup were almost nil. Rather, as Claudio Coutinho so perceptively noted, his outburst 'seemed more like a cry for help'.[20]

It was a cry that was exacerbated by his inability to put together a concerted run of games in a white shirt. His Paulista campaign started well, with three goals in the first three games in early July, but he missed large parts of the season because of injury and international duty, and both he and the team were frustratingly inconsistent during the second half of the year.

They did enough to qualify for the second phase of the Paulista at the top of their group, but they failed to convince and a last-day defeat by Internacional de Limeira at the Pacaembu was the final straw for hard-core fans, some of whom tried to climb into the directors' box and make their feelings known to Vicente Matheus.

The fury was typically Corinthians and largely undeserved. Although they started the year inconsistently, they had improved and qualified comfortably for the next stage of the competition. But the players' decision to take their foot off the pedal and preserve their strength for the second round did not sit well with supporters who demanded 100 per cent effort every game, as well as a clearer return on the 20 million cruzeiros invested on new players. Coach José Teixeira was one of the main targets of abuse – as were his children – and he resigned.

Sócrates, too, was one of those singled out. After a dazzling debut for Brazil, his club form had dropped off and he had been hindered by niggling injuries. He came back too early from his ankle knock and played several games (badly) in fear of doing it more damage. A persistent cough – 'something smokers get from time to time' – did not help matters and neither did the fixture list, with the Campeonato Paulista so ridiculously stretched that Corinthians opted not to play in that year's Brasileiro because their players were so exhausted.[21]

He was tired and stressed and unhappy, and he openly admitted that the credit he built up in his good first year had been washed away by a few bad performances. During one not untypical week in late October, he went to Paraguay for the Copa América semi-final on a Wednesday, was back in his home state to play for Corinthians in Bauru the following Sunday, and then three days later he was in Rio for the return leg against Paraguay. The fixture congestion and the non-stop matches meant that he and other São Paulo-based players 'turned up at the CBD in a deplorable state', Coutinho said. Sócrates 'is dead, killed by the disorganisation of Paulista football'.[22]

Corinthians fans knew he did not have the same stamina as the other players, but they were angry at seeing him excel for Brazil and then disappear for Corinthians and their patience wore thin. Some of them believed he was deliberately not giving his all in order to get back at Matheus in the salary war and they gave him more abuse than he'd ever got before. The 'Doctor', whose incisive passes had cut opponents to shreds, was now taunted as the 'Nurse'.

A large part of the problem was Sócrates' failure to understand Corinthians' famously passionate fans. Palhinha warned him soon after his arrival that Corinthianos needed to believe their players loved the team as much as they did. Like insecure girl-friends, they demanded public displays of affection.

'Right at the start, I said to him, "Sócrates, when you score a goal, you have to celebrate,"' Palhinha said. 'He had this habit of being more reserved, he never showed emotion. I told him, "You have to change. If you play badly but run your heart out and give your all they might recognise that, but Corinthians fans can sense if you are not fighting for the team."

'One time we lost a game and we were leaving the Pacaembu and we got in his car. And the fans surrounded the car and lifted it off the ground. We lost, and they were demanding guts and determination. And I said to Sócrates, "You see what I mean? When you score, run to the fans, jump up and down, celebrate with them because Corinthians fans like that." After that, he changed the way he celebrated. He ran to the fence.'[23]

Corinthians have the second largest support in Brazil after Flamengo, but their fans believe they are different in ways that go beyond mere numbers. More than any other side in Brazil, Corinthians fans love players with *raça*, a Portuguese word that implies both commitment and guts. At Corinthians, the fancy dans and pretty boys are suspect and the hard-working right back who runs 50 yards to make a crunching tackle gets a bigger cheer than the classy winger who beats five players before split-ting the defence with an inch-perfect pass.

Unlike at some other clubs, the collective is also more important than the individual. Although stars such as Rivellino,
Sócrates and Ronaldo have all enjoyed happy periods at the
club, Corinthians, unlike Flamengo with Zico, Santos with Pelé
or Botafogo with Garrincha, do not have one special player who
overshadows all others in their history.

Their belief that they are different stems largely from a 1976
game in Rio de Janeiro, when an estimated 60,000 supporters
travelled to the Maracanã for the Brazilian championship semi-
final against Fluminense. Corinthians had not won a major title
since 1954 and their fans hoped this was the year they would
finally end the drought. Supporters drove 270 miles from São
Paulo to Rio in a mass convoy to see them qualify for the final
on penalties. They lost the decider to Internacional a week later
but the event was immortalised as the 'Corinthians invasion' – a
name that would also be given to the presence of more than
10,000 supporters in Tokyo for the final of the 2012 Club World
Cup against Chelsea.

Inversely proportional to their devotion was their patience.
When Corinthians had possession the samba drummers who
stood on the terraces would hammer away at a fast pace, calling
their players to action. When they lost the ball, the sounds would
slow and a lone drummer would beat out an angry one-note
rhythm on a big bass drum. It put tremendous pressure on the
home side and visiting teams knew that if they could keep things
tight early in the match, Corinthians fans would get restless.

The world first noticed Sócrates at the 1982 World Cup and not
just because he passed the ball better than everyone else. The
Brazil side were cool and Sócrates was the captain of cool. The
socialist Doctor Sócrates was largely unknown to foreign viewers and he had yet to establish himself as a champion of the poor.
TV commentators told us he was a doctor who smoked like a

chimney and enjoyed a beer, but the cool quotient was probably more down to the fact that he looked good. While the other 21 players on the pitch scurried around like their lives depended on it, Sócrates was laid-back and languid and he only seemed to exert himself when he really had to. To put it bluntly, he looked like he couldn't give a toss.

There was a good reason Sócrates looked that way. For the whole first half of his career, through eight years at Botafogo and even after a year at Corinthians, Sócrates really didn't care. In 1979, still struggling with the demands of a new club and new city and not yet at ease with his decision to abandon medicine, he saw football as a game that was below him. It was somehow unworthy of his attentions, a pastime that was more about brute force than mental agility. Sócrates regularly tried to convince people that football was played with the head as much as with the feet, but he was always looking for ways to spice it up with intellectual challenges.

He knew that the Corinthians fans were demanding and he knew they wanted blood and guts. But this Corinthian remained casual and he wasn't going to change his unhurried style just to suit a few million football fans. Ruling on how the team played was almost a battle of wills and he set his mind on changing the long-established mentality. Brazilian football was in a rut after failing to win the World Cup in 1974 and 1978, and a vocal group blamed the move towards the slower and more cultured style personified by Sócrates and Palmeiras' midfielder Ademir da Guia. Flamengo centre half Rondinelli declared the game needed more hardmen and Botafogo's Búfalo Gil blamed the middle-class players he said lacked the desire and commitment of those who came from dirt-poor backgrounds.[24]

Sócrates made no apologies for his middle-class upbringing and pointed out that iceman Björn Borg was every bit as effective as the screaming and shouting John McEnroe. Sócrates compared himself to the Swede and believed that, with him controlling things in the centre of the park and centre half Amaral bringing a touch of class to the defence, Corinthians had the makings of a team that need not rely on an all-or-nothing style. If football was music, Corinthians were heavy metal and Sócrates wanted to produce something more pleasing on the ear.[25]

He spoke with Amaral, who also wanted to change direction, and together they sat down with the players and backroom staff and formulated a plan. They were both Brazilian internationals who had reached the top by playing patient possession football and they convinced their team-mates that keeping the ball would win them more games than chasing it.

They agreed to give it a go and training was adapted to concentrate more on one- and two-touch football and less on physical conditioning. Slowly but surely they began to evolve and, to reinforce his message, Sócrates went out of his way to teach the fans patience. When Corinthians lost a goal, the momentary silence would be followed seconds later either by howls of outrage or a roar of defiance. Sócrates shut them all out and picked the ball from the net and walked slowly to the centre circle to restart. It allowed him not just to take the heat out of the moment but also to have a word with players as he passed them. When things threatened to get too frenetic, he would make the 'cool down' gesture with his hands, pushing his flat palms up and down and mouthing the words 'Calma, calma'. It was meant first and foremost for his team-mates but it was a message that was never missed on the terraces.

The players understood but the fans took more convincing. Not only were Sócrates and Amaral trying to change a style that had been forged over decades, the slower, more cultured game was too similar to that of hated rivals Palmeiras. Groups of hardcore supporters gathered at the side of the practice ground after each training session and demanded explanations. Sócrates and Amaral, the two most articulate players in the squad, would stand a few metres back from the fence and listen to the club's notoriously irrational supporters sound off.

'Why has the team changed since you two arrived?' one supporter shouted accusingly at the pair. 'Corinthians used to be a team of fighters, now we're all about technique.'

'We're not changing, we're just trying to make the team evolve,' Amaral replied. 'We can't play the same way forever; we can't be content with scraping out one-goal wins. We need to show that we have a great team, one that is worthy of respect. This is a team that can go far. Even if you win all your home games playing average football you won't get any respect when you play away. You need to win respect.'

'We don't want to see that kind of football, at least not all the time,' another fan screamed. 'We want players who will run for the jersey.'

'You can't play one style in one game and another style in another,' Sócrates told them. 'Little by little the team is changing and you'll see our new style. Tell us in a year's time if it was for better or worse.'[26]

The anger that bubbled up in the second half of 1979 was diminished by a typically Brazilian series of events that worked beautifully to Corinthians' advantage. Corinthians were one of 12 teams who qualified for the second stage of the Paulista and in mid-November the Paulista Football Federation took the unusual decision to schedule a double header of games at the Morumbi. Vicente Matheus refused to let his team play Ponte Preta, arguing that Corinthians had more fans not just than Ponte, but of them, Palmeiras and Guarani (the game scheduled to take place before) combined. He didn't want to share the gate money with his rivals and went on the television and radio telling Corinthians fans not to go to the stadium because Corinthians wouldn't be turning up. The federation ignored his appeals for a cancellation, which led to a farcical Sunday when 11 Ponte Preta players lined up for kick-off waiting in vain for their rivals to come down the tunnel.

The issue went to court, causing the semi-finals of the 1979 Campeonato Paulista to be delayed until late January 1980. Until the break, Palmeiras were the form team, going unbeaten and scoring almost twice as many goals as their nearest rivals. But the enforced stoppage halted their momentum and handed the advantage to Corinthians. The teams drew 1-1 in the semi-final first leg, before Corinthians won the second leg with a goal that went in off Biro-Biro's shin.

The final was a best-of-three against Ponte Preta and Corinthians won the first 1-0 and then drew the second 0-0. They needed just a draw to clinch their second title in three years, but they ended up winning with ease, Sócrates and Palhinha getting the goals in a 2-0 victory.

It was the biggest triumph of his career so far but Sócrates was characteristically unenthusiastic about the whole thing. He ran to the fence when he scored the opener after 56 minutes, but he did not do a lap of honour or even acknowledge the acclaim of the crowd when the final whistle went. His promised his shirt to a young supporter, but fans grabbed it as he left the field so he ran to the dressing room, picked up another top and then sprinted back outside to give it to the kid.

He sat calmly in the dressing room afterwards and fought back tears as if trying to maintain his image of coolness person-ified. The win meant a lot to him, but it was tempered by the tough times that had preceded it and the friction with Corinthians fans. 'I have this sensation that I've done my duty,' he told reporters after the game. 'I feel whole, as if I've been doing my job well for a long time.'[27]

They were curiously inscrutable words from someone who had just won a major trophy. Sócrates felt vindicated by the win and the medal was a reward for seeing out those dark days of late 1979. But if he thought it would be blue skies from now on, he still didn't know Corinthians. The club was famous for making its fans and players suffer and 1980 would be a year that tested not just his resolve but whether or not he was truly cut out to be a Corinthiano.

6

'He used to say that football is an intellectual activity.
You use your body but you play with your head. If he was
100 per cent fit but his head wasn't in the right place then
it didn't matter, he didn't play well.'

Wladimir

When Sócrates got pocket money from Seu Raimundo one of
the first things he spent it on was LPs. It was the era of the
Beatles and the Rolling Stones and youngsters were rebelling
across Europe. But Western rock'n'roll was seen as imperial trash
by many Brazilians and at that point in his life Sócrates was one
of them. He would later choose John Lennon as one of his
heroes, but as a young man what he really loved was the music
that spoke to him directly, the music whose lyrics in Portuguese
expressed what he saw and felt in the changing world around
him.

Brazilian music is as varied as it is beautiful, with different
styles marking out different regions. There is samba and bossa
nova from Rio, *forró* in the northeast (which was then brought
south by huge numbers of migrant workers), *frevo* from

Pernambuco, and *sertanejo*, the Brazilian country music that was hugely popular in Ribeirão Preto and the rural heartlands. There are many more, and different styles dominated the airwaves in different regions and all of them competed for airplay with what was known as MPB, *música popular brasileira*, or Brazilian pop music, an all-encompassing genre that was essentially pop songs sung in Portuguese.

Sócrates' parents enjoyed traditional Brazilian folk music and it was these authentic if unsophisticated sounds that encouraged him to end four unproductive years of piano lessons and pick up a guitar. Throughout his life, Sócrates loved nothing better than to sit around with friends, nursing beers and cigarettes and strumming away at the head of a singsong.

'He was the first person I ever saw with a huge LP collection,' said his brother Raimar. 'He had everything, from *sertanejo*, to samba, to MPB; he liked anything and everything. He always had music in him. He knew the songs, he bought them, and he sang them all. He always knew all the words, all the singers.'[1]

In early 1980, the artistic director of RCA Records approached Sócrates with a novel idea. Osmar Zan frequented the same karaoke bar where footballers hung out after matches and, unlike everyone else who heard him sing, Zan thought Sócrates had potential. He offered Sócrates a recording contract and the chance to make an LP of whatever *sertanejo* and traditional Brazilian folk tunes he liked.

'I was close to the Corinthians players and also to the players at São Paulo,' recalled Zan. 'And I knew that Sócrates was from Ribeirão Preto and was very into *sertanejo* music. I was open to doing new things so I asked if I could meet with Sócrates. He came to RCA and we talked over some ideas and I proposed that we do a *sertanejo* LP. He liked the idea and said, "Sure." So we chose some songs. We called a few musicians. And we recorded.'[2]

The LP was called *Casa do Caboclo* and had 12 tracks, most of them *sertanejo* classics or traditional folk ballads he knew from his childhood. *Caboclo* in the indigenous Tupi language means the offspring of an Indian and a white person and has also come to signify a humble, dark-skinned person from the countryside who lives a simple rural life. Written in 1928, the title track spoke to Brazil's poor country folk and it became a standard that is still being recorded by artists today.

His growing popularity at one of Brazil's biggest clubs had given Sócrates a confidence to try these new things and a truly awful singing voice was no obstacle. The record company arranged for a voice coach to prepare him, but they had not bargained for Sócrates' powers of persuasion. On both occasions the coach turned up at his house, Sócrates talked him into having a few drinks before they got started, and sessions that had nothing to do with recording and everything to do with drinking ensued. He struggled when he first entered the studio and merely approaching the microphone left him trembling with fear. He calmed down as time went on and he got used to the equipment, and he was soon confident enough to request retakes and alterations to the production.

Around 50,000 copies of the record were made but it didn't sell and it wasn't a big hit. RCA deleted it from their catalogue just two years later and Sócrates typically never even owned a copy. He had neither the time nor the inclination to promote the album, and once the tracks were done he promptly forgot about it. It was all about trying something different and confounding the conformists. 'I decided to do it because I wanted to break urban prejudice against *sertanejo* music,' he explained.[3]

Sócrates' voice may have been dodgy but he was on song when he got back to playing football.

Corinthians started well in the Brasileiro, winning seven of their nine games and qualifying easily for the next stage, and they continued their good run in the following group stage, losing just one of their six games and progressing to the third round. Sócrates scored 11 goals in 13 games.

The third stage comprised four groups of four, with the teams playing each other just once and the top side going through to the semi-finals. Corinthians had the disadvantage of playing two of their three games away from home and they got off to the worst possible start when Vilson Tadei hammered home a spectacular strike from 35 yards out to give Coritiba (the club's name was spelt differently from that of the city they played in) a 1-0 win.

The loss meant that Corinthians had a mountain to climb to reach the semis, and their task was made harder by post-match comments from president Vicente Matheus. Matheus said that Jairo, the Corinthians keeper who once played for Coritiba, had made a 'strange mistake' and should have stopped Tadei's shot. Some players thought the insinuation was racial, others that Matheus was hinting that Jairo, Curitiba born and bred, had deliberately helped his local club. Whatever the meaning, his comments caused outrage in the squad.

Jairo stayed in Curitiba after the game to see family and so missed most of the immediate controversy. When he arrived back in São Paulo the next day, he was besieged by reporters wanting to know what he thought of Matheus' comment. Jairo was furious and went directly to Matheus' house to have it out with him, but he wasn't at home so it was left to his wife Marlene to promise that her husband would get in touch. Matheus asked Jairo to come by his office, but Jairo refused and the atmosphere at the club worsened. Jairo declined to meet him the next day as well, and it was only on the Wednesday, a full three days later, that the keeper got a much-deserved public apology.

The real story, however, came that night in Corinthians' must-win tie against Grêmio. The home side took the lead in the second minute through Geraldão and then Sócrates got a second 14 minutes later. When the ball hit the net, Sócrates turned and made a beeline towards his own goal. He had organised a special tribute and he ran the length of the field to give Jairo a hug. The rest of the players and the substitutes piled on to the field to join in.

'All the players knew what was happening but I didn't,' Jairo said. 'It was very emotional. They were all jumping on me. The *Gaviões da Fiel* [organised fan group] applauded me, even when I picked up a back pass. And they chanted my name throughout the game. I didn't have much to do but they chanted my name, all because Sócrates had organised this show of support.

'Neither Sócrates nor anyone else explained anything. I went and asked him afterwards and said, "Magrão, you're a piece of work," and he said, "Jairo, this is the least you deserve." And he had some choice words for the president. When Matheus called him to talk about what happened he never went either, he just said, "I'm not going to talk to him. Fuck him." And so he [Matheus] gave an interview saying that Sócrates was trying to turn the fans against him. Which was the same thing he said about me. Sócrates didn't care. He just said, "Fuck him." He was so cool.'[4]

Coritiba's 1-0 win over Botafogo the same night meant Corinthians had to win at Botafogo in their last match and hope that Coritiba lost away to Grêmio. Coritiba went down 1-0 but Corinthians couldn't quite take both points from the Maracanã. Another error from Jairo cost them a goal and although Vaguinho equalised, the draw meant they finished third in the table and fifth in the overall standings of the 1980 Brazilian championship.

*

There was less than a week between the end of the national championship and the start of the Paulista state league and in that time the atmosphere at the Parque São Jorge worsened even further. Jorge Vieira, who had replaced José Teixeira, left the club after the Botafogo game and goalkeeping coach Julinho looked after the team while a new manager was sought.

Jairo was forced to train on his own after Matheus called out his mistake against Botafogo and claimed the keeper had threatened him. Matheus also took aim at Wladimir, the strong-willed full back who was a leader of Brazil's nascent black-power movement and a man who Sócrates quickly identified as smarter than the average footballer. Wladimir said Matheus had promised the club would pay the tax on his signing-on bonus, and when the money was taken from his account he called Matheus a liar. Matheus demanded a formal retraction and Wladimir was out in the cold while the club's lawyers looked for a way to settle the issue.

So, just five days after they were knocked out the 1980 Brasileiro, Corinthians lined up against Botafogo-SP for the opening match of the Paulista. They came away with a 1-1 draw thanks to a late equaliser from Toninho, but if they thought the result might offer them a semblance of stability they were mistaken.

The crisis deepened three days later at home to XV de Piracicaba. Corinthians were awful in a 2-1 defeat and sections of the crowd turned on the players. The main targets were Sócrates and Amaral, who, with unfortunate timing, were pictured the day before holding Roma and Lazio shirts. It was nothing more than a mistimed photo op which came about after fans had asked the pair to pose. But it was easy to misconstrue their intentions given the team's abysmal run of form. Within minutes of the game kicking off, fans were abusing them and calling them mercenaries, and with only 12,000 people at the

Pacaembu stadium the players could hear every insult and every volley of abuse.

Things got even worse after the final whistle. A large group of supporters stayed behind to remonstrate with the players at the back of the stand. Sócrates and Amaral bravely poked their heads out of the door, but the car park was filled with fans baying for their blood and they retreated to the safety of the dressing room. Both of them had come in their own cars and Corinthians' directors thought the mob might be distracted or lose interest if the rest of the team departed in the coach. If they weren't, at least Sócrates and Amaral could sit it out for a while and let the anger subside.[5]

Instead, they were held captive and when they did finally manage to escape, several hours later and under police escort, their cars had been vandalised. A terrified Amaral was so afraid of further attacks that he told reporters he was going directly to pick up his wife and kids and get out of town.

Both were indignant at what were, even by the irrational standards of Corinthians fans, protests out of all proportion to the result. Amaral called it the most humiliating moment of his life and Sócrates declared himself 'deeply hurt'. The accusations of mercenary were especially stinging given that he was earning less than the squad average and around a tenth of what his peers Zico and Falcão were getting. Sócrates lashed out at them for their lack of respect and was forced to backtrack a day later to avoid alienating the vast majority of supporters who had nothing to do with the abuse. He blamed a small number from the organised fan groups for causing trouble, but he could not hide his pain and he once again threatened to quit.

'I always think about packing it in when these things happen,' he told reporters. 'This is a life choice. I am not rich but that's not important. If I earn 8,000 cruzeiros [$160] as a medical resident then fine. Of course, my standard of living will fall but if I need money I can get it, I have two arms and two legs. I know it's only a small number of fans but these guys get to me, you know what I mean? It's really easy to say pay no attention, but it's not just the ego that answers. The kind of person I am, it's truly shocking to me. In this case they are hurting the man. If it was just the professional I wouldn't mind so much.'[6]

But that wasn't the end of the matter. Sócrates' most memorable response came four days later in São José do Rio Preto. Corinthians travelled 270 miles to face América and needed a win to stave off a full-blown crisis. They got it thanks to a Sócrates goal in the 35th minute. But instead of celebrating, Sócrates turned towards the centre circle, lowered his head and walked away. His team-mates went to congratulate him and he shrugged them off, stony-faced.

It was a calculated protest, but his reaction barely registered because the game was played on a Wednesday night in the provinces and was not televised. Sócrates knew he needed to repeat the gesture on a bigger stage if it was to have the desired effect. So exactly a week after he was hounded out of the Pacaembu, he returned to face his tormentors with the intention of sending a message. He did so in style, scoring a hat-trick against Comercial in a 4-2 win.

He refused to celebrate his opening goal, a spectacular free kick fired into the top corner almost from the left-hand touchline. He lifted his arm slowly and deliberately after scoring the second, and repeated the reluctant gesture – and asked to be substituted – after getting the third from the penalty spot after he himself had been felled.

'It's normal for players not to celebrate sometimes but he went even further,' recalled Basílio, one of the senior players in the team that day. 'He just walked away. And we were jumping up and down and Magrão was like, "Yeah, cheers." But he was cool because that was his way. He was always sure of himself.

'We were all surprised by it. We said to him, "Magrão, that's over." And when we were in the changing room after the game he said, "It's about time we showed them that they need to give us more respect." That was his way of putting it. He thought he was right. But I said to him, "Magrão, get it into your head that it's not all of them. It's just a part of the organised fan group that was criticising you and abusing you. So, get it into your head, you need to celebrate. Fine, you're cold and calculating but you need to get the fans on your side." And that was what he did.'[7]

It wasn't the first time Sócrates had conspicuously refused to celebrate a goal, but it was the first time he had done so in response to fans' behaviour. It reinforced his image as a player who lacked emotion and it brought him an undeserved reputation as a joyless man who didn't care about scoring. However, his reaction was anything but typical and Sócrates would later explain that his celebrations could usually be measured in proportion to a goal's importance. In his early days, they were more spontaneous and he often ran to the crowd with his arms thrown high and wide. He later became famous for coolly raising his clenched fist in a militant salute. But by overtly refusing to celebrate his goals against América and Comercial he was deliberately sending a message to fans, and particularly those with the *Gaviões da Fiel*, the main organised fan group.

'Not celebrating goals started as a reaction against the fans' attitude,' he later told Jorge Vasconcellos for his book *Recados da Bola*. 'We lost a game and in the next match when I scored I didn't jump up and down. It was my way of saying, "Look, I didn't like what you did in the last match." The fans had reacted aggressively so I wanted to show them on the pitch that I was not happy with that reaction. It was as if I was saying, "Let's both be clear about this: this is the way I am, when I think something isn't right I'll show you, it's my way of expressing myself."

'When you work with the public you have to know how to deal with them, otherwise you're throwing away a great potential. The fans have a say in who wins: that's why it's necessary to work with that collective psychology, that collective energy. I had to create a way of communication with my public so that in one way or another I worked with them and not against them; if I didn't do that I'd be putting my work and the team's work in jeopardy.

'You need to be aware of the importance and the power that the fans have. They can knock a team down or lift it up; you have to know how to work with that, people on the pitch need to know that's the way it is, because if you manage to create a communication and harness that energy it's much easier. At Corinthians, there's this emotional thing going on, a real madness. It needs to be put into perspective. My perspective was "harness this and we're going to work properly". For me it was critical to establish that communication.'[8]

Sócrates had been mobbed after his starring performance against Comercial but he was in no mood to declare a unilateral ceasefire in his war with the club. Both he and Amaral reported for international duty and missed the next match, a 2-0 win over São Bento in front of just 6,571 people, Corinthians' lowest crowd of the season. Coincidentally or not, their absence coincided with a grim few weeks for the club as they embarked on a dismal run of six consecutive draws, four of which were goalless.

Even while on international duty Sócrates was turning the incident over in his head. He had invested almost two years at the club and did not want the time and effort to be in vain. He was getting used to living in São Paulo, with people he now considered friends. He was one of the best-known footballers in the country and he wasn't planning to let a few abusive fans spoil it all.

What he decided to do was to seek some sort of reparation when he negotiated a new contract the following month. Sócrates wanted to stay at Corinthians because of the massive platform it gave him to speak to an entire city, and he knew a transfer made little sense because fans could be just as fickle elsewhere. He said he now had 'a connection' to the club and that he had 'created a base there and that can't and shouldn't be thrown away'.

But if he was going to stick it out and risk further abuse, he at least wanted to be properly recompensed. He gave another long interview while on international duty, repeating his alarm at the fans' treatment and committing himself to Corinthians. But the interview was interesting because it contained the first hint that he wanted a role off the field. Corinthians Democracy was still a long way off but Sócrates was starting to fantasise about running the show.

At the time, no one gave his comments a second thought. Players had never sought control of a football club and a man like Matheus was never going to cede power, especially in a country that hadn't seen democracy for a generation. But in hindsight Sócrates' message was clear. He saw himself as more than just a footballer.

'What I want is to demonstrate that I am important to the club and vice versa,' he said. 'Maybe there are already signs of that. I have a sense the president is closer, independent of the fact that I am looking to get closer to him. I want to warm relations inside the club, do more, participate more in the decisions. Returning to the group will be immediate and things won't be just financial. Players need to feel an emotional connection and I am looking for that in a role for myself. Then maybe my rationality – which at the root of things is the biggest barrier between myself and the fans, although I think they should adapt – might change. If I could take part in the decisions within the club my behaviour is going to change in a lot of ways.'[9]

Before he could even begin to think about his role off the field he needed to guarantee his place on it with a new contract. Sócrates had been angry at Matheus' refusal to renegotiate his existing deal the year before but he had taken a pragmatic and ruthless approach. He decided to keep his head down and continue playing. He believed his performances would improve and that his price would rise. He was right, and now he wanted to make Matheus pay for his intransigence.

Sócrates good-naturedly dubbed Matheus 'the old man' soon after arriving at the club and he was one of the boss's favourites during his first few months there. Sócrates thought Matheus 'one of the most honest people I ever knew' and respected him as a professional administrator who not only had the best interests of the club at heart but who also 'took responsibility for his acts', a rarity in the opaque world of Brazilian football.[10]

Matheus, however, was also one of the most intractable people Sócrates had ever met, and for a man who valued compromise that caused no end of suffering. Their stalemate the previous year had perplexed Sócrates, who saw his proposal as a good deal for both sides, and he found it hard to forgive Matheus for his stubbornness.

Sócrates' contract ended on 3 August 1980 and negotiations to renew it turned into a weeks-long soap opera that kept the Brazilian press titillated and the fans on tenterhooks. Sócrates contested four internationals in June – against Mexico, the USSR, Chile and Poland – and he returned to his club as the new Brazil captain, having been installed as official leader in the 2-0 win over Mexico. But he wasn't at the Parque São Jorge for long.

Corinthians finished fifth in the league table and missed out on the semi-finals of the Campeonato Paulista in July, and their enforced three-week break gave both parties a chance to sit down and resolve the situation. But attitudes had hardened and neither side wanted to give an inch, even after his absence was felt in the 4-0 drubbing by São Paulo in the first match of the second half of the Paulista. Once again, Sócrates threatened to retire if he wasn't paid what he thought he was worth and, when asked what his chances of staying with Corinthians were on a scale of one to 100, Sócrates replied, 'None.'

Two days after the defeat by São Paulo, Sócrates' father tried to kick-start negotiations, with a proposal worth 33.6 million cruzeiros ($1.24 million) over two years. After consulting Flamengo and Internacional to find out how much they were paying Zico and Falcão, the two highest-paid players in Brazil, Corinthians came back with a top offer of 28.4 million cruzeiros ($1.05 million).

Sócrates had three factors working in his favour against the famously stubborn Matheus. The first was that Corinthians were struggling and obviously missed their midfield general. They had won just three of the nine games they had played since the start of July and lost three of the four *clássicos*, including two to São Paulo, a team that hadn't beaten them in the previous four years.

The second advantage was the return of Osvaldo Brandão, who replaced Orlando Fantoni after a hapless 13-game spell. Brandão had left Corinthians a few months before Sócrates signed in 1978 and had had mixed success at Ponte Preta, Portuguesa and Palmeiras. But he had a wealth of experience and he knew a good player when he saw one. He wanted Sócrates back in a Corinthians shirt and one of the first things he did on returning to the club was to lobby both Sócrates and Matheus to end the impasse.

A third factor was that other teams were watching the soap opera with increasing interest. São Paulo publicly asked to speak to the player – reportedly offering future World Cup striker Serginho in a swap deal – and Flamengo were prepared to hand over 30 million cruzeiros ($1.1 million) and international midfielder Adílio. Internacional sent scouts from Porto Alegre, and Santos and Botafogo also registered interest. Matheus was crazy but he was not stupid and he knew what the fans' reaction would be if he sold their best player to a rival side.

Matheus rejected his initial terms and Seu Raimundo came back with a new offer that included the right to use the Corinthians logo in publicity deals, as well as 10 per cent of the gate money from friendlies played in Brazil and 15 per cent from those played abroad. Matheus accused Sócrates of wanting 'half of the Parque São Jorge' and leaked his demands to the press, blatantly telling a radio show that Sócrates was asking for a percentage of all the club's gate money, not just from friendlies. That lie infuriated the player even further.

Sócrates was sensitive to the fact that many of the fans who came to watch him earned the minimum wage of 4,149 cruzeiros ($78) a month, and he was worried that even if he did return he would lose their backing once and for all. Supporters who called radio phone-ins and took part in local polls felt he was asking too much. He had already faced unfair accusations of being a mercenary and the last thing he wanted was more grief from the terraces. So after going to Ribeirão Preto to talk with friends and family he returned to São Paulo with a new attitude. He went back to training on 19 August and called on fans to support him.

'No player can be unwelcome at his own club,' he said. 'The biggest stimulus for an athlete is having the fans on his side. If it wasn't for that then I wouldn't agree to stay with Corinthians. And for that to happen I am going to need a solid psychological base.

'I can't assume sole responsibility for the whole team,' he added. 'I just think that I need to be a conscientious professional and show my value on the pitch. If the club pays me X or Y it's because of what I can do. I am not going to play good or bad according to what I earn, but because of what I can do. I think a guy should earn according to what he can give the company.'[11]

It was a pre-emptive ploy. Sócrates had had enough of the uncertainty and mind games. He turned up unannounced at Matheus' house the next day and the two of them quickly hashed out a deal. When they were done, they phoned Sócrates' father to come and work out the details. Once they'd put pen to paper, Matheus ordered a takeaway and they ate fried chicken and drank wine and whisky for several hours more.

Although the terms of the deal were not made public, newspapers speculated he would get a 12 million cruzeiro ($219,000) signing-on bonus and then 500,000 a month ($9,100) for the first year and 700,000 a month ($7,100) for the second year. [Exchange rate fluctuations account for the US dollar reduction.] Matheus said Sócrates was now one of the best-paid players in Brazil, and Sócrates declared he no longer needed to worry about money.[12]

Sócrates also said the promise of a bigger say in how the club was run was a key factor in him putting pen to paper. But he still had a problem. In the midst of all the negotiations, he had admitted he didn't yet love the club and said he saw himself much like an employee at a multinational. He was merely being honest, but he knew such candour was dangerous when discussing Corinthians. He was anxious about the reception he would get against América and was nervous as he made his way to the Pacaembu.

He needn't have worried. Fans outside the ground chanted 'Doctor! Doctor!' as he got off the team coach and his name was cheered loudest when the line-ups were announced. It was his first game for almost seven weeks and he repaid the 37,000 fans with an outstanding performance in Corinthians' 2-1 victory. When América took the lead from the spot three minutes into the second half, he picked up the ball and walked slowly back to the centre circle in what was a gesture calculated to give the players confidence and show the fans that, in spite of all the controversy, he had not changed. Five minutes later he was fouled inside the box and put away the penalty himself. He even had a hand in Toninho's winner 17 minutes later.

Mobbed by reporters and TV cameras after the game, he tried to explain what it all meant to him but it soon became impossible. Around 200 ecstatic fans fought their way into the dressing room, chanting his name. Good-naturedly barging past the press and players, they lifted him above their heads and deliriously celebrated his return to the fold. Finally, he could contain himself no longer. Finally, he cried.

The new contract made him one of the highest-paid players in Brazil and brought with it a further raft of responsibilities. Paramount among them was the need to prove to the supporters that he was now one of them, that his hard-fought signing of a new deal committed him to the club not just in body but also in spirit.

He celebrated his penalty against América by running to the fans, both fists held aloft and his arms outstretched. It was the kind of celebration his team-mates had been urging him to do for years, but Sócrates didn't feel comfortable pretending to love the team as much as those lifelong fans who had watched them through thick and thin. He tried to tell them that being dispassionate did not mean he lacked passion, but rather that he was able to control his emotions for a greater good, or, in his words, that he had an 'indispensable composure at the crucial moments'.[13] He understood that fans were emotional. He understood that he was different. And he understood that not all of them would relate to him. It was their refusal to accept him for who he was that bothered him, and he repeatedly urged fans to get behind the team and transform their anger into something more positive.

His appeals were heartfelt and Matheus' promises to give him more of a say in club affairs were key in convincing him to make more of an effort. He was now on one of the biggest salaries at the club, and friends convinced him it was vital to give more in return.

He enjoyed a short honeymoon after signing the new deal. Corinthians beat Marília, Santos and XV de Jaú by the same 3-0 scoreline, put four past Guarani without reply, and lost just once in 14 games to resuscitate their chances of qualifying for the semi-finals.

Sócrates grabbed a hat-trick against XV and scored both goals in Corinthians' 2-1 win over Palmeiras as he hammered home 10 goals in 14 games. But the schizophrenia that plagued Corinthians was never far away and it inevitably came to the fore in October after a 1-0 loss to Portuguesa at the Morumbi. Corinthians created chance after chance but couldn't put the ball in the net and then watched their opponents charge up the pitch to score a winning goal in the dying minutes.

The fans went mad and Sócrates was once again singled out as the main target. With shouts of 'Mercenary!' ringing in his ears, hooligans tried to assault him as he emerged from the dressing room and, although the police made sure he didn't come to any harm, his car wasn't so lucky. Supporters lobbed a rock through the windscreen, smashed the headlights and bashed in the doors and bonnet.[14]

He had grown almost sanguine about the behaviour, having realised that he had nothing to gain by hitting back. He publicly admitted he had maybe treated football as a hobby for too long and he vowed to be more professional in the future. Corinthians still managed to qualify for the semi-finals, due in no small part to Sócrates' double against Noroeste in their penultimate game, but they were no match for Ponte Preta, who hammered them 4-1 over two legs.[15]

That meant they would round out the season with three weeks of meaningless friendlies. They were especially meaningless to Sócrates, who was looking forward to a break from the irrationality. He had bigger battles to fight. A new start with a new manager awaited at the seleção. Preparations for his first World Cup were about to get under way.

7

'The one with the gift for leadership is Sócrates. He is intelligent, a serious professional and humble in his dealings with us. He acts as a kind of magnet for the group; he attracts the problems and takes it upon himself to resolve them.'

Zico

On 30 March 1980, Sócrates walked into the Paineiras Hotel in Rio de Janeiro to prepare for a friendly against a Brazilian youth select. The hotel was stuck high on a hill overlooking the statue of Christ the Redeemer and parrots and monkeys hooted and honked in the lush green forest that surrounded it. Sócrates ambled in nervously and greeted his team-mates with smiles and embraces. Sitting further back on a sofa was coach Telê Santana, who got up and gave him a warm handshake to welcome him to the squad.

'I was apprehensive when I arrived as this was the first time we had met,' Sócrates recalled. 'I don't exactly know why but I always feel a little uncomfortable when I come across new situations or people. Fortunately, I already knew most of my team-mates well. When I walked into the foyer, I saw some people seated to the right. I walked towards them to say hello. Telê was there. I could see he was simply dressed and sitting there comfortably and discreetly. When he saw me he gave me a long but timid smile and he made a point of getting up to greet me. We shook hands. His look was profound and incisive and filled me with complete confidence. His rough, pock-marked skin told the story of his life so far.'[1]

'Although he was small, he gave the impression that he was strong and secure. I couldn't help but compare him to my father. I knew instantly that we would get on well. People who count sensibility and sincerity among their virtues are easy to deal with, even when they have a higher rank or superior position. With them, relationships are always transparent and honest.'[2]

One of 10 siblings born in a rural mining town in Minas Gerais, Telê, as everyone in Brazil came to know him, was interested only in football. He began his career at local club Itabirense and moved from there to América de São João del Rei before eventually signing for Fluminense, where his skinny build and never-say-die attitude won him the nickname 'Thread of Hope'.[3]

After winning a series of titles with the Rio club in the 1950s, the winger spent shorter spells at Guarani, Madureira and Vasco da Gama before hanging up his boots and getting into coaching. He won state championships with Fluminense, Atlético Mineiro and Grêmio before being appointed Brazil manager in 1980, the first man ever to be given the job on a full-time basis.[4]

Telê was a football man who lived and breathed the game. He would turn up at his club's training grounds to weed the pitch and cut the grass because he knew that good players love to play on a pristine surface. Training was more about ball work than running, and when he took over at the seleção he brought in youth teams and local sides to play friendlies so that his team would have a chance to get to know each other in a match environment.[5]

He was a notoriously hard taskmaster but his players loved him because he was fair and because he gave them free rein to play football. He picked the best 11 and told them to get on with it, never worrying too much about tactics, preferring to focus on maintaining a balance and a spirit he trusted the players themselves to nurture.

Telê was also insistent that his players play to win and to win with style. To him, the most important qualities in both a footballer and a man were hard work, discipline and integrity.

'A guy scores a goal with a handball in the 47th minute of the second half and wins the game, does that satisfy me?' he said. 'No. I'll get my win bonus but I'll be ashamed to win a game that way. I want to see good football and I am not alone. Everybody wants to see good football. Isn't that better than seeing punts up the field? It's much better. I don't go to football to see that.'[6]

Telê took over the reins at the seleção in February 1980, just a fortnight after his Palmeiras side lost to Corinthians in the delayed semi-final of the 1979 Paulista state championship. Brazil's elimination by Paraguay in the 1979 Copa América meant that Claudio Coutinho had failed to win a second tournament in succession and such failure was unforgiveable for Brazilian coaches. Fresh ideas were required.

The night after bringing his first squad together for the match against the youth select, Telê made it clear that Sócrates would not be an automatic first choice, which surprised many given that he was one of the outstanding footballers in the country at the time. The manager explained that he wanted to see his players playing in their club positions and that Sócrates was playing in a deeper midfield role for Corinthians. He wanted a more orthodox centre forward and gave Reinaldo the nod.

Sócrates replaced Falcão at half-time in the match (one of seven substitutes including, curiously, Baltazar, who played for both sides) and brought a sense of fluidity to the team. After going in 2-0 up at the break, Brazil improved in the second period and eventually won the match 7-0.

Telê's decision to start Sócrates on the bench was a half-hearted attempt to test him. Telê didn't know Sócrates personally but he had heard the same gossip as everyone else and he had doubts about whether he possessed the discipline necessary to play for one of his teams.

Friendly journalists had warned Sócrates he needed to gain the new manager's confidence and Sócrates played the good soldier. He calmly accepted his place on the bench and passed the test with flying colours. Telê picked him to start the next game a month later, another unofficial match at the Maracanã, this time against a Minas Gerais state select. Sócrates got the third in a 4-0 win and obviously impressed. When he chose his team to play Mexico in June, Telê made Sócrates captain, a move he said came as 'a pleasant surprise'.

'I knew that he was placing a tremendous responsibility on my shoulders,' Sócrates said. 'Playing for Brazil was always my dream and it was what made me delay my medical career, but I had never imagined that one day I would assume such a prestigious position. That yellow and green armband on my left arm was a weight and an honour and I had to quickly understand exactly what it represented. However, even though I was frightened by the news I felt proud and confident. I knew that from then on in I would have to do more than ever to live up to the faith he had placed in me.'[7]

The year 1980 was a period of transition for the seleção. After the two bounce games against youth and state selects they played nine official friendlies, losing just one, a 2-1 defeat by the USSR in June. Played out of position on the right wing, Sócrates had his worst game yet for the seleção and was booed off after being subbed, justifiably, he said, because both he and the team hadn't performed to anything like the best of their ability.

That, though, was their only hiccup. Chile, Uruguay, Paraguay (twice) and Switzerland were all vanquished, and Poland came away from the Morumbi with a 1-1 draw. Sócrates was an ever-present and captained the side in all the games.

The friendlies were a lead-up to the end of the year's Gold Cup, a tournament organised to commemorate the 50th anniversary of the first World Cup held in Uruguay in 1930. Also known as the *Mundialito*, or Little World Cup, it featured all the previous winners except England, who turned down the invitation and were replaced by Holland, the finalists at the last two tournaments.

For Brazil, the *Mundialito* was to be reminiscent of two of their most memorable World Cups, but for very different reasons. As in 1970, they went to the competition with few fans believing they could win. But just as they did in Mexico, they defied both the pessimistic forecasts and the odds. They were without two of their best players, Zico and Reinaldo, both of whom were injured and never even travelled with the squad, and first choice goalkeeper Carlos went home early after dislocating his shoulder in the opening match.

Brazil were drawn in Group B, along with Argentina and West Germany, with the winner of the group going through to the final to meet the winner of Group A containing Uruguay, Holland and Italy.

Sócrates went into the tournament in fine form, scoring freely for an inconsistent Corinthians side.

He recovered from a knee injury picked up in training and was declared fit for Brazil's opening match against Argentina.

The Argentines hadn't beaten Brazil since March 1970 and they went all out to break that streak. It was a typically tumultuous South American *clássico*, with Diego Maradona opening the scoring on the half-hour, before Edevaldo lashed home an equaliser right after the break. Brazil had several great chances to score and had one goal erroneously chalked off for offside, while Argentina hit the post and missed an open goal. At the final whistle, instead of trading shirts, the players traded punches in the centre circle.

The result meant Brazil needed to beat West Germany – who had lost their opener 2-1 to Argentina – by two clear goals if they were to pip the Argentines to a place in the final.

Once again Brazil went behind after Klaus Allofs put away an easy cross in the 54th minute. But Brazil fought back and steamrollered the European champions. Júnior equalised with a beautiful free kick on 57 minutes, Cerezo put their noses in front three minutes later, and after 75 minutes they got the goal that counted when Sócrates, with his only real contribution of the game, got away from defender Bernard Dietz and rolled the ball across goal for Serginho to tap home. Zé Sergio put the icing on the cake with a fourth in the 81st minute.

That set them up for a final against the hosts, who had delighted the home fans by beating the weak Dutch and Italian sides by the same 2-0 scoreline.

The final, however, was more reminiscent of a less happy World Cup game for Brazil, the 1950 *Maracanazo*, when Brazil lost 2-1 at home to Uruguay. As 30 years previously, Brazil were favourites but they were surprised by Uruguay's fight and determination. The home side took the lead after 50 minutes, when defensive dithering allowed Jorge Barrios to fire home from close range. After a powerful run from the centre circle, Sócrates was felled inside the box 12 minutes later and he got up to coolly side-foot home the penalty. But Uruguay bounced back and took the lead with 10 minutes remaining thanks to another lapse in defence.

That was it, with the 2-1 scoreline not just repeating the famous result in 1950, but also marking Uruguay's first victory over Brazil in more than 20 years.

The tournament gave Sócrates vital international experience, but he looked unprepared for the increased physical demands of playing against the best in the world. Without Zico and Reinaldo, Telê played him out of position as a target man and his real impact came when he dropped deeper to make way for Serginho at centre forward. If the tournament was memorable for anything, it was the Mexican moustache he wore in the opener against Argentina but shaved off the next day after his team-mates ribbed him mercilessly.

From Uruguay, the seleção went on a Latin American tour that encompassed two friendlies and two World Cup qualifiers. Brazil were lucky to have been drawn in the easiest group, alongside Bolivia and Venezuela, but they were worried about playing in La Paz and so travelled to Colombia and Ecuador to prepare at altitude for what they considered the key match in the group. They drew 1-1 in Colombia, before edging Venezuela 1-0 in the qualifier and then defeating Ecuador 6-0 in the mountains of Quito.

The game against Bolivia was the hardest of them all, but Sócrates played a blinder and justified Telê's decision to make him leader. Although there was serious doubt about whether he was fit enough to handle the rarefied air of the Bolivian city, he turned in a command performance, scoring Brazil's opener and then feeding Reinaldo for the winner. He was given oxygen at half-time and again on the sidelines as Brazil fought to contain Bolivia following Cerezo's dismissal on the hour. Brazil should have had the game wrapped up by then, hitting the woodwork three times, but they held out in the end, as did Sócrates' legs.

He lost four kilos through his running and when he returned home his prestige was higher than ever.

After easy home wins against Bolivia and Venezuela guaranteed their place in Spain, the seleção went to Europe to test themselves against the best in the world. The two-week tour to play England, France and West Germany was Sócrates' first trip outside South America, and he was captivated by reporters who briefed him about London and Paris and the galleries and museums there. Seeing the *Mona Lisa* at the Louvre was his priority, he said, but the most memorable picture of the trip was him beaming with delight as he stepped off a red London double-decker bus.

Instead, the culture came on the field, where Brazil outplayed all three of their opponents. A 1-0 win at Wembley marked the first time that England had ever lost to South American opposition at home; France's 3-1 defeat three days later was their first loss at the Parc des Princes since 1975; and the 2-1 win over West Germany was more comprehensive than the scoreline suggested.

The victories restored some of lustre Brazil had lost in the dismal decade after their last World Cup win, with the Germans calling them 'the best team in the world' and British bookies making them 5–2 favourites to win a fourth World Cup a year hence. The successes had fans back home believing another title was almost a formality, while the European media were only slightly less congratulatory in elevating Sócrates and Zico to a select group of world greats alongside Karl-Heinz Rummenigge, Ruud Krol, Diego Maradona and Kevin Keegan.

Sócrates was flattered by the compliments but, contrarian as ever, said it might have been better had Brazil not won all three games so convincingly, because their superiority could lull them into believing there was no room for improvement ahead of the main event.

'The only danger we have is ourselves,' he said prophetically. 'There's no one better than Brazil. We have to believe that because that was what we saw in Europe. But we can't relax and think that no one is going to beat us. I think that is going to be our big challenge from now on.'[8]

After Brazil beat West Germany to make it three wins out of three, the players hit the town in Stuttgart for a celebratory *bier*. Reporters found Sócrates surrounded by team-mates and beer bottles and asked if they could film an interview. Sócrates agreed and a reporter went to clear the empties from the table in front of him.

'What do you think you're doing?' Sócrates asked.

'I don't want to compromise your image . . .' the reporter replied.

'Put them down!' Sócrates barked. 'I drink when I want to drink. I'm an adult with children. I've already got one father and I don't need another one.'[9]

Neither the harsher spotlight at Corinthians nor taking centre stage at the seleção led Sócrates to drink less. He refused to hide his fondness for the bevvy and he wanted people to know he was a professional footballer who could play at the highest level and not care what anyone thought of him.

Winning after drinking was better than just winning because it provided the perfect rebuttal to those who said football players should treat their bodies as temples. 'When people give me compliments no one says that I smoke my cigarettes or that I like to drink my beer,' he said. 'It's funny, why do they only say that when I am not playing well?'[10]

Sócrates had been in São Paulo for almost three years and he was starting to gain the reputation that his drinking deserved. After spending his early years in the city drinking either discreetly or at home, he had by now made friends and the metropolis no longer scared him like it once did. Footballers had their hang-outs and reporters knew them, but they didn't make a big deal of it because to do so would mean an end to their access. Occasionally, *conselheiros* or others inside the club would complain about players' excesses, but Sócrates thought they were fools for not understanding that the footballer's drink of choice was not beer but the more potent *cachaça*. Drinking beer was the lesser of two evils and he thought they should be congratulated for taking it relatively easy and not hiding what they were doing.

His refusal to apologise brought him grief at Corinthians, but even there he preferred to confront the critics rather than hide. There were bars scattered throughout the Parque São Jorge and before Sócrates joined the club the players rarely dared to drink in them because fans could see what they were up to. If they lost a game the day after drinking openly, they knew the backlash would be quick and nasty.

After establishing himself as the club's predominant player at the start of the decade, Sócrates took pleasure in leading groups of players to the Bar da Torre (Tower Bar). Located at the bottom of an old water tower just 50 yards from the players' dressing room, the Bar da Torre was a humble little café-cum-bar that sold snacks and drinks. In the years to come, the players would nickname it 'The Senate', the place where they debated Corinthians Democracy, but at first it was simply somewhere to relax after training.

'When we finished training on a Saturday morning we would all go to the Bar da Torre and have two or three crates of beer,' said his team-mate Basílio. 'The critics and the *conselheiros* saw us – we called them the old men – and they went crazy. They said, "What are you doing drinking? We have a game tomorrow! This is anarchy, you're having a laugh! If you lose tomorrow we're going to come after you!" And we couldn't have cared less. No one got drunk because there were a lot of us. We knew we had to play well the next day so that it wasn't used against us. And when we were on a winning streak the critics appeared and said, "Hey, don't worry, I'll get this round."'[11]

Drinking in public was about challenging authority but it was also about camaraderie. Sócrates was a social animal and never happier than when surrounded by friends; drinking, laughing and mercilessly taking the mickey. The dark side of that sociability, however, was a fear of being alone. It was a typically Brazilian weakness that could be both comical and infuriating, and it sometimes led to clashes with his friends. Sócrates would often hold parties that lasted until dawn. He had no problem drinking the whole night but not everyone found it so easy. Wimping out was fine, but leaving him to drink alone was not, and if the party started to wind down before he was ready to call it a night he would hide the front-door key so his guests couldn't get out. In São Paulo, he would close the cloakroom at the Hilton where he held birthday parties so that the wives couldn't get their coats and handbags to leave. In Rio, where he lived in a mansion behind a massive wall, he would lock the door and then throw the key away.[12]

'Once everyone had arrived he'd toss the key over the wall and the wall was high,' recalled Leandro, his team-mate at Brazil and Flamengo. 'The first person who wanted to leave was the one that found out. He'd say, "I have no idea where it is, someone must have taken it – maybe it was one of the kids," as there were always kids running about. I loved it. I was single and if I had to stay until six or seven in the morning then that was fine. But there were married guys and they had to leave. One in the morning came round and he wouldn't let them go. There were people sleeping on the sofas. Some people never came back. They'd say, "I love you, Sócrates, and you can come to my house, or we can go out to a restaurant, but I'm not coming back here to get locked in again."'[13]

'What he was doing with the key thing was saying, "It's great that you're here, I love being around you. It's important to me and I am going to keep you around as long as possible." He was happy when he was surrounded by people. He had two sides; he liked to read and to be alone, but he much preferred to be with a lot of people, chatting, drinking his beer, having a laugh.'[14]

Sócrates never intellectualised football. In fact, he never even spoke much about it. He believed that football was a game to be played and watched, not to be discussed. He patiently listened to fans when they talked about games or goals, but he found the conversations boring. He had little time for analysis and even less time for nostalgia. Like many great players, he couldn't explain how he did what he did, and he had no intention of trying.

Sócrates never even watched games after he'd played in them. Early in his career, he had the chance to review his performance on video tape and he came away thinking that he remembered the game better from his own vantage point on the pitch. After that, he almost never watched videos of himself again.[15]

Instead of talking about football, Sócrates talked about everything else. His public persona, especially after he had hit the headlines for his political and social activism, was that of a serious man with a gruff voice, who casually imparted wise words on weighty issues. But to people who spent time with him, to family, to interviewers, to those who listened to his talks and presentations after he'd retired, he wasn't serious at all. He was funny and self-deprecating and he took the mickey every chance he got, out of both his friends and himself.

'His sense of humour was cutting,' said Mauro Beting, a Brazilian media personality who worked with Sócrates on TV and then chaired corporate presentations he gave a few years before his death. 'But hidden in among the jokes, in the middle of the wicked humour, he'd come out with some erudite concept. He'd be taking the piss and he'd get something in his head and he'd get going on some really serious subject, and then he'd jump right back to taking the piss.

'He could talk about absolutely anything, it was very impressive. No matter what he talked about, he talked with passion and conviction. And even when it was nonsense, it was Sócrates speaking, and so it came with an air of erudition. Sometimes he'd be drunk and his arguments were even more brilliant, and the drink made it funny and unthreatening.'[16]

His caustic wit also shone through in another of his hobbies – that of giving people nicknames. Brazil's everyday informality means that everyone has nicknames, irrespective of their background or social standing. Such informality is especially prevalent in football, where no one knows Edson or Arthur or Manuel, but everyone recognises Pelé, Zico and Garrincha. Sócrates gave team-mates nicknames as a way of creating an instant connection with them and he didn't care if the target objected. In fact, he prided himself on being able to hit a nerve.

Wladimir never liked being called 'Saci', after a mythical black creature of Brazilian folklore, and Zé Maria, the Corinthians captain, wasn't unhappy that his name 'Bocão' (Big Mouth), given to him because of the beaming smile that filled his face, never caught on.

Some of his ideas were more creative than others. His good friend Ney was only ever called 'Asshole', and the receding hairline of compact midfielder Elzo won him the name 'Carequinha', or Little Baldie. Maurinho Saquy was forever called 'Cripple' because of the persistent injuries that forced him out of the game at an early age.

Júnior was 'Helmet', because of his Afro hairdo, President Lula was 'Beard', and Botafogo team-mate Marinho was christened 'Sloth' because he hated training. One of his most memorable designations came at Fiorentina, with the arrival of a teenager from Vicenza with the half-perm, half-mullet of a 1980s pop star. 'Your name is Boy George,' Sócrates told the kid, who smiled shyly at being singled out. His real name? Roberto Baggio.[17]

When Sócrates returned from Brazil's jaunt around Latin America in April 1981 he found a club in crisis. Corinthians started 1981 in much the same form they had ended 1980, winning just four of the 15 Brasileiro games they played without their leader. After going down 4–1 at home to Santa Cruz, their second three-goal loss in a week, Matheus took drastic action, transfer-listing a handful of first-team players that included Amaral, Geraldão and Vaguinho. Players' representative Wladimir wanted Sócrates to intervene, but he was on the other side of the continent and by the time he returned three weeks later the purge was complete.

Sócrates' football had improved greatly over the previous year and his experiences with the seleção had been hugely beneficial. Telê trusted him enough to let him tweak the side or their tactics during a match and he thought about the game more than ever before. His shooting had improved – he was standing closer to the ball and getting more power in his shots – and his passing and positioning were still better than anyone else in Brazil. He was more of a team player than at Botafogo and, having reached a new level of fitness, he was more consistent. The improvements, he said, were down to the maturity and personal responsibility he had found at home. A second son, Gustavo, was born in 1979 and Marcelo followed a year later and, while Sócrates often acted more like a big brother than a father, he believed the increased responsibility had an effect on the way he played.

'It's very clear to me that my game has improved as a conse-
quence of me maturing personally,' he said. 'Life experience,
inner peace, and self-confidence are all factors that have influ-
enced my performances. You know why? Because I had to do
a lot of things very early. When I was 17, I was already at university around older and more interesting people. By the time
I was 19, I was a professional football player and making a living.
By 20, I was married, and I didn't need to ask my family for
money. By 21, I was a father. By the time I made the Brazil
team, I was 25 and my head was already in the right place. And
that made things much easier.'[18]

But even with Sócrates back in the side Corinthians didn't
do much better in the Paulista. His form was decent and in June
he scored two of what he considered the best goals of his career
so far, a back-heel against Guarani in Campinas and a stunner
a week later against Botafogo, when, on the edge of the box
and with his back to goal, he flicked the ball up and over the
defender behind him with his right foot, and then spun around
and volleyed the ball home with his left.

Unfortunately for Corinthians, he wasn't dominating
matches for them like he had for Brazil a few weeks earlier,
and it took him a while to get back into the groove at club
level. He defended his lack of influence as temporary, a phase
brought on by his four months away from the club. Sócrates
was surprised at how much the team had changed in the time
he had been away. Corinthians had signed a bunch of players
to replace those released by Matheus, and Sócrates was worried they would resort to the full-blooded charges of old. He
had yet to form a bond with the new men and found it harder
to play with them and for them. The Brazil players were his
friends, men he respected greatly because of their international caps, and that made a big difference to his performances.
He believed that he played better alongside friends than

strangers. 'Football is fleeting,' he said. 'Friendships are what matter.'[19]

Sócrates was also a big-game player, one of those men who had the knack of raising his performance level for the fixtures that counted. He enjoyed the matches in big stadiums, with wall-to-wall media coverage and intense pressure from fans. Ever the contrarian, it wasn't simply that he enjoyed those games; he thought that playing against the likes of Argentina at a packed Monumental in Buenos Aires was easier than turning it on against São Bento in front of a few hundred people in Sorocaba.

The Paulista matches should have been easy for the Corinthians players, but their struggles continued into the second half of the year. Sócrates played in 19 of their 25 Paulista fixtures between August and November, and the tournament was more important than ever as it had been designated a qualifying competition for the 1982 Brasileiro. The top seven teams in state tournaments qualified for the national league, but Corinthians won just eight times to end up in eighth position, one spot outside the qualifying places. The result meant they would begin 1982 in the Taça de Prata (Silver Cup), a competition that was effectively the second division.

The turmoil was in part a reflection of what was happening off the pitch. On the managerial side, Osvaldo Brandão, the latest incumbent, resigned after the club drew 3-3 at home to Juventus on 15 July and he was replaced by former goalkeeping coach Julinho. Julinho lasted just three months in charge and Mário Travaglini took over in late September. Travaglini would become a key ally for Sócrates in the year to come, but the most important changes took place at boardroom level.

The club's constitution prevented Vicente Matheus from running for a third consecutive term as president, but the wily Matheus did a deal with his friend and vice president Waldemar

Pires. Matheus didn't want to step down and Pires was quite happy being number two, so although they swapped roles on the ballot paper they planned to continue as before, with Matheus in charge and Pires his assistant. The ruse was apparent to all and sundry, but no one really cared and they were handy winners when the votes were counted in early April. The new arrangement worked fine throughout the early winter months, but it went awry in memorable style when the famously dictatorial Matheus went too far. Not only did he refuse to give up the president's office or parking space, his security men at one point blocked Pires from sitting in the directors' box at a game.

The humiliation stung Pires into action and in August he surprised everyone, and particularly Matheus, by demanding his rightful place as president. Matheus at first baulked, then retreated; and, when he realised that Pires was not going to back down, he resigned, leaving the new man to put his own team in place.

That directorial merry-go-round would have a profound impact on the club's future, but Sócrates' present was more about changes in his own outlook and frame of mind. He had struggled to adapt at Corinthians but now, two and a half years later, the worst was over and he was ready to admit he had developed feelings for the club.

Maybe it was his exalted position with supporters. He was the only Corinthiano in a Brazil squad that contained six players from São Paulo, five from Atlético Mineiro and three from Flamengo, and Corinthians fans could see that he was the standout member of an otherwise unremarkable group.

Maybe it was attrition. Team-mates had long told him to embrace the fact that Corinthians fans could go over the score and, after signing a new contract, he had decided to accept the fans' lunatic passion and try to see the positive side. Maybe it was all that time spent with the Brazil squad and absence had made the heart grow fonder.

Whatever the reason, while stuck in the frigid mountains of Colombia watching Corinthians go from one embarrassment to another, he wrote what for him was an impassioned love letter to Corinthianos, appealing for more of a role at the club and declaring that he was finally not just a Corinthians player but now also a fan.

'I discovered a very important thing here in Colombia,' he said in the two-page statement dictated to *Placar*. 'If I was to stop playing right now for whatever reason, I would cheer for Corinthians (and a little bit for Botafogo de Ribeirão Preto) until the day I die. That must be why I am dying to get back again and wear the shirt that I learned to love thanks to you.'[20]

It was just as well. Because the boardroom changes were a harbinger of revolution at the Parque São Jorge. How Sócrates reacted over the next year would define his career.

8

'It was one of those rare coincidences in history where suddenly, all at the same time, people who were completely different came together behind a common cause right at the moment when they were desperately needed.'

Juca Kfouri

In 1977, when Botafogo were playing well and the win bonuses were piling up, Sócrates went to his team-mates with a novel idea. He was still uninterested in politicians and political parties but he saw injustice and inequality all around him, and he decided to speak up for the men and women who helped the club perform on match day. He thought the masseur, the laundry woman and the stadium janitor played almost as important a role as the right back, the reserve goalkeeper and assistant coach, and he proposed that they take a percentage of the win bonuses.

'Look,' he told his team-mates after training one day, 'Dona Palmira washes the strips, let's include Dona Palmira because we're here in nice clean shirts and that's down to her. Compadinho has the keys for all the rooms and the gates; he's always here to help us when we need him. Sebinho is one of us and doesn't get anything and that's not right. We're doing really well. Let's share it with everyone.'[1]

His team-mates embraced the idea and they decided to offer the ancillary staff around a fifth of the bonus given to players. They took the idea to the directors and it was approved.

Sócrates successfully fought the same battle not long after arriving at Corinthians, and a year or so later he led another campaign. The players got just two shirts a month from sponsors Topper and when they asked the company for more they were turned down. If they wanted an extra shirt to auction off or give to a friend, they had to pay for them.

Sócrates got the players together and suggested they turn their training gear inside out so that Topper's name wouldn't appear on TV or in the newspapers. They all agreed and it instantly had the desired effect. Topper complained to the club, who said it was an issue for the players, and two days later the company agreed to give each player 10 shirts a month for their own use.[2]

'I remember that as being the first time he took a leadership role,' said goalkeeper Jairo. 'Nobody had thought of Corinthians Democracy at this point but that was the start for me. For us, the players, the respect that he had for us and that we had for him didn't change at all, but he started to take on more of a leadership position. He decided more.'[3]

A few months after that, in February 1981, Sócrates made his most explicit appeal yet for more of a say in the running of the club. Corinthians were going through a shocking run of form and Sócrates, who was in Colombia for the World Cup qualifiers, was sorely missed. For him, the root of the crisis was not to be found in the players or the tactics, but in the exaggerated hierarchy that kept players subservient. At the same time as he professed a love for the club, he appealed for more of a role. The key to success came with scoring goals, he said, but the key to scoring goals came with solidarity.

'What is needed in Corinthians football – and not just at Corinthians, nor even just in football – is to close the gap between the boss and the employee,' he told *Placar* magazine. 'In our specific case the employee, the player, has duties that are very well-defined. That's as it should be. But the relationship ends right there. You never stop being anything other than an employee. The human being doesn't exist. Personal questions are never taken into account.

'When faced with a mentality like that, what is a professional going to do?' Sócrates went on. 'He is going to do the essential; he clocks in and then goes home when his shift ends. He has no incentive to do anything more, to create, to love his work environment. Honestly, I respect and admire companies with the capacity to get their employees publicly declaring, "We, the workers, at whatever company . . ." How I'd love that our team says, "We, from Corinthians" or, "Us Corinthianos". Instead of, "Me, whatever my name is." What I want – and I know that other team-mates want it, too – is that Corinthians becomes an extension of each of our families.'[4]

Those were the seeds of Corinthians Democracy and Sócrates had been planting them for more than a year. When they finally started to blossom at the end of 1981, it was in the appropriately hot-house conditions of the Caribbean basin.

Corinthians could only finish eighth in the 1981 Paulista, a tournament that was used as a qualifier for the following year's Brasileiro. The top seven teams qualified for what was called the Taça de Ouro (Gold Cup), with the rest going into a 48-team tournament called the Taça de Prata (Silver Cup), to all intents and purposes the second division. The Silver Cup ended in late February and the top four jumped immediately into the Gold Cup that began just days later.

Corinthians' early elimination from the Paulista meant they had time to kill at the end of the year, and they filled it with a lucrative three-week tour to Mexico, Guatemala and Curaçao. They won the Feira de Hidalgo trophy in Pachuca by beating Argentine side Independiente 2-1 and Club América of Mexico 2-0. Then they flew south to Guatemala, where they beat Comuncaciones 1-0 and drew 0-0 with Aurora. They wrapped things up in Curaçao with a 6-0 win over the island's national team.[5]

Many of the players had never spent such a long time away from their families and they struggled to cope with the alien atmosphere, the foreign languages and the long spells of boredom that come with being on the road. Sócrates was upset at missing his son's birthday, César made plain his frustration at not being a first-team regular, and the hulking Caçapava cried when he heard *mariachis* sing weepy romantic ballads in Mexico City.

But instead of allowing the trip to break them, it brought them closer together. They saw things they had never seen before and talked about them. The conversations stretched far beyond football and, over cold beers and the occasional exotic cocktail, they bonded.

One of the most memorable incidents involved Paulo César Caju, a flamboyant attacking midfielder who had spent much of his career at Botafogo and Olympique de Marseille and who played in four of Brazil's six matches at the 1970 World Cup. Although Caju's talent was undeniable, he was also famously supercilious and his attitude infuriated his new team-mates. One night during the tour, players were drinking in the hotel lobby when Caju sat down to join them. While the rest of the lads downed beers, Caju demanded something less ordinary. Sócrates remembered him ordering two bottles of champagne; Wladimir recalls it was four shots of Grand Marnier.[6]

Whatever it was, Caju disappeared without paying his share of the bill. The other players, few of whom had Caju's spending power, were not happy. They sensed that Caju was out for himself and their suspicions were confirmed in Caracas airport. The flight home from Curaçao was via Venezuela, but bad planning and penny-pinching meant they had a 14-hour stopover and tempers frayed as they waited it out on the plastic chairs and hard floors of the departure lounge. Players argued with players, players argued with directors and directors argued with directors. At one point, the players discussed splitting their income from personal sponsorship deals and they all agreed except Caju.

The incident led to a debate about what kind of players were best suited for Corinthians, and they came to the conclusion that they would be better served by hard-working journeymen rather than selfish individuals. It was the final straw for both parties, and the players got together and decided to force Caju out. Caju, knowing he was not wanted and appalled by inheriting a locker infested with cockroaches, left the club a few weeks later after wearing a Corinthians shirt just four times.[7]

'Caju didn't fit in,' said Wladimir. 'We decided that we wanted players who would give the club something back. Caju thought he was better than everyone else so we voted him out.'[8]

'When we went on tour we were like pieces from a jigsaw all scattered about,' Wladimir added. 'During that trip, the pieces either came together or they were out.'[9]

The other hugely important factor in finally turning Sócrates' progressive ideas into something more concrete and more political was the appointment of Adilson Monteiro Alves as director of football. The son of Waldemar Pires' vice president, Adilson gave up running the family biscuit factory to join Corinthians at the start of November.

He was an unusual choice, not least because he was a sociologist who made no secret of his inexperience. His first meeting with the players was supposed to be a short talk to introduce himself, but it turned into a hours-long debate in which he candidly admitted he knew nothing about running a football club, and the players – led by Sócrates – seized on the opportunity to tell him exactly what was wrong and what could be done to change it.

The meeting touched upon the unheard-of ideas of ending the *concentração*, diminishing the huge salary discrepancies in the squad, and giving players a percentage of the gate money.[10]

Adilson's willingness to consider such radical ideas was just one reason the players took to him so quickly. He was still in his thirties, barely older than some of those he would be leading, and he was open, ambitious and down to earth. He had been a student activist in his younger days, he had a wicked sense of humour and his bushy beard was the unmistakable sign of a liberal in a country where beards were still exclusive to rockers, hippies and communists. His opening gambit, telling players, 'I know about biscuits and sociology, not football, so tell me where we're going wrong', was music to Sócrates' ears and he immediately fired back, 'We have a solution – let's put it into place.'[11]

Even before the trip to the Caribbean, Adilson had laid out his ideology for all to see. A lifelong Corinthians fan, he was cheered by the thought of democracy returning and dreamt of using the club as a vehicle to speed the process up. He publicly told the players they should question what was going on around them, and further endeared himself to Sócrates when he declared that football clubs were not 'capitalist enterprises there to make a profit'.[12]

He had an important ally in Travaglini, who was not your typical Brazilian coach. A journeyman centre half who retired at 29 and moved into coaching, Travaglini was one of those rare people in the parochial world of Brazilian football who was as welcome in Rio de Janeiro as in his home state of São Paulo. He took Palmeiras to Paulista and national titles in the late 1960s and then completed a notable double by going to Rio and leading Vasco to the Brazilian league in 1974. A confirmed bachelor who lived with his sister and extolled Italian family values, he was one of the most popular men in the game and famous for his insistence on treating players with respect and dignity.

Travaglini rejected the conventional wisdom that footballers were either children to be mothered, idiots to be indulged, or delinquents to be brought into line. While Adilson told the players they were employees like any others and should enjoy the same rights and respect, Travaglini declared they were adults who were more than capable of telling the difference between right and wrong. He encouraged them to set up their own system of fines and punishments and to use it every chance they got.

'Very quickly they realised that they all had power and that they didn't want to be punished,' he said. 'They disciplined themselves or they punished themselves.'[13]

The overall effect was to bring the players and management together, and they talked and talked and talked. It was no longer them and us, bosses and workers, masters and servants. For the first time in ages, Corinthians were a team.

The players returned from their Christmas break in January and the new atmosphere was apparent from day one. They would normally go through a battery of tests to evaluate their fitness, but Adilson wanted to keep the momentum going and he organised a barbecue instead. The players were warned in advance and César drove 1,500 miles from his home state Maceió with a 19-kilo golden dorado fish in the boot of his car. The club laid on racks of beef and chicken and they didn't skimp on the beer. Sócrates and Paulinho brought a couple of guitars and hours later led their team-mates in an impromptu singsong.[14]

The squad was small but such bonding sessions meant it was increasingly united, and Adilson, with Sócrates and Wladimir his lieutenants in the dressing room, moved quickly to put their ideas into practice. The new system was based on participation and they decided that important decisions concerning the football club should be put to a vote and approved by a majority. Although some of the players had never voted before, Adilson convinced them they had to discuss their aims and intentions and take decisions not as individuals but as a team. Every week or so – or more often if someone called an emergency meeting – they would sit in the dressing room or the gym and debate whatever topic was raised.

The initial aim was to get players to talk to each other, but any issue was open for discussion: they voted on what day to fly to games in distant states, what time they should start and finish their daily training sessions, and whether or not to stop the coach for a toilet break on the way back from away fixtures. Everyone involved with the first-team squad, including reserves and support staff, was given the chance to say their piece, although in practice it was usually Adilson, Sócrates and Wladimir who shaped the debate. They were all aware of the club's financial position and took that and other realities into account when making decisions.

One of their first rulings was to let players check in at the airport, a small point that was all about trusting them to do things for themselves. It didn't take long, however, for Sócrates to move his ideas to the front of the agenda and force a debate over the *concentração*, the age-old institution that was based around the premise that footballers couldn't be relied on not to drink and party every chance they got.

Sócrates hated the *concentração* for a lot of reasons, some more noble than others. He thought that when players were cooped up for days, they focused not on the game but on the final whistle that signified freedom. He loathed being treated like a criminal who had to be locked up for his own good, and was outraged that a 28-year-old adult was not allowed to come and go as he pleased. He had a wife and young children at home and he wanted to be with them. He was also a hedonist who wanted to be out drinking and having fun.

The discussion over the *concentração* was the most important one of all for Sócrates, and it encapsulated the reason he threw himself so fully into the new movement. Sócrates' biggest goal – the one he spent his entire life fighting for – was not democracy but freedom. He hated anyone telling him what to do and, when they did, his first instinct was to rebel.

'All his life he tried to adjust the structure of professional football to his life as a bohemian,' said his brother Raimundo. 'The end of the *concentração* was not about ideology. He wanted to be at home on a Friday or a Saturday night drinking his beer, and to do that he needed to end the *concentração*. And he knew he couldn't do that alone, so he thought, "I am going to create Corinthians Democracy." It's not that he did it consciously, but his motivation was: "I am going to adjust everything in my life to the way I want it."'[15]

Sócrates knew the institution was entrenched and that changing it would require time, and so although he wanted its immediate abolition he was convinced to take it step by step. He suggested making the *concentração* optional for all, but Travaglini wanted an exception made for the unmarried and younger players, many of whom either lived alone or at home in sometimes precarious conditions. Staying in a luxury hotel the night before matches gave them peace and quiet and ensured they would eat and sleep properly.

It took them a few months to reach a decision and at first the *concentração* was reduced to one night from the usual two. That proved a success and, before the year was out, they had voted to let married players avoid it altogether. It wasn't obligatory and many of the married men preferred a quiet night in a nice hotel to the potential hassles of a night in with the wife and young children. By the end of the year, Sócrates himself was so involved in making the movement grow and so at ease with the other players that even he sometimes chose to stay in the hotel with his team-mates.

Another key decision that was turned over to the players was who to sign. When Corinthians needed a new player, the directors would come up with a list of three possible targets and the squad would debate which of them to recommend. The football world was tightknit and they knew which players carried their weight, who was injury prone or unfit, and who would embrace or reject their democratic project. When they reached a decision, they took the chosen name to the directors, who, if they thought the club could afford him, did their best to make it happen.[16]

The players were encouraged to discuss their problems openly, whether it was about money, tactics, playing time or personal issues. But this was Brazil in the early 1980s, almost two decades into a repressive and authoritarian regime. People were unaccustomed to having a voice and it took a while before they felt comfortable speaking their minds. Some of them were afraid of a backlash if they said what they thought, others were afraid of sounding stupid. Defender Mauro said many of them simply decided to indulge Sócrates and play along. The players were not intellectuals. They knew little about democracy and cared even less, and they believed it was only a matter of time before either the club cracked down or the military put an end to it.[17]

The old order was similarly sceptical and afraid that a loosening of restrictions could give the players – many of whom were, not coincidentally, poorly educated and dark-skinned – a chance to end up running the game. Corinthians' *conselheiros* equated democracy with anarchy and almost every day – and particularly after a bad result – they complained bitterly, loudly blaming the new openness and declaring the movement little more than an excuse for the players to run wild.

Sócrates and his *companheiros* tried to neutralise those concerns by stressing that they always put football first and that the game's strict demarcation lines would not shift. In a bid to allay fears of a revolution, they came up with the clarifying motto: 'Freedom, with Responsibility'.

'What was different was the way that players participated,' explained Hélio Maffia, the club's veteran trainer. 'It wasn't just a manager saying, "You do this and you do that." We all still had our responsibilities. The medical department decided what treatment each player needed. And the coach showed the players how it was going to be.

'It made my life a lot easier,' Maffia added. 'The players normally can't be bothered to train. You tell them to run that way and they run that way, you tell them to run the other way and they run the other way. With Corinthians Democracy, if a player tried to avoid training his team-mates would pull him up and say, "We're trying to win something here." There was a consensus; they all wanted the same thing.'[18]

One of Sócrates' clearest childhood memories was of his father building a bonfire in the back yard when he was 10 years old. The military coup was under way and Seu Raimundo was tossing books on the fire. Sócrates was too young to understand why and, when he asked his dad to explain, his father batted his questions aside with a flippant, 'Ah, they're just old books, son.' Sócrates didn't quite grasp what was happening, but as he watched the flames leap into the night sky he instinctively knew that something wasn't right. Something serious must be going on for his father to be destroying his most prized possessions.

The incident replayed itself in Sócrates' head for years and, when he had time to read the classics and the philosophers, he would occasionally do a double-take on looking down at the book in his lap and realising it was by an author whose work he'd seen being burnt in his garden. Eventually, having picked up clues from his dad and having got to know the likes of Plato, Nietzsche and Orwell, he understood what had happened.

'He was afraid because of the civil service job he had,' Sócrates recalled. 'He had Marx's *Das Kapital*, he had Engels, he had everybody, he read everything, from the left and the right, Gramsci, Machiavelli, and he burnt them because he thought it could cause him embarrassment. And that was shocking to me.

'Later, I wanted to read that literature and I got on at him and asked him, "What was all that about, why did you burn those books, what kind of books were they?", and I pieced it together over time. So even though I never understood what those books were about, it had an effect on me. When I was able to understand what he had shown us, I went after much more stuff.'[19]

One of the people who introduced him to 'more stuff' was Adilson, the brains of the new movement and a man who had read more books than the entire Corinthians squad put together. Adilson – like the players he was known by just one name – felt an immediate affinity with Sócrates and quickly recognised that if the movement was to succeed then he needed the support of the team's best player.

Adilson was a political animal and a former student leader, and it was his influence that helped turn the conscientious citizen into a political provocateur. He gave Sócrates books to read, loved nothing more than schooling the younger man in philosophy and sociology, and introduced him to politicians, academics and artists who broadened his horizons even further. He did it all while encouraging Sócrates to drink and enjoy himself, and he participated in the hedonism whenever he got the chance.

Sócrates' other big influence was Juca Kfouri, the editor of *Placar*. Kfouri studied sociology at the University of São Paulo a few years after Adilson and had worked as a driver and messenger for the leftist rebels who were preparing to launch an armed rebellion in the late 1960s. He entered journalism in the 1970s and got to know Sócrates when he put together the 1979 *Placar* special edition on his life. Even though he was only four years older than the player he wrote about, Kfouri took Sócrates to task after an interview in which he gave top marks to dictators and right-wing politicians. Sócrates wasn't used to hearing people criticising the regime so openly, but he took it all in and Kfouri was soon hosting him for dinners of spaghetti alfredo that were followed by hours and hours of drinking and debating. The older man was amazed at how hungry Sócrates was for information of all kinds and how easily he soaked it up.

'He asked me all the time, "What books are you reading, what films have you seen?"' Kfouri said. 'He heard about what was going on and he wanted to know more about it, where it all came from. I'd tell him stories about what was happening or had happened and his eyes opened wide. He was like, "Are you sure?" or, "Did that really happen?" And I told him all the details. When he was interested in something, he dived right in, and when he came back to you later, he knew all about it.'[20]

The other key factor in the politicisation process was his new surroundings. São Paulo was both a catalyst and a crucible for Sócrates, the place where he came of age. Brazil's biggest city was filled with musicians, intellectuals, artists, writers, politicians, unionists and activists of all different types, and as the biggest name at the city's biggest football club Sócrates had access to all of them. He took full advantage and spent nights and afternoons at cinemas, theatres, art galleries, nightclubs and openings. He thrived on the knowledge and the debate and, even more than playing football, he adored spending long hours discussing politics and philosophy around a table littered with empty beer bottles.

From the very first day, Sócrates was the face of the club's new movement, the player who, along with Wladimir, articulated their ideas to the fans and the media. It was a position that brought him the acclaim and adulation of those who were with him, and aroused alarm and anger among those who were against.

Sócrates accepted the role with characteristic insouciance. He knew that few of his team-mates had the intellectual capacity – much less the desire – to repeatedly face the press and explain what they were trying to do. Many of the players had only a primary education and, while they might have liked having more freedom, this wasn't their fight and they were not ready to place themselves in the firing line. Taking the lead was natural for Sócrates and it came with the additional advantage of allowing him to dictate the agenda.

He also knew that success on the field was absolutely vital if the movement was to prosper, and the victories came, albeit slowly. Corinthians began their Silver Cup campaign with a 2-0 win over América and then stuttered to draws against minnows Colatina and Catuense, poor results that meant they would have to win their remaining two games to stand any chance of progressing. They managed it thanks largely to Walter Casagrande, an 18-year-old striker who scored four goals on his debut in the 5-1 win over Guará and another in the 3-1 victory against Leônico.

Sócrates had injured an ankle in a pre-season friendly and missed that jittery opening stage, but he came back to partner Casagrande for the first time in the next two games, against Fortaleza and Campinense. Wins would take them back into the top flight and they got them thanks in no small part to the understanding the pair quickly worked up. Sócrates scored in the 4-2 triumph at Fortaleza and then laid on goals for Casagrande and Eduardo in the 2-1 defeat of Campinense.

The wins lifted Corinthians into the Gold Cup and, just days later, they kicked off that next stage in a group with Atlético Mineiro, Flamengo and Internacional. All three opponents were former Brazilian champions and few people gave Corinthians a hope of progressing into the last 16.

But the changes going on inside the club had brought the players together and instilled in them a sense of unity and purpose. They drew 1-1 with Flamengo, a team who just two months previously had crushed Liverpool to win the Intercontinental Cup, and then won 2-0 away at Internacional and 3-1 in Belo Horizonte, with Sócrates and Casagrande scoring in both games. The away wins were huge for the players, who had transformed the team almost overnight from a hapless second division outfit that couldn't beat minnows at home into a confident and free-scoring side able to win away at two of the biggest clubs in the country.

The wins against Atlético and Inter were followed by repeat victories at home, which meant they had already qualified for the next stage before going to Maracanã and losing 2-0 to Flamengo.

They maintained their form in the last 16, beating Bahia 6-3 on aggregate and then overcoming Bangu on a better group record after their home and away ties ended two goals apiece. They fell at the semi-final stage, losing 5-2 on aggregate to Grêmio, but a place in the country's final four was nevertheless a remarkable achievement for a team that hadn't even started the season in the top tier.

The future at Corinthians was filled with promise, both on and off the field. Sócrates was playing well and feeling both energised and optimistic about where the club was headed. But he was forced to put it all to the back of his mind after the loss to Grêmio. The moment he had been waiting for was almost upon him. He was off to Spain to lead his country in the World Cup finals.

9

'I am sure about only one thing. I am going to be world champion in 1982. Whatever it takes.'

Sócrates

Sócrates arrived at Brazil's World Cup training camp promising to play goalkeeper if it would help them win. He was still on a high after his brilliant early season with Corinthians and he was prepared to do anything for his country. Playing goalkeeper was unlikely, as was giving up beer and cigarettes. But this was, he thought, his best and perhaps his one and only shot at glory, and he decided it was worth kicking the habits of a lifetime.

One of the main reasons Sócrates had chosen football over medicine was to play in sport's most glamorous tournament, and he took a conscious decision to make every sacrifice necessary. Although his dad had nagged him for years to give up smoking, it wasn't until the middle of 1980 that he even considered cutting back. Until then, he was smoking up to two packs of Minister a day, but he had managed to cut down to around half a pack by the middle of 1980 and he felt much better for it. He put on weight, found training less of a struggle and he was enjoying his football more.

His bad habits were a constant irritation to Telê Santana, who himself gave up smoking in 1965 and turned evangelical about the harm it does to players. Two years before the World Cup came around, Telê openly told his captain that tobacco was what stood in the way of true greatness.

'If Sócrates looked after himself like Zico, who doesn't smoke, he would be the best player in Brazil,' Telê said. 'For now, Sócrates makes up for his physical deficiencies with youth and an undeniable class. But time marches on and the way he smokes I don't know if he'll manage to keep that up by the time the World Cup comes around.'[1]

Telê singled out Sócrates but he was far from being the only footballer of the time to enjoy a puff – much less a drink. One in five of all Brazilian players admitted to smoking – the true number was undoubtedly much higher – and Júnior, Luizinho, Serginho and Batista were just a few of those in the World Cup squad who also enjoyed a cigarette.[2]

Almost all the players enjoyed a beer and Toninho Cerezo used to take a quick nip of *cachaça* after a shower because he thought it helped him avoid catching a cold.[3]

Sócrates took what was for him the traumatic decision to give up cigarettes at the start of 1982 after a long conversation with trainer Gilberto Tim. A staunch nationalist like Sócrates, Tim was the great motivator in the Brazil camp, and he told the captain that if he stopped smoking and cut back on the bevvy then he could take the world by storm.

Sócrates loved Tim's intensity and conviction and he was eager to make his mark. After returning from his summer holidays eight kilos overweight, Tim, with the help of Corinthians trainer Hélio Maffia, put him on a strict fitness regime designed to turn that fat into muscle. He quickly shed some pounds to stabilise his weight at 84 kilos, which was more appropriate for someone who stood six-foot-four. After five months of hard work in the gym and on the training ground, his chest, biceps, thighs and hamstrings all got bigger, while his waist stayed the same size.[4]

The changes transformed him into a stronger and quicker footballer. When team doctors measured the players' physical performance before the tournament began, Sócrates did especially well given his history. He could jump higher than any of them from a running start and no one covered 30 metres quicker than he did. Only Edinho had a stronger shot with his right foot.[5]

Telê announced his squad in three stages, with Sócrates joining up on 20 April after Corinthians had been knocked out of the Gold Cup. The last group of players from finalists Flamengo and Grêmio arrived at Cruzeiro's training centre in Belo Horizonte six days later, and Falcão and Dirceu were set to join them when their club commitments with AS Roma and Atlético Madrid were completed in May.

Concerned about the effects of the Spanish heat, Tim had prepared an ultra-rigorous training regime for the whole squad, with sprints, laps of the pitch and stretching exercises. It was nothing less than torture for Sócrates, who dragged himself to the side of the field to throw up several times. But his dedication to the cause inspired those around him. His team-mates could see their captain was putting the group's interests ahead of his own and they feigned disbelief.

'What's this? Magrão at the front of the group doing laps of the pitch!' Zico shouted, to the sound of laughter from behind. 'What's going on?'[6]

'He always talked about how hard it was to look after himself and stay in shape but that wasn't the case at that World Cup,'

Zico recalled years later. 'From the moment we started our preparations he gave up everything and was one of the fittest guys we had at the tournament. He trained and he set a real strong example for that generation. At that World Cup he was focused on being in top form and that was what happened. He proved that there was an athlete inside him. And that was an abiding memory that stayed with everyone who was there with him.'[7]

The squad was a fairly settled one, the main question being who would fill the central striking role. Reinaldo had been favourite, but Telê questioned his off-the-field behaviour and an injury sealed his fate early in the year. The battle to replace him was between Serginho and Careca, the 21-year-old Guarani marksman. Careca started the final two friendlies before the squad headed to Europe and would have been first choice up front, but he tore a thigh muscle in training and was ruled out on the eve of the tournament. That left Serginho to get the nod, with Vasco da Gama's Roberto Dinamite coming in as his understudy.

The other dilemma came in midfield, where Telê was unsure whether to play a 4-4-2 with Falcão, Cerezo, Sócrates and Zico together in the middle of the park, or whether to withdraw one of them and opt for more width up front by playing Grêmio winger Paulo Isidoro alongside Serginho and Éder.

He appeared to be going for the latter option in the final warm-up games in May, with Paulo Isidoro starting all three and the quartet only managing 20 minutes of the final game, a 7-0 drubbing of Ireland that could have been twice that.

But it didn't really matter who started. Brazil were brimming with confidence and were certain they were going to be world champions. Since early 1980, when Telê's reign as manager began, Brazil had played 33 games, three of them against state or youth selects, and lost just twice, to the Soviet Union and Uruguay, both times by a single goal. They scored in every game bar one, at an average of 2.5 goals per game. The football they played was quick and one-touch, with all of the players comfortable on the ball and most of them eager to get forward.

It was scintillating stuff, reminiscent of both Brazil in 1970 and Holland in 1974, although Telê arrogantly rejected any comparison with the Dutch masters, saying, 'The way we play is similar to that of Holland in 1974 except we have more skilful players and we don't miss as many chances.'

No one had yet come up with a name for their style or their system, but Sócrates, with his customary dry wit, eventually took it upon himself to give it a moniker. He described their football as 'organised chaos' and quintessentially Brazilian in that it was unscripted, creative and unpredictable.

'Everyone has the freedom to play how they wish as long as they perform certain basic functions. As amazing as that might seem, it works. It comes . . . from improvisation, but also from the knowledge that was acquired in two years of working together,' he said. 'I play on the wing, I am a centre forward, a sweeper, holding midfielder . . . it depends on how the game is going. Even if we don't win the title, we'll have altered the traditional schemes of 4-2-4 and 4-3-3 and whatever else they have invented.'[8]

When Sócrates led Brazil on to the turf at the Ramón Sánchez Pizjuán stadium in Seville, it marked the end of one personal odyssey and the beginning of another. He was finally fulfilling his long-held dream of appearing in the World Cup finals. When he looked to the stands and saw thousands of Brazilians singing along to the first strains of the national anthem, he felt prouder than at any time in his life.

The opening match was against the USSR and the conditions

in Seville clearly favoured the South Americans. A party atmosphere pervaded the city, with the Brazil fans turning the terraces yellow and the late afternoon sun playing its part, bathing the ground in a golden sheen. The temperature was still in the 80s and the Brazilians lined up with their usual nonchalance as the samba drums hammered out a musical accompaniment. In their short blue shorts and iconic yellow jerseys, they even made sweating look elegant.

The Soviets, however, were unperturbed. Not only had they qualified for the tournament unbeaten, they were also one of only two teams to defeat Brazil since Telê had taken over. They attacked from the off, creating three good chances in the first quarter of an hour and having a clear penalty shout ignored by the Spanish referee. The Soviets were easily the better team and they got the goal they deserved after 34 minutes when Waldir Peres allowed a 30-yard strike from Andrei Bal to squirm through his hands.

With Cerezo suspended, Sócrates started the match on the left side of midfield, playing deeper than at club level, and he struggled to make much of an impact, at one point in the first half even being nutmegged. He spent much of the half-time break calmly reassuring the players that the game was not lost, and they were given a boost when Telê introduced Paulo Isidoro to replace the ineffective Dirceu. The move brought some width back to the side and the second half was a different story, as the tricky little winger made his presence felt and Sócrates and Falcão started to dominate the midfield. Sócrates pushed forward more and more as the Soviets tired, and when Brazil finally got some reward for their efforts it was thanks to their captain.

With 75 minutes gone, the Soviets struggled to clear a throw-in and Sócrates picked up a weak clearance around 35 yards out. He glanced up, before skipping past one tackle and shimmying to the right to avoid another. He was about 25 yards from goal and didn't even need to look up. He knew exactly where he was and he let fly with a glorious right-foot shot that sailed over the outstretched hands of Rinat Dasayev into the top left-hand corner of the net. Thirteen minutes later they got a winner and again it came from a screamer from outside the box. Éder had sent half a dozen long-range shots high and wide, but this time he made no mistake. Paulo Isidoro passed the ball along the 18-yard line, Falcão cleverly let it run through his legs and Éder flicked it up and volleyed home.

Brazil were off to the perfect start, but they were lucky and they knew it. The Russians wilted in the heat and were denied a clear penalty in the second half when Luizinho threw up an arm to handle a cross into the box. But a win was a win and, going by his unpublished memoir, it was one of the most important days in Sócrates' entire career. He devoted more time to the game than any other, with the emotion, the pride and the release of the goal making the occasion unique.

'We had to deal with the anxiety of being behind for most of the game,' Sócrates recalled. 'We tried everything to get near the Russian goal. A sure defence and a magnificent goalkeeper looked like they would stop us from making our dream come true. And then the ball fell to me. There was a wall of red shirts ready to spill their own blood to stop me. I feinted to shoot and jinked to the right. A space opened up. I feinted again and an even bigger space appeared. I put everything I had into my shot. And the scream came: Goooallll. No, not a goal. An endless orgasm. It was unforgettable.'[9]

The Brazilians celebrated with paella after the game and then some of the players enjoyed a rare day off in the centre of Seville. Sócrates wanted to see the city, and took the opportunity to meet up with his friend Raimundo Fagner, one of Brazil's best-known pop stars, and together they sat around and played guitar before heading off to meet the rest of the team and watch their next opponents.

Scotland beat New Zealand 5-2 and the Brazilians were divided on whether the Scots would pose more problems than the Soviets. Zico thought Jock Stein's men were faster and more creative, but Sócrates wasn't so sure. With typical inconsistency, one day he called them 'better than the Soviets' and the next day 'time wasters' who played a traditional British game of high balls and were therefore not to be feared.[10]

The game was important for Brazil because it marked the return of Toninho Cerezo to the side. Zico, who took a knock against the USSR and didn't train, knew his role would change with Cerezo back alongside him and Brazil took time to find their feet.

David Narey put the Scots ahead after 18 minutes, to the shock of almost everyone in the ground. Zico got one back shortly before the break with a sublime free kick, but the Brazilians weren't happy and there was a lot of disgruntlement in their dressing room at half-time. Zico criticised Sócrates and the other midfielders for leaving him alone on the right side of the park and he pointedly told Telê and his team-mates that if he didn't get more help then he wanted to be subbed.[11]

They all agreed to rotate more and Brazil came out and dominated the second half. Oscar rose to head home a corner within three minutes of the restart, and then Éder lifted a sublime chip over Alan Rough on 63 minutes to put the game out of Scotland's reach. The fact that the bar was mistakenly set 3cm lower than the regulation height made no difference. A lovely 25-yard daisy cutter from Falcão three minutes from time put the gloss on a fine performance.

Sócrates once again started deeper than he was used to but moved further forward after Serginho was replaced by Paulo Isidoro 10 minutes from the end. He had a good game but the highlight of the evening was yet to come. He was selected for an anti-doping test, but having played 90 minutes in the searing heat he was severely dehydrated and in need of a drink before he had any chance of providing the required urine sample. Officials had kindly prepared a row of well-stocked fridges and Sócrates' eyes lit up when he saw the liquid feast in front of him. There was beer, champagne, wine, and shelf upon shelf of water, juices and sodas. He did not need to be asked twice to partake in what he called 'celebratory diuretics'.[12]

'When the guy opened the fridge I tried to hide my smile,' he recalled in his memoir. 'It was filled with all kinds of drinks. It was beautiful! I was drinking my second can of beer when I realised that the others had already completed their mission. And I didn't feel at all ready. To be honest, I didn't want it to end. I drank all the beer they had and then I moved on to cham-pagne. And still nothing. Wine, nothing. Soft drinks, nothing. It was only almost three hours later that they got their sample. When I left the stadium the rest of the team had already gone but I was the happiest of men. It was one of the best days of my life.'[13]

Sócrates was delighted with the way they had beaten Scotland and brushed off the criticism of their first-half performance as teething troubles with their new formation. But while things were progressing on the field, they weren't quite as delightful off it as the players began to chafe at the long time they had spent away from home. Most of them had not seen their families since leaving Brazil a month earlier and *saudades* – a quintessen-tially Brazilian word that evokes an emotional mix of longing and nostalgia – were kicking in.

They got just five minutes to phone home each day, and Sócrates was both happy and sad to speak to his son Rodrigo on the day he celebrated his seventh birthday. He missed his family and he wanted to be at home with his children. The players enjoyed very little free time, with their days structured around training and other team events. Management set up pinball machines and arcade games in the foyer, but Sócrates preferred to read. He had a room overlooking the sunflower fields that surrounded the town of Carmona and he lay on his bed with a pile of books that included Frank Kafka's *The Trial*, Ernest Hemingway's *The Sun Also Rises* and a signed copy of the new Jorge Amado novel sent to him by the author.[14]

Every day he would take the hotel stationery or rip pages from a notebook and scribble down his thoughts for his daily diary that appeared in *Placar*. He wrote letters to family and friends, played cards and chess on the electronic game he had bought in Europe the year before, and read the papers and letters that were delivered each day from Brazil. Pelé sent his best wishes and some fans sent telegrams suggesting new line-ups and formations, encouragement that had him chuckling, 'In football, Brazilians really do want to participate.'[15]

The players also organised parties whenever they could, especially for birthdays, and because all three games in the group stages kicked off at night they seldom went to bed before 1 a.m. On 15 June, they celebrated Dirceu's 30th with a small bash at the hotel and five days later they had a cake for Oscar's 28th.

Saudades notwithstanding, they were settled in Seville and the early results boosted Sócrates' confidence to the point where he was openly discussing how he might lift the trophy 19 days hence.

'I have confidence in this group,' he said. 'Sometimes I think about winning the title. And about lifting the trophy. I don't think it would be fair to the other players just the captain lifting the cup. It has to be everyone. I wouldn't want to reproduce the gesture of other Brazilian captains who were immortalised in photos from other World Cups holding the Jules Rimet. I think it would be better to find a way for everyone to hold the trophy and pose for photos with everyone together. All 11 of us or more, everyone that can fit in, substitutes, the backroom staff . . .'[16]

His comments sounded very much like someone putting the cart before the horse, but Sócrates was attempting to gauge public opinion over what any celebration should look like. It was partly about making the celebration collective rather than individual, but it was also because the act of lifting the World Cup had such a special significance in Brazil. With the exception of Mauro in 1962, almost every Brazilian captain who lifted the World Cup did it his own particular way, starting with Bellini in 1958 and ending with Cafu in 2002, who scribbled a message across his shirt and stood on the podium to hoist the trophy high after a 2-0 win over Germany.

In Sweden in 1958, Bellini was handed the cup by King Gustaf VI Adolf on the pitch just moments after the game ended. A photographer shouted at him to lift the trophy up so that everyone could get a better picture, and the resulting picture of Bellini coolly raising the Jules Rimet trophy above his head with both hands became an iconic image in Brazil.

Mauro repeated the gesture in 1962, and eight years later in Mexico City Carlos Alberto Torres added a bit of Brazilian panache by kissing the cup. In 1994, Brazil hadn't won the competition for 24 years, but they were playing ugly football and fans and the media were not slow to make their distaste clear. No one expected the drought to end and, when they beat Italy on penalties in Los Angeles, captain Dunga took the cup from Vice President Al Gore and screamed, as much to the team's detractors as in joy, 'Four-time champions, fuck!' The outburst prompted journalist Marcelo Barreto to memorably quip, 'Bellini invented lifting the cup. Carlos Alberto invented kissing the cup. And Dunga invented swearing at the cup.'

Sócrates may have been thinking of these iconic celebrations and how to outdo them, but talking so early in the tournament about how he might lift the cup was at best presumptuous and at worst tempting fate. It was not, however, out of character. Sócrates loved the psychological side of the game – he often said football was played more with the head than the feet – and with time on his hands and the world's media at his beck and call, he enjoyed being able to toss ideas back and forth.

Among the big questions that preoccupied him ahead of the competition was how to incorporate so many big egos in the one side. Sócrates, Zico and Falcão were considered the three stars of the squad, with Cerezo not far behind. This quartet represented four of Brazil's biggest states and the media sometimes succumbed to the parochial temptation to play them off against each other. Sócrates the psychologist believed that if his team lined up behind one player, it would prevent infighting and jealousy. He could have chosen to elevate any of them, not least himself, the team captain at the peak of his game.

But Sócrates preferred to take on the assistant's role, once saying he was happier being the co-pilot rather than the rally driver. He ruminated for weeks over what to do and eventually came to a decision. Although Falcão was in the best form of his life, he was based in Italy and the distance meant he had played for Brazil just twice in two years. He didn't know his team-mates as intimately as the other contenders. Zico, meanwhile, knew everyone and was respected for both his skills and his integrity. Sócrates and Zico were close and the captain made a conscious decision to put him on a pedestal and urge his players to support his choice.

'The question that people kept fucking asking us was, "Who is better, Zico or Sócrates?"' he recalled. 'I could have been political and said, "Ah, each player is important and they are all great," but I wasn't doing that, I had to put one man above everyone else and that was him. Why did I do that? Shit, if you stimulate an internal competition you will never have a great team, so as captain I did that to help diminish the intrinsic rivalry. That was the basic objective – put one guy above everyone else because that is the concept I have for a football team. If you don't have a reference point, one great player, the best player, then the team is never going to play well. If you don't have one man who's better than the others in a football team, you have a bunch of guys who will be fighting each other. If you put all 11 at the same level, they won't play; you have to have one who is better so that the others fight to get closer and the benefits are collective.'[17]

Zico's bicycle kick was the most memorable moment in the 4-0 win over New Zealand in their final group game on 23 June. Zico was playing well and the win ensured them top spot in Group 6, which meant they would bid farewell to Seville and fly to Barcelona, where they would face Argentina and Italy in the second round.

All three teams would play each other in a round-robin system, with only the group winner qualifying for the semi-finals. Brazil were hot favourites and, with the best record in the early stages, they sat out the first match and waited to play the loser of the Italy–Argentina game, on 2 July. They would then face the winners on 5 July, with both games taking place at Espanyol's 44,000-capacity Sarrià stadium.

The Brazilians moved to a hotel around 50 kilometres outside Barcelona along a road that was so narrow and winding that some of the players complained of nausea every time they got off the bus. The hotel was spartan, but Sócrates didn't care about his new surroundings. What bothered him more was the isolation. He was getting tired of being so far from home and was anxious about the birth of a fourth child he had convinced himself would be a girl they would name Mariana. Not for the last time, he complained of missing Brazil and wrote in his *Placar* diary, 'I want to go home.'[18]

The move to Catalonia also marked an important change in schedule for the players. For their first three weeks in Spain, they would get up late and go to bed late because their group games were played at night. Both their upcoming matches in Barcelona were afternoon games, and so they were now forced to rise earlier and take part in training sessions both morning and afternoon.

The Brazilians watched Italy beat Argentina 2-1 on 29 June and they were not impressed with either side. What did strike them was the violence, and Brazil were expecting Argentina to continue the rough stuff at the Sarrià, where César Luis Menotti's men desperately wanted to end a 12-year run without a win against their South American rivals. Enzo Bearzot called the Argentines 'bulls who attacked them on the blind side' and Edinho said Brazil were preparing for 'a real war'.[19]

'You run the risk of getting hit in every game. This one won't be any different,' Sócrates said. 'There's no doubt they go in hard and nasty, as the Italians witnessed. Don't expect them to be soft or nice. It's going to be a hard game, and probably a violent one, and we have to be up for it and make sure we don't lose our heads if we want to win.'[20]

An estimated 13,000 Argentines lived in Barcelona and Maradona had just signed for Barça so they knew the home crowd would be against them. Moreover, the gap between the New Zealand match and the Argentina game was a seemingly endless nine days, which were marked by solitude and mind games.

Maradona had been winding the Brazilians up since day one, studiously ignoring Zico and Sócrates in naming Éder, Falcão and Júnior as the three most impressive Brazilians in the opening stages and then declaring Karl-Heinz Rummenigge a 'much better' player than the Flamengo star. Menotti said it would be easier to beat Brazil than Italy as they had an inferior defence, and Maradona declared that Italy were the favourites to win the group and make the semis.

Sócrates called on his team-mates to ignore the provocations, but tensions were starting to show across the board as the tournament entered the knockout stages. The Italian players weren't speaking to the press because of reports they were fighting over their bonuses and stories that two of them were having an affair. In the Brazilian camp, meanwhile, Edinho declared he was a better player than starter Luizinho, and Batista and Roberto Dinamite were complaining they weren't getting a chance to show what they could do. The much-vaunted solidarity was clear among the first team but the fringe players were restless.

Sócrates, again, was despairing of his isolation far from the heat and hustle of central Barcelona, where fans from the world over were congregating to drink and sing along the famous Ramblas. He wanted to be involved in the World Cup not just as a player, but also as a citizen of the world. His inability to engage with players and supporters led him to launch one of those periodic outbursts he would later disavow.

'I am a bit depressed,' he wrote in his *Placar* diary of 30 June. 'All my life I've wanted to play in a World Cup. I am here now and I am conscious of the fact that I am not doing badly but there's no doubt I am frustrated. The World Cup isn't what I imagined. It doesn't permit an exchange with people from other countries, each one is on their side and that's it. I think it's better to watch it than play in it. That's why I have no doubts at all. Another World Cup? Never again. Who knows, maybe I can watch the next one with Rê and the kids. It will be much more fun.'[21]

In the end, the match against Argentina was more of a cakewalk than a showdown. Sócrates predicted that Argentina would create more chances but that Brazil would win the game in the second half due to their superior fitness, and his analysis proved spot-on. Argentina needed to triumph, preferably by a good few goals, to have any chance of progressing to the semi-finals and they started the stronger side. But they were dealt an early setback when Brazil scored with their first shot of the game. Éder's free kick thundered against the underside of the bar from 35 yards out and Zico was the quickest to react as he nipped in to poke the rebound home from under the despairing Ubaldo Fillol.

Argentina continued to have more of the ball, but when they lost possession they always looked vulnerable. Júnior was outstanding, Zico and Éder were always dangerous with the ball at their feet, and Brazil's change of pace in the last third of the field caused the Argentine defence all sorts of problems.

Brazil got a second after 66 minutes, after Daniel Passarella got caught in possession in the centre circle. They swept forward and Falcão beat the offside trap before crossing to Serginho, who was unmarked at the back post and headed down and into the net. Júnior put the result beyond doubt nine minutes later when he got on the end of a defence-splitting pass from Zico and slipped the ball under the advancing keeper.

Until this point Argentina had remained composed, but they soon lost the plot and with 10 minutes to go Passarella clattered Zico so hard he was forced to go off. Just five minutes later, Maradona stamped his foot into Batista's groin and got a well-deserved red card. Ramón Díaz's goal in the last minute was no more than a footnote.

Sócrates had his quietest game so far, particularly in the first half when he seemed a little off the pace. But he was still one of Brazil's outstanding performers, with several Spanish newspapers selecting him as one of the players of the tournament.

Not everyone, though, was quite so sanguine. The day of the

Argentina game a friend arrived with letters and cards from Ribeirão Preto. One of them brought the customary tough love from his dad and Sócrates couldn't help but have a giggle at his father's expense. 'I was delighted [to get the letters] in spite of the bollocking I got from my old man. He thinks I am not playing as well as I can. He wants me to be more active and take more shots at goal. It's funny, a Spanish paper rated me the best player in the tournament, calling me the "brain of Brazil". I think they're blind. Seu Raimundo, watching on TV, can see things much more clearly.'[22]

The fans, too, could see that Brazil were the outstanding side. One of the cultural events held in parallel to the football was a festival featuring dance performances from the participating nations. A poster outside one of the host venues in central Barcelona advertised Scottish Highland dancing and below it a Brazilian had scribbled his own advertisement: 'Brazil will dance around the opposition on July 2 and 5 at the Sarrià stadium' – the dates of their games against Argentina and Italy. That first night got rave reviews. The final performance was to feature an all-star cast and was one of the most eagerly awaited in years.

10

'I think football is work and our work is always important. But it's never the most important thing. It's not a matter of life and death and that's what we are trying to transmit. We could lose. We can't be afraid of losing. But we could also win, as we've prepared for it.'

Sócrates

The Brazilian players beat on tambourines, shook their match-boxes like maracas and hammered out rhythms on the roof of the coach as they sambaed their way towards the Sarrià stadium to face Italy. The atmosphere started out joyful but then turned sour as the bus inched its way slowly around tight mountain roads. Organisers were worried that terrorists with the Basque separatist group ETA or the Italian Red Brigade, both of whom were active in Europe at the time, would attack a team on their way to a stadium, and before they set off coach drivers had to pick a route drawn randomly from a hat. The journey to Espanyol's ground took almost an hour, so long that the Brazilians ran out of sambas to play. Some of the players stepped off the coach feeling nauseous because of the windy roads and were delighted to finally be back on terra firma.[1]

Brazil's 3-1 win over Argentina gave them an advantage over Italy, who had beaten the Argentines 2-1, and they needed just a draw to qualify for the semi-finals. The Italians had started the World Cup poorly, drawing all three of their group games, against Poland, Peru and Cameroon, and they only qualified for the second stage because they had scored two goals in three games, one more than Cameroon, who also drew all three of their matches.

Less than two months before the tournament Telê Santana had rubbished the Italians' chances, saying they thought they were the best in the world and therefore didn't need to change their antiquated style of play. He criticised their adherence to man-marking and suggested that Roma were the only Serie A team to play modern football because they had Falcão in their ranks. And, although his spies had warned him that Italy were one of the best teams in the tournament, he was no more circumspect on the eve of the game, boldly declaring, 'The Italian marking won't work against Brazil. Our team doesn't depend on just one player like Argentina does with Maradona.'[2]

His players were equally confident. Brazil had scored 13 goals in four games, compared to the Italians' four, and they were the toast of the tournament so far. Their performances had filled the squad with a dangerous euphoria and too many of them were treating the game as a foregone conclusion. Before the groups for the second round were known, the Brazilian players had prayed to get Italy because they looked like a soft touch. Their prayers were answered and, after sitting through the Italy–Argentina match, their confidence soared even further.

'We watched Argentina against Italy,' recalled Oscar. 'Italy beat Argentina and played really poorly. Then we played Argentina and beat them 3-1 and we thought, "Fuck, Italy can't play, we're going to destroy them." We were certain we were going through.'[3]

CBF officials felt the same way, and nothing exemplified the overconfidence more than the discussion over prizes. The issue of prize money had annoyed Sócrates since before the tournament even began. The players met before arriving in Spain to discuss how to approach the CBF about prize money and Sócrates wanted to take a hard line. After some discussion, the players decided to ask for $100,000 in prize money and Sócrates convinced everyone it should be all or nothing. If the CBF tried to negotiate down, as was the norm, Sócrates would stick to his guns. If they baulked at paying $100,000 then they would take the moral high ground and play for free. It was a risky strategy but the other players went along with it. Sócrates was both furious and disappointed when the CBF made a counter offer of $35,000 and several players accepted straight away.[4]

The issue of prizes from the team's sponsors was even more divisive, arising as it did right before the all-important game. The CBF president arranged to meet with the squad the day before the Italy match to update them on the status of sponsors' freebies. Sócrates and Zico thought it was madness to discuss such things just 24 hours before the most important match of their lives and they refused to take part. With the two most important players in the squad absent, the meeting was adjourned after just five minutes.[5]

Officials, however, did not let the matter drop. On the morning of the game, centre half Edinho arrived for the team talk to be met by Giulite Coutinho, the head of the CBF. In Brazil, the team talk takes place several hours before the game, not in the dressing room just before kick-off, and a function room was set aside in the hotel for the players to hear Telê give his final instructions.

'Edinho,' Coutinho said excitedly as they waited for the others to arrive. 'We got the prizes. The motorbikes, cars, the other stuff. The sponsors have agreed.'

'President, I don't think this is the time to be talking about these things, not at the team talk,' Edinho replied. 'We've got our minds on winning the game.'

Coutinho didn't care for humility and was soon regaling the players with promises of video cameras and household appliances. 'People's eyes opened wide right there and then,' Edinho said. 'On the coach to the stadium, many good people could only talk about the money.'[6]

The team talk was also notable for a brief discussion about tactics. Falcão's AS Roma team-mate Bruno Conti spoke to him after they beat Argentina and said, only half-jokingly, that Italy had their bags packed because they expected to lose. They had seen how well Brazil were playing and so planned to sit tight and try to hit them on the break. Falcão wondered aloud if Brazil should play it tighter than usual for the first few minutes while they got the measure of their opponents. They discussed having the full backs stay deep to stop Italian counterattacks, but the suggestion was drowned out by team-mates who didn't think they should change a style that had served them so well. Many players were afraid that if they abandoned their attacking ways and lost they would be massacred at home for betraying their ideals. If they did go out, they wanted to go out true to themselves and their glorious attacking style.

Monday, 5 July was another gorgeous day in Barcelona and when the teams walked from the tunnel just after 5 p.m. the sun was still high in the sky. Smoke from terracing flares wafted down on to the pitch and yellow and green kites danced above the field. Behind Waldir Peres' goal to the left, people in the blocks of flats gathered on their balconies to watch the spectacle unfold.

The game turned out to be one of the most exciting in World Cup history and was barely five minutes old when Brazil suffered their first setback. Antonio Cabrini swept in a cross from the right and an unmarked Paolo Rossi darted in at the back post to head past Peres. Rossi had been the surprise name in the Italy squad, returning to action after a two-year ban for his involvement in the *totonero* match-fixing scandal, and the goal was his first at international level for more than three years.

Going behind startled Brazil, but they pushed forward the only way they knew how and Serginho should have brought them level moments later. Instead, he scuffed the ball past the post when he had only Dino Zoff to beat. The equaliser came quickly, however, and it was thanks to some nice interplay between Sócrates and Zico. The Flamengo man took a pass from Sócrates in midfield and then performed a brilliant turn before threading a return ball for him to run on to in the box. Sócrates had kept going down the right-hand channel and he got behind his marker, took one touch to steady himself and then side-footed the ball between the keeper and his left-hand post. He ran to the fence beaming in delight as first Zico, then Júnior, Falcão and Luizinho, piled on top of him to celebrate.

But their joy didn't last long and 13 minutes later Italy were ahead again. Cerezo had the ball in the right-back position but he played a sloppy pass across the middle of the pitch and, as three Brazilian defenders hesitated, Rossi darted in to steal the ball and crash a second past the helpless Peres.

Sócrates had a powerful header saved on the line by Zoff in the 35th minute and Zico should have had a penalty after Claudio Gentile ripped his shirt while pulling him back just inside the box. But the scoreline stayed unchanged up to the break and Sócrates went in at half-time with a strange sensation. Before the tournament started, he had told Juninho Fonseca of a premonition he had, that he would score Brazil's first and last goal in the tournament. After he got the opener in the first match versus the USSR, Juninho joked that he shouldn't even think about scoring again until the final. They both laughed about it as the competition went on but it made Sócrates feel uneasy and, when he got the equaliser against Italy, a chill went through his body and he said to himself, 'Oh no, we're fucked.'

The sensation, though, was fleeting and the dressing room at half-time was unusually confident for a team that was just 45 minutes away from being knocked out of the World Cup. Every man in the squad thought they deserved to be level, and not one of them believed that the second half would fail to bring them the goals they required. They all geed each other up, with Júnior, Sócrates and Zico, the three strongest personalities in the dressing room, urging their team-mates to stay focused and keep playing their usual game.

The second half was unforgettable. Brazil almost drew level within seconds of the restart when a shot from Falcão flashed across the face of the goal and narrowly past the post. A powerful drive from Leandro went straight to Zoff and then the keeper was quick off his line to stop Cerezo capitalising on a nice through-ball from Sócrates. Serginho cheekily tried a backheel that Zoff managed to block and Cerezo hit the outside of the post with a volley from a tight angle. Italy too had their chances. Bruno Conti should have done better than poke a shot wide in a dangerous counterattack, and Rossi should have grabbed his third after Francesco Graziani set him free but could only shoot past.

Brazil were clearly the better side and, in the 68th minute, they got the goal their efforts deserved thanks to Falcão. Júnior skipped past Conte and cut inside from the left, and his crossfield pass found the Roma midfielder on the corner of the penalty box. With Cerezo pulling defenders out of position to give him space, Falcão drifted along the 18-yard line. A big hole opened up in front of him and he let fly with a vicious left-foot shot that gave Zoff no chance. The Brazilian TV commentator was every bit as cocky as the players and wasted no time in declaring that the goal would 'allow Brazil to think about winning and not just drawing'. But once again the Italians bounced right back. Six minutes later Rossi pounced on a loose ball from a corner kick to whip a shot past Peres from six yards out. It was 3-2 to Italy with 15 minutes left.

Sócrates moved to centre forward after Serginho was replaced by Paulo Isidoro straight after Falcão's goal. He had the ball in the net with 11 minutes remaining, but the linesman had his flag up and he struggled to make much headway against a superb Italian defence. As Brazil pushed forward, spaces opened up at the back and Rossi fed Giancarlo Antognoni to score a fourth that was incorrectly chalked off for offside. Then, with two minutes left and in what was the last clear chance of the match, Oscar watched despairingly as Zoff got down to smother his thumping header on the goal line. Brazil kept pushing but it wasn't enough. Zoff had made 18 saves compared to Waldir Peres' four, but Brazil were out.

Sócrates was not just the best Brazilian on the field, he was one of the few to keep a cool head when all around were losing theirs. Cerezo actually cried when Falcão got the equaliser and Júnior threatened to punch him if he didn't man up. Sócrates, though, never for a second believed that Brazil wouldn't go through. Right up to the final whistle he was a study in calm, urging his team-mates to play their usual game, even as a draw looked increasingly unlikely.

When the final whistle blew, Sócrates walked dejectedly to the tunnel and almost immediately came face to face with Telê

Santana. Sócrates felt the pain of defeat and he felt it not only for himself, but also for the man who had become a second father to him. Telê got a standing ovation when he appeared for the press conference after the match, a gesture as touching as it was unexpected. Criticism that he should have played for the draw dragged on for years afterwards but he remained unrepentant. Brazil were an attacking side and his players couldn't play for the draw even if he ordered them to. Sócrates, like most of the players in the squad, agreed wholeheartedly and said that if they replayed the game 100 times, Brazil would win 99 of them. The result was just one of those things and he exempted Telê from blame. When the two men met, they hugged at the edge of the field and no words were needed, or even possible.

'The first person I saw after the game was him,' Sócrates recalled. 'His face was etched with the pain that we all felt. Yet he tried desperately to console us. He waited for us at the side of the pitch and he showed his appreciation to each and every one of us. In the dressing room, the anguish was immense. Some cried uncontrollably while others suffered in silence. He gazed towards the horizon and appeared calm, in spite of the blow. I think he felt comforted by our efforts. But that didn't mean he wasn't suffering. I really wanted to hold him, to protect him. I didn't have the strength. Once again I thought of my father. I felt that the pain they were both feeling was equally intense. I cried for them much more than for anything else, but the tears did not come easily. I felt destroyed and impotent in the face of what had happened. I only really understood exactly what that feeling meant when my old man passed away many years later. I wanted to work miracles and bring him back, just like I wanted to recapture that world title for the man who deserved it most.'[7]

*

On the other side of the world, Sócrates' father was suffering every bit as much. Back in Ribeirão Preto, dozens of people – including some friendly reporters – crammed into the Vieira family living room to watch the match live and there was a deathly silence when the final whistle went. Seu Raimundo was distraught and, after chatting with Sócrates on the phone later that evening, he spent much of the next few days holed up in his room, too upset to face the world. Raí, who watched the game with friends, was so shocked that he stormed out of the house. His brothers discovered him hours later sitting in a nearby square, his face still red with tears.[8]

The disappointment had subsided a little by the time the squad arrived home on 7 July, and the anger Brazilians often reserve for World Cup losers was mercifully absent. Most fans recognised the defeat was just one of those things and that their team had done everything possible to win. The little rancour that existed was reserved for individuals, and even then it was half-hearted. Cerezo came under fire for the second goal and for being emotionally suspect; Serginho, Waldir Peres and Luizinho were often singled out as the weak links, and the pragmatists blamed Telê for not playing for a draw.

'We lacked humility,' Luizinho acknowledged years later. 'We wanted to win the game but we only needed to draw. In football, there are days when no matter what you do, you're not going to win. That just wasn't our day and we should have played for the draw. And there was no leadership on the field; someone out there on the pitch should have said, "Leandro, Júnior, stay back. Let's tighten up in midfield, let's make sure of the draw that will get us through." No one said that and we had experienced players and an experienced coach and yet no one changed the way we played. Someone should have said this just isn't our day. Let's play for the draw when it was 1-1 or 2-2. No one ever imagined we would lose; we always thought we'd come back.'[9]

Sócrates thought it silly to look for scapegoats or point the finger of blame, but he did harbour a quiet grudge against one player. He never mentioned him by name in public but for years he was resentful of Éder, the left winger who had been one of Brazil's best players throughout. Years later, Éder was accused of celebrating goals during the 1982 tournament in front of certain advertising billboards in return for a $1,000 payment. He denied that charge but Sócrates had another reason to question his commitment.[10]

Sócrates felt that Éder was playing for himself more than the team because he was jealous of the midfielders who were getting all the praise. The captain believed that individualism was one of the decisive factors in their loss to Italy. It wasn't just that Éder had insisted on taking most of the free kicks, missing the target and blasting five out of six into the wall. It wasn't even that he tried to score a goal direct from a corner in injury time. In the 69th minute of the match, just seconds after Falcão had equalised for Brazil, Éder picked up a loose ball 25 yards from the Italian goal. He had one defender in front of him and Sócrates coming up on the right. But instead of slipping the ball to Sócrates for a free shot on goal, he attempted to dribble past the defender and was dispossessed.

Éder had been greedy in a similar situation in an earlier game, and Sócrates was so concerned that he asked trainer Gilberto Tim to raise the matter with Telê. He never found out if Tim took it to the coach, but he was convinced that Eder's selfishness was a defining moment and he couldn't get the irritation out of his head. He broached the issue not only in his unpublished memoir 20 years later, but also in the conversations about his prospective biography with Juca Kfouri.[11]

Sócrates liked Éder and the two men remained friends, but it was a lesson in ego that he never forgot.

*

The Italy game was the greatest Sócrates had ever played in, but he openly confessed that he was 'never brave enough' to actually sit down and watch it. He was brave enough to replay it, joining his old team-mates to take on their Italian counterparts for Júnior's farewell match in Pescara in 1990. (Éder was the only one of the 11 starters who didn't take part in Brazil's 9-1 victory.)

Then one night in the mid-1990s, he was sitting in a bar in Tokyo with his friend Ruy Ramos. Sócrates was on a two-week trip to Asia and he arranged to meet up with Ramos, a footballer who had moved to Japan and played for their national side. They decided to go out for the night in the Roppongi neighbourhood. Roppongi was famous for its pubs, clubs and karaoke bars, and the two friends hung out in a Brazilian bar called Amazônia. They were laughing and joking when, long after midnight, some familiar faces flickered on a TV screen above them. It was Brazil vs. Italy.

'I was chatting away and the game came on and I started to glance at it and then watched the whole thing,' Sócrates recalled. 'I was transfixed. I thought it was fucking brilliant, an amazing game, fantastic, I think the best game that I had ever seen in my life and I had never watched it before. What a game. I don't like to look back ... but there it was and I watched it.'[12]

Long before that point Sócrates had come up with an alternative assessment of what the result meant. The rest of the world lamented the defeat and picked over both the reasons and the consequences, but Sócrates quickly made peace with Brazil's premature elimination. The loss shocked him and in the days and weeks that followed he struggled to focus on anything else. But he had considered the ramifications of being a world champion long before he had even played for Brazil and he was ambivalent about them. Winning the World Cup would rob anyone of motivation, he said, and once you had reached the summit of international football the only way to go was down.

Sócrates (right) with his brothers and their pals made a fine five-a-side line-up.

Sócrates could occasionally be persuaded to leave his football behind. Here he is (right) with his parents and brother Sóstenes.

A family trip to the park, in 1960 when Sócrates (second right) was six years old.

Even as a child, Sócrates (third right) enjoyed a good party. (All Vieira de Oliveira family collection)

Lining up (front row, third from left) with the Botafogo amateur side in 1972. (Marinho private collect

A useful recruit to any university football team, Sócrates (back row, third from right). (Vieira de Oliveira family collection)

Sócrates' graduation ceremony.
(Dr Said Miguel private collection)

Cigarette and two drinks in hand, Sócrates enjoys his graduation party. (Dr Said Miguel private collection)

Sócrates, Fagner and Regina (Fagner private collection)

Best man at Maurinho Saquy's wedding, with his wife Regina (Maurinho and Regina Saquy personal collection)

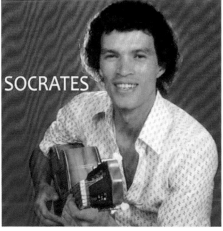

Always willing to try something a little different, Sócrates' album – most of them sertanejo classics or traditional folk ballads he knew from his childhood – wasn't a huge hit. (Katia Bagnarelli personal collection)

Sócrates celebrates after Corinthians score. (Archive of Sport Club Corinthians Paulista)

Sócrates in action for Corinthians against São Paulo – always a key contest. (Archive of Sport Club Corinthians Paulista)

Sócrates became famous for celebrating goals with his militant clenched-fist salute

(Estadão)

There was so much more to Sócrates than being a footballer.

e was a qualified doctor. (Estadão)

He was a symbol of democracy. (Estadão)

nd he was a fearless activist. (Estadão)

Sócrates hurdles a challenge from Ray Wilkins in Brazil's May 1981 encounte with England at Wembley, which they won 1-0. On that trip, Brazil also beat France and West Germany and were soon installed as favourites for the 1982 World Cup. (PA)

In one of the most exciting matches in World Cup history, Brazil were just edged out 3-2 by Italy. Here Sócrates confronts Dino Zoff.

(Getty Images)

His performances in the World Cup inevitably attracted the attention of wealthy European clubs, and in 1984 he signed for Fiorentina, but it was not a happy time for him. (PA)

fter a race to be fit for the 1986
'orld Cup finals, Sócrates scored the
inning goal against Spain in their
'st match of the tournament. (PA)

Nearing the end of his career, Sócrates turned out
for his boyhood favourites Santos. (Estadão)

There was one final – bizarre –
outing for Sócrates in November
2004, when he came on as a
substitute for Garforth Town in the
Northern Counties East League
Division One. (PA)

After retiring from the game, Sócrates remained an influential figure in Brazil. In 2005, he joined President Lula for a game of football in the presidential residence. (Getty Images)

Third time lucky? Sócrates marries Simone, 16 years his junior, in May 1997. (Simone Corrêa personal collection)

Holidaying with his partner Adriana in Paris.
(Maria Adriana Cruz personal collection)

Celebrating his wedding to final wife Kátia. (Kátia Bagnarelli personal collection)

He made those same arguments the day after losing to Italy but he would go even further in the future. As the months and years wore on, Sócrates argued that losing was a good thing because the massive demands made on a World Cup winner would have been too hard to handle. In truth, no one in Brazil's 22-man squad was more capable than he was to deal with those demands, but he used the excuse to rationalise the most painful defeat of his career.

'I think we deserved to win, I wanted to be champion of the world, of course I did, but I wouldn't change a thing,' he said. 'It would be much harder to deal with it all; it would be immense. I was already carrying a bomb around with me; it would have been an arsenal of bombs. [Those bombs] were how to manage that shit in my head, because that's really complicated, dealing with the popularity and the fame that goes with it. It's fucked up; imagine what it would be like if that team were world champions. Winning is never good; it is always harder to deal with. Losing hurts but when you hurt you grow.'[13]

Sócrates had always spoken about retiring after the 1982 World Cup, but that idea was contingent on him winning and he had not foreseen the rise of Corinthians Democracy or his political awakening. The morning after the Italy game he was already talking about returning for a second World Cup four years later, egged on by Zico, who had immediately vowed to be back for another tilt at the title.[14]

But as he sat drinking beers by the pool in Catalonia, the next World Cup was still a long way away. For now, his focus extended only to days and weeks. His fourth child was due any minute and he was going home to be a father again. If that wasn't enough to get him excited then a return to Corinthians Democracy was an enticing prospect. The movement was about to enter a decisive second phase and Sócrates couldn't wait.

11

'Corinthians Democracy helped take the message of change and democracy to lots and lots of people. Corinthians is one of the biggest teams in Brazil and seeing players putting democratic ideas into practice showed how important that fight was.'

Luiz Inácio Lula da Silva, former president of Brazil

The disappointment of the Sarrià was still fresh in the memory but the national side's brilliance was of little concern to those running Corinthians. The revolution that threatened to transform the domestic game was almost over before it began thanks to another outbreak of hostilities at the Parque São Jorge. Brazilian clubs were run by enthusiastic amateurs elected by fans, and the presidents spent as much time constructing their own little empires as they did building a winning football team. Vicente Matheus was still furious at being deposed and he went all out to get his revenge on Waldemar Pires. Before July was out, he had launched a move to oust Pires over the club's proposed sponsorship deal with Bradesco, one of Brazil's biggest private banks.

The government had legalised shirt sponsorship and Bradesco were negotiating a deal with Corinthians that would put their name on the team's jersey. Matheus' lieutenant, Mário Campos, claimed the deal was arranged without fully consulting the club's *conselheiros*, and Matheus called an extraordinary general meeting to discuss impeaching his rival. Although fewer than a third of the club's 300 *conselheiros* turned up, they were mostly pro-Matheus and they voted to remove the president.[1]

It was a questionable move on many levels, and both fans and players were incensed. Supporters expressed their backing for Pires with chants and banners when the club played Juventus at the Pacaembu, and Casagrande and Zenon took a leaf out of Sócrates' book by refusing to celebrate their goals in the 2-0 win. Sócrates, whose contract expired the next month, sent an even stronger message by vowing to leave the club if the coup held firm and Matheus returned.

A court soon ruled Pires' ejection illegal and he was restored as club president just a few days later. The coup attempt turned out to be a boon for Sócrates as fans threw their support behind his and Pires' progressive march. Adilson, with vocal backing from his captain, took the rejection as a sign they could push on with their ambitious plans to transform the club.

Adilson unabashedly laid out his plans for world domination, declaring that Corinthians would try to sign the big-name players who could win them first the Brazilian league, then the Copa Libertadores, and then the Intercontinental Cup in Japan. Off the field, they would explore new revenue fields through commercial partnerships and sponsorship deals the likes of which had never been seen before in Brazil.

As the biggest star at the club, Sócrates was a key part of the project, and he had no problems with the club's commercial aims. He could see that football was moving into a new era of commercialism and that the principal issue was not whether or not to embrace it, but how to do so with integrity. He was open to shirt sponsorship, unlike many who didn't want to see the club jersey sullied with adverts, and was flattered by plans to produce a Corinthians doll that came in two versions, one wearing a football kit and the other dressed as a doctor. Becoming an action figure to be bought and sold wasn't about him being famous, he insisted, it was about being good enough to merit the honour and still remaining a team player. If being good brought benefits to both himself and the club then that was just reward, he said.[2]

Sócrates was already Corinthians' highest-paid player and he took one-fifth of the fee from overseas friendlies, the same portion that all the other players shared between them. His team-mates accepted that arrangement because his outstanding performances helped them pocket win bonuses and boost their own transfer value. With him in the team, Corinthians were paid 20 million cruzeiros ($100,000) per match; without him the fee fell to just over half that.[3]

Fans, meanwhile, accepted his embrace of commercialism because they had come to trust their biggest star. His declaration of love for the club the previous year had not gone unnoticed and neither had his commitment to it on the field of play. Supporters sensed the transformation and stopped calling him the more formal 'Doctor' and started addressing him as the more familiar 'Magrão'. He was no longer the aloof outsider who arrived at the club claiming football was just a job and Corinthians was a club like any other. Now he was one of them.

With the seleção not returning to action until April 1983, Sócrates was able to spend nine months devoting himself exclusively to Corinthians and he took full advantage. It was his longest uninterrupted stint at the club since early 1979 and it turned into one of the busiest periods in his career.

His personal life notwithstanding – a fourth son, Eduardo, was born just days after he returned from Spain – Sócrates spent every waking hour thinking about Corinthians and the revolution he had helped start. When he wasn't playing or training, he was debating or publicising the movement and its aims. Corinthians players soon got used to the wall-to-wall coverage by Brazil's sports media, but Sócrates was transcending sports. The democracy movement, coming so soon after his outstanding performances in Spain, elevated him to a whole new level of stardom and he revelled in the attention.

Sócrates positioned himself as a spokesman for Brazil's poor and he spent as much time talking about democracy and social justice as he did about football. Radio and TV interviews started off with questions about fixtures and line-ups, but Sócrates' answers soon veered into politics, education, public health and the economy. The expected two-minute interview on the next day's game often turned into a half-hour debate on public policy.[4]

He met with politicians and took positions on matters that were startling not just for being sensible, but for being ahead of their time. Proposals to expand the number of trade schools, increase the reach of preventive medicine and grant favela residents title deeds for their homes were ones that would be implemented by future governments years, and sometimes even decades, later.[5]

His activism coincided with an increasing clamour for change from all sectors of Brazilian society. The good times had ended, with the economy shrinking for the first time in more than 30 years and annual inflation leaping to 100 per cent. The dictators looked more and more anachronistic and the longer they clung to power, the more anger grew. By 1982, the government was printing more money than ever before and had even banned imports of many foreign products in a bid to protect local industry. Rents doubled, food prices soared and petrol rationing was once again on the front pages. Change was on everybody's lips and Sócrates was one of the voices that spoke most loudly and most directly in favour of it. For the first time in Brazil's history, a sportsman had a megaphone and fans were listening.

At the end of September, not long after signing a contract that made him the highest-paid player in Brazil, Sócrates went to the US to play in Carlos Alberto Torres' farewell match for the New York Cosmos. Flamengo were invited as guests of honour and the Cosmos, in the spirit of a British testimonial, invited a number of current and former stars to line up alongside their regular first-teamers. Their side included superstars like Franz Beckenbauer and Johan Neeskens, and Sócrates – who, thanks to his World Cup performances, was now attracting increasing attention from foreign clubs – was one of the special guests who played more than an hour of a thrilling match.

Flamengo dominated the first half and went in 3-0 up at the break through goals from Zico, Wilsinho and Júnior. But the Cosmos delighted the 37,000 home crowd by storming right back into the match in the second half, and Giorgio Chinaglia grabbed a hat-trick to bring them level within 12 minutes of the restart.[6]

The game was memorable, but not as memorable as the flight home, at least not for Sócrates, who joined the mile-high club with an air stewardess somewhere in the skies between New York and São Paulo. The real bombshell for his personal life, though, came later in the year after a game at the Morumbi. An event with local singers and musicians had been organised for the same night and, as the biggest names in Brazil's sports and entertainment worlds mingled in the foyer of the brutalist old stadium, Sócrates clapped eyes on Rosemary Pereira Gonçalves.

Rosemary – she went by one name just like footballers – was a stunning petite blonde who hit the big time in the 1960s with a string of hits. She was a successful actress whose mellifluous voice won her an invitation to sing for Jimmy Carter at the White House, and her blonde bombshell looks got her on the cover of *Playboy* not once but twice. They never got a chance to talk as reporters hassled them non-stop for interviews, but they exchanged phone numbers and Sócrates' bedevilling look left her in no doubt as to his intentions. 'He looked at me and I looked at him,' Rosemary recalled demurely. 'There was something there.'[7]

Sócrates' marriage to Regina had cooled after eight years and four children, and the gorgeous little crooner left him spell-bound. Their busy schedules meant it was three months before they actually met up, but he called her every spare minute and they chatted long into the night, creating a solid bond that went deeper than the obvious lust they both felt.

Sócrates had never been faithful but until he met Rosemary the other women in his life had rarely been more than one-night stands. He slept with secretaries at the companies he visited, waitresses at the bars he frequented, and sisters, cousins and friends of his friends. (One possible illegitimate son appeared in São Paulo in 2016 asking for a DNA test.) He would even pick up girls at the start of Corinthians' international tours and take them along with him for the rest of the trip.

With Rosemary, though, it was different. She was seven years his senior and had a maturity that appealed to him. Unlike Regina, who was a homebody never much interested in fashion, Rosemary was a superstar who oozed sex appeal. She under-stood what it was like to be constantly in the spotlight and Sócrates was prepared to risk everything to be with her.

Rosemary lived near the beach in Rio, 270 miles away, but distance was no obstacle when Sócrates was in love. He would send her tickets to come visit, arrange for her to be in the towns where Corinthians played away matches, and one day he even took four 50-minute flights back and forth between the two cities just to spend an hour or two alongside her.

'I got up early in the morning to have breakfast with her,' he wrote in his memoir. 'Straight afterwards I flew to São Paulo for a morning training session. At midday I returned to Rio to have lunch with her. At the start of the afternoon I was back in São Paulo. A few hours later I went back to have dinner with my sweetheart. When I got off the plane in Congonhas airport in São Paulo on what was to be my last trip, I got this longing in my heart. A crazy, impossible desire to lie beside her. I felt this need, this desire, this madness and I had to sleep with her. And almost without thinking, I flew back to her arms.'[8]

Their affair started out discreetly but it didn't take them long before they were planning their lives around it. On at least one occasion, he was so desperate to see her that he got himself subbed at half-time and rushed from the ground to be with her. Friends and team-mates would cover for him and they would cajole or coerce the press into not writing stories or photographing them together. Regina either never suspected or turned a blind eye and Sócrates was never short of alibis. He was always training or on the road with Corinthians and Brazil, and when he wasn't, any one of his commercial sponsors had events and meetings lined up for him. Rosemary would sometimes work out where he was playing and surprise him by having a suite booked when he arrived.[9]

Carrying off such deception wasn't easy but they managed it, and if he ever had any doubts his form on the field was a reminder that the affair was good for him. Sócrates believed that people – and particularly footballers – were more creative when they were relaxed and it was perhaps no accident that he produced some of the best performances of his career during the time they were together.

'Love makes us stronger than we could ever have imagined,' he said. 'Love is the most energising and entrancing feeling that we can experience. When we are in love, everything else is secondary.'[10]

After an uneven start to the Paulista state championship in July, Corinthians' campaign took off against city rivals Palmeiras on 1 August. Casagrande had been showing the same lethal form as at the start of the Silver Cup earlier in the year, getting key goals in the wins over Santo André and Juventus.

But against Palmeiras he was sensational, scoring three goals in four minutes to guarantee the 5-1 victory. Sócrates put Corinthians 2-1 ahead from the penalty spot midway through the second half but, with just 10 minutes remaining, Casagrande secured the points with classic poacher's goals, all three of them tap-ins from less than five yards out.

He scored two more later that week in the 2-0 win over Francana, grabbed another brace in the 2-1 win over Ferroviária and got yet another couple in the win over Internacional de Limeira on 11 August to take his total to nine goals in four games.

Earlier in the year Sócrates had told reporters he was going to help Casagrande become the best centre forward in the country and he openly declared he would dedicate himself to helping his team-mate win the Golden Boot. He passed to him when he could have scored himself and let him take penalties when the result was beyond doubt.

The two players gelled on the field and they soon became inseparable off it as well, with Sócrates taking on a role as Casagrande's calmer, elder brother. Born and raised in Penha, a working-class neighbourhood close to the Parque São Jorge,

Casagrande grew up a Corinthians fan. He had been expelled from school and brought his fame as a restless young trouble-maker to the football field. He made his name by scoring four of Corinthians' six goals in the 1980 São Paulo Youth Cup, but coaches never quite trusted the combustible teenager to step up to the first team. Osvaldo Brandão came close but after calling him into the squad for one game and then unceremoniously dumping him on the eve of the match, Casagrande threatened to punch him and he was farmed out to Caldense, a small club in neighbouring Minas Gerais state.

He scored a barrowload there and was recalled by Travaglini at the start of 1982 to be given his chance. Casagrande was the most visible of a new generation of players who were coming of age just as Brazil and football was changing. Brazilians were no longer quite so scared about speaking their minds and foot-ballers were starting to earn ever bigger sums thanks to the rise of consumerism and advertising.

Casagrande was not the intellectual that Sócrates was but he was clearly more thoughtful and independent than most. He dressed like a typical teenager, in jeans and T-shirts and Converse high tops, and he completed the rock'n'roll look with cool shades below his shaggy mane of hair. The six-foot-three Casagrande liked to stand out on the pitch, too, with his socks around his ankles and his Corinthians top untucked and flap-ping around behind him as he loped across the park.

Sócrates loved Casagrande's energy and identified with his youthful rebelliousness. He was a younger, higher-voltage ver-sion of himself and he could see that Casagrande had a natural affinity with the disaffected youth he wanted to communicate with. Casagrande, meanwhile, was able to use Sócrates to deflect some of his own controversies and at the same time learn from the older man's experience.

Sócrates' ability to identify with and mentor a working–class teenager nine years his junior was indicative of his remarkable ability to bond with the disparate personalities in the Corinthians dressing room, most of whom were light years behind him intellectually.

In the 1980s, Brazilian football was still played almost exclusively by the poor and underprivileged. Brazil's middle class hadn't started to grow, and the elite who ran the nation still saw the sport as a refuge for delinquents who had no other way to escape the country's grinding poverty. At Corinthians, Sócrates was surrounded by players who knew nothing other than football. They'd never had the chance of a proper schooling or they'd flunked out early and football was their only hope in life. When he talked about political theories or personal improvement, they laughed in his face.

'He had a drink and came with all these ideas, you have to read, you have to have some culture,' said Ataliba, one of the jokers in the squad and one of the most down to earth. 'Listen, fuck that, let's play football. Am I going to read a book? No chance. Forget it. He wanted us to but, Magrão, for fuck's sake. Give it a break.'[11]

Sócrates managed to connect with people like Ataliba thanks in part to a throwaway comment made by a former team-mate more than a decade before. He was still playing for amateur side Raio de Ouro and one of the older men in the team praised his performance with the words, 'It's a pity you're not the son of a brickie.' Sócrates interpreted the comment as a warning – the soft middle-class boy wouldn't make it in a world populated by men who were hard and ruthless. The words stayed with him for years and inspired him to try to be like that brickie's boy, or at least to always try to understand him.[12]

In spite of the intellectual gap between him and players like Ataliba, Sócrates never once lorded it over them. The doctor, with his books, his fancy words and his *Playboy* lover, could easily have come across as arrogant or snobbish. Instead, Sócrates made a point of helping the other players when they weren't playing football, and he emphatically played up their contribution to the side when they were. Biro-Biro said Sócrates would sometimes sit with them after they gave interviews and help them with their vocabulary and diction. Whenever someone praised his performance or his goals, he immediately responded with his own interpretation that shifted credit to his colleagues. Sócrates may have won the game but without Biro-Biro's running or Ataliba's crosses or Paulinho's tackling none of it would have been possible, he said. The upshot was that even though his team-mates thought he was weird and distant, they were always fiercely loyal.

'He was different,' said Ataliba. 'As a man, as a father, and especially as a player, on and off the field. I have this image of him, I wouldn't call it gratitude ... but in the two and a half years we were together, I don't have a bad word to say about him.'[13]

One of the characteristics that most struck his team-mates was his confidence. The Corinthians players were either poor or black or both, and like their impoverished and dark-skinned countrymen they were used to being treated as second-class citizens. Experience had taught players like Ataliba and Biro-Biro that they couldn't get away with what the middle-class doctor did — whether it was the affairs, the drinking before matches or the way he boldly spoke his mind. But everything that Sócrates did and said let them know he was on their side.

'He knew what he was doing and he was aware of it and that transmitted a real confidence to us all,' said Biro-Biro. 'You'd get to the hotel and he'd be with a group of four or five people [drinking]. And the next day he played exactly the same way. I thought it was wrong but it never had any effect on him. And as he passed that confidence on to us, I thought, "Oh well, then, fine." Even when he wasn't playing well or playing for 90 minutes, he'd play for 30 minutes or even two or three minutes and do something.'[14]

Players at winning teams – and sometimes even at losing teams – love to pretend that the squad are all best mates on and off the pitch. It's usually nonsense, for as Sócrates never tired of pointing out, while football is a team game, every player is an individual competing with other individuals for more playing time, more money and more recognition.

The Corinthians team of 1982 had its divisions, but they were minor and it was the most united of all the club sides Sócrates played in. The team coach would bring players back to São Paulo after away games but the vibe was so great that the players didn't always head straight home. Sometimes they extended their weekend, going out together or sitting around for a few last beers rather than running back to wives and families. They were winning, which always makes for a happy atmosphere, and they were playing well, with Zenon, Wladimir, Biro-Biro, Paulinho, Casagrande and Ataliba among those playing the best football of their careers. What was once heavy metal had evolved into power pop and was now approaching something more like jazz. It was, in the memorable words of novelist and Corinthians fans Marcelo Rubens Paiva, 'Earth Wind and Fire football'.

The team of strong characters, each of whom had assumed their own distinctive personality, were a godsend to the media. Sócrates was the thinker, gladly imitating the pose of Rodin's sculpture for the front cover of *Placar*. Biro-Biro was the most recognisable man on the pitch, with his socks rolled down to his ankles and a mane of blond curls that was unsurpassed until Carlos Valderrama came along. Zenon had a Beatle-ish mop top, a jet-black moustache and played with his shirt untucked, a rarity for the times; while Casagrande was the rebel, with his wraparound shades, white boots and opinions about everything. Veterans Wladimir, with his long-term commitment to both the club and Brazil's black-power movement, and Zé Maria, the tireless warhorse, were the archetypal, and therefore hugely popular, Corinthianos.

Such flashiness had always been the antithesis of Corinthians' solidly blue-collar ethic, but Sócrates changed that, too. The fans loved their irreverence and, as long as they were winning, they could do as they pleased.

And they did. During the second half of 1982, they tried things that no Brazilian football team had ever tried before. Brazil has an image as a country where anything goes, a nation that, according to two local sayings, is not for beginners and where there is no such thing as sin. But Brazil in the 1980s was still closed and conservative, even in a relatively cosmopolitan city like São Paulo. Those boundaries were what Sócrates hated most and the more power he had, the more he tried to push them back.

At his behest, Corinthians hired a pop psychotherapist famous for his newspaper columns on personal relationships. Many of the players thought Flávio Gikovate peddled self-help mumbo jumbo – he said Brazil lost to Italy because the Brazil players were afraid of being world champions – but Sócrates loved it and for a while the two became friends.

One of Brazil's most creative minds joined to boost their marketing department and Corinthians fanatic Washington Olivetto formed a lifelong friendship with several players, none more so than Sócrates. Olivetto was as well connected as he was charismatic, and he reached out to his friends in the music business and in television to help promote the new movement.

The players got actively involved in the resurgent music scene, with Casagrande leading groups of players to concerts every week. The garage band, do-it-yourself ethos had reached Brazil and a new wave of angry rock'n'rollers were taking their frustration out on their guitars. In one pre-planned outing just days before landmark elections in November, Sócrates, Casagrande and Wladimir took to the stage during a concert by Rita Lee and sang along to her song 'Vote For Me'. Casagrande had planned to give Lee a Corinthians shirt to wear but forgot to bring one along and had to beg someone in the crowd to give him theirs. Sócrates walked on stage with the strip on over his T-shirt and then pulled it off to give to Lee, who was a Corinthians fanatic. The four of them danced around joyously and then Sócrates lifted one of the performing dwarves on to his shoulders and pranced off, drunkenly falling off the stage as he left, fortunate to do neither himself nor the dwarf a serious injury.[15]

Several of the players became politically active outside the dressing room, with Zé Maria joining the centrist opposition group the PMDB and Casagrande and Wladimir among those who signed up to the Workers' Party, the leftist party started by future president Lula. Contrarian as ever, Sócrates preferred to remain above party politics, a stance that disappointed those on the left who wanted to claim him as one of their own.

Still, he kept hammering home his message of change. In one of their most daring challenges yet, the Corinthians players walked out for a November match against Juventus with the words 'Dia 15 Vote' on their shirts. The message to encourage people to vote in state elections scheduled for 15 November was too political for the powers that be and they were forced to remove it, but the job had already been done.

There was a downside, too, as the praise started to go to their heads. Sócrates insisted on hosting a party before one crucial game and laid on a full *feijoada*, a notoriously heavy meal of black beans, rice and cheap cuts of meat and sausage. They lost the next day and some of his team-mates were furious at his lack of professionalism. More seriously, Casagrande got involved with drugs and was arrested for cocaine possession just before Christmas. Although the charges were later dropped for lack of evidence, it drew more attention to the team and every game became an event. The spotlight on Corinthians was constant and they weren't playing for themselves any more, or even just for their fans. The whole country was watching and results took on a significance that went beyond football.

'Our responsibility grew,' recalled Biro-Biro. 'We created a democracy that had an effect on the whole country and every game was a final. We had to win every game and the fans and the people gained confidence, and politically our responsibility got bigger and bigger. Whether we liked it or not, people took that to the stadiums. If we lost, it would have been difficult for Corinthians Democracy to survive. There was a lot more pressure, without a doubt.'[16]

Sócrates enjoyed the pressure but he was not immune to it. He had no superstitions in the dressing room but he had a peculiar way of coping with the stress of big games. When he was happy, his mind wandered and he found it harder to concentrate. So if he arrived at the ground in a good mood, he tried to make himself sad. It wasn't always a conscious decision, but he instinctively switched the computer upstairs into sleep mode before big games.

'When I was happy it affected my concentration so I brought it to a quick halt, I always shut it down,' he said. 'It was intuitive; I didn't know I was doing it. Being sad helped me concentrate. When I was sad for some reason, or angry, I blocked the world out and went into my shell. I would even sleep in the dressing room before a game. I would be much more focused on the game, or rather not on the game, I was focused on me and that gave me a certain inner strength and in time I started to manipulate that.'[17]

His team-mates and friends began to notice how important the mental preparation was to him and they began to act accordingly. 'When he arrived in the dressing room and was quiet, I'd say, "Don't bother him, he's going to blow them away today,"' recalled Biro-Biro. 'Magrão, when he was quiet, when he lay down and rested, he played much better once he got out on the pitch than if he arrived all fired up. When he concentrated, he was something else.'[18]

Gikovate also believed Sócrates played better when he was preoccupied and Olivetto, spotting his need for intellectual engagement, set up events to help take his mind off football. Before important games, Olivetto would invite an architect or a musician or a novelist to dinner, and they would sit around drinking and debating long into the night.[19]

Their efforts worked and Corinthians breezed through the Paulista state championship, which had returned to a more sensible format, with the winners of the first round of home and away fixtures meeting the winners of the second round in the final in December. Corinthians walked the first half of the season, finishing five points ahead of reigning champions São Paulo with a goal difference that was twice that of their rivals. They came very close to equalling that feat in the second phase, but two defeats in their last two games handed the honour to São Paulo and set up both teams for a final showdown over two games.

Corinthians won the first thanks to a goal from Sócrates in a match so scrappy he said it barely resembled football, and then they gathered ahead of the decider three days later in what Sócrates promised would be the last obligatory *concentração* before its abolition the following year. It was their 76th and last match of the season and they clinched the title with a 3-1 win.

The triumph for Corinthians was a triumph for democracy and for the footballing neutrals who wanted an end to the regime. It was also a high point for Sócrates, who played in 13 of the 19 first-round games and in all 19 of the second. He scored 18 goals to finish second in the goalscoring table, 10 behind Casagrande who waltzed away with the Golden Boot in his first full season as a professional.

The victory was notable for Corinthians as their first Paulista title for three years and they celebrated their success by directing the team bus to Waldemar Pires' mansion and surprising him with demands for an impromptu victory party. The president couldn't say no and the players piled up the steps into his front room – and then downstairs into his wine cellar – to drink to their success.[20]

It was also significant for Sócrates and not just because he capped the best year of his career so far with a trophy. He celebrated his goal in the first leg by holding his right arm aloft, his fist clenched in a militant salute. Although he was never sure about what led him to adopt the celebration, it became his trademark. He later cited the Black Panthers on the podium in Mexico City in 1968 as one of his influences and he was surely aware of its anti-Fascist history. It wasn't the first time he had used it – he celebrated goals with a clenched fist as far back as 1978 – but its appearance fitted perfectly with the new progressive agenda and he took to using it more often.

Perhaps the most memorable decision during those final few months of 1982 was made at a university, and not by a player, manager or even director. Although it was almost a year old, the movement still didn't have a name. People referred to it as 'player power', or they called Corinthians 'the democratic team', or the goings-on the 'Corinthians revolution'. That began to change in November after a debate at São Paulo's Catholic Pontificate University.

Olivetto, Sócrates and Adilson sat on stage in front of hundreds of students and fans to discuss the movement and its aims, aided and abetted by moderator Juca Kfouri, who at one point in the evening wryly summed things up with the comment: 'So if the players keep participating in decisions at the club, if the directors don't stop them, and if the enlightened media give them support, then what we'll see here is a democracy, a Corinthians democracy.'[21]

It was one of those moments that PR man Olivetto has never forgotten.

'As soon as he said it I thought, "My God, that's it,"' he said.

Olivetto grabbed his pen and scribbled down the words 'Corinthians Democracy'. He turned to Adilson in the chair next to him and whispered, 'I've got a name!'[22]

Sócrates thought the title was accurate but unfortunate, because the word democracy served as a red rag to the conservative bulls who were working to maintain the status quo. But it stuck and went down in history as the name of the most transformative movement ever to rock a major football club.

Sócrates believed that winning the Paulista title in December was proof that openness brought rewards, and he headed to the beach for his Christmas holidays with big plans to expand the movement in 1983. His optimism, however, was to prove excessive. As their ambition grew, so did their problems. Democracy was now their name but its meaning would come under increasing scrutiny. The coming months would teach Sócrates that democracy meant different things to different people. It could be used in varying ways. Or, when it suited him, it didn't have to be used at all.

12

'In 1982 we were all happier, freer. 1983 was more
difficult for us all, more of a struggle. We thought that
the atmosphere would be the same as in 1982 but things
are never the same.'

Casagrande

On a drizzly afternoon in early February 1983, Adilson called
the Corinthians players together for a team meeting in the gym.
The two dozen or so participants moved the benches into a
square and Adilson started talking.

'We're thinking of hiring a goalkeeper and we're thinking of
Leão,' Adilson told them. 'What do you guys think?'

Émerson Leão was one of the most controversial footballers
in Brazil, a brilliant goalkeeper who had won four league titles
and been to three World Cups but whose outspoken individualism had made him enemies everywhere he went.

Many of the Corinthians players were happy to welcome
Leão, for his goalkeeping ability if not for his personal skills.
But some were vociferously against, with the three goalkeepers
in the squad, plus Casagrande and Wladimir, all expressing their

opposition in no uncertain terms. Voices were raised in the debate that followed, with half the team fearing his arrival would jeopardise the harmony they had fought so hard to create, and the other half prepared to risk that harmony to sign the best goalkeeper in the country.[1]

'Let's vote on it,' Adilson said when the debate died down, and after Leão's signing was approved by his casting vote, he did something that no one in the room expected.[2]

'Well, now that we've voted in favour I am going to introduce him to you, he's here right now,' he said.

The stunned silence was quickly broken by a chorus of disbelieving voices asking, 'What do you mean he's here right now?'

'He's here,' said Adilson, and he shouted out for Leão to come and meet his new team-mates.

Leão, who had been next door listening to the arguments about whether it was more important to sign a great goalkeeper or reject a potential troublemaker, walked into the room and introduced himself. The exercise had been a sham, and Leão was coming to Corinthians whether or not the squad voted yes.

Adilson later explained that unlike previous signings, which were agreed ahead of time by the whole squad, this one was decided beforehand by a coterie of senior players. Sócrates, Wladimir and Zé Maria, all of whom had played with Leão at the seleção, were quizzed privately as to their thoughts, as were Travaglini and trainer Hélio Maffia, who knew him from their time at Palmeiras. All five agreed that the pros of signing such a great keeper outweighed the cons of signing such a divisive personality. That was enough for Adilson, who did the deal. Only then did he take it to the full squad, where, thanks in part to Sócrates' powers of persuasion, they narrowly voted yes, thus avoiding a potentially fatal split.

But even after putting it to a show vote the decision infuriated more than just the goalkeepers in the squad. Casagrande was so outspoken that he was handed a 40-day suspension and tensions rose sharply as the season got under way.[3]

The deceitful way the transfer was handled focused an uncomfortable spotlight on the movement and leaders Adilson, Sócrates, Wladimir and Casagrande. Their outsize influence led critics to dub it a 'Four-man democracy' or 'Corinthians aristocracy', claims they laughed off, even while acknowledging that in democracies some people got more involved than others. The episode, though, was an affront to the whole concept of democracy and it called the movement's ethos into question.

They got away with the chicanery for the simple reason that most of the Corinthians players neither cared how Leão's signing was arranged nor knew enough about democracy to object. The movement was only a year old and of secondary importance to most of the squad. They were unsophisticated football players with minimal experience of voting or collective ethics, and they were unaware that true democractic leaders did not circumvent ballots they ran a risk of losing.

'We knew very little about democracy,' admitted Zé Maria. 'We wanted a democracy but we didn't really understand it, we weren't aware what it was.'

Sócrates knew they were committing an injustice but he signed off on it because he was convinced they must sign the best players if they wanted to challenge for the Brazilian championship. Winning was more important than he cared to admit and, although he would privately tell friends he had erred, he was not so noble in public. In a book he co-authored on Corinthians Democracy in 2002, he feebly claimed not to remember the exact circumstances of Leão's arrival.

The controversy came at a sensitive time. The Brazilian

media were split over Corinthians Democracy: a few well-known journalists supported their aims but the majority of big publications were openly hostile. Ordinary people, meanwhile, were watching closely and debating its importance at a moment that was starting to feel like a crossroads. Brazil in early 1983 was increasingly on edge, as shrapnel from the economic boom came raining down. The currency was devalued by 30 per cent at the beginning of the year, inflation rose to its highest monthly level in two decades, and the government introduced price controls to try to keep the economy going. Unemployment was rising, as was government debt, and the tensions spilled out on to the streets, where strikes and looting became more and more common.

At Corinthians, Leão's signing was followed soon after by a vital election between Pires and Vicente Matheus. Maintaining Pires in charge was crucial if the movement was to continue, and Sócrates got more involved than ever before. He didn't just threaten to leave Corinthians if Matheus returned; his name was down as a candidate for *conselheiro* alongside that of Wladimir and Zé Maria.

The election was held on Sunday, 6 March, the day Corinthians were to play Fluminense at the Maracanã, and Sócrates wanted his team-mates to participate. He tried to convince them to delay their flight by a day and go to Rio after depositing their ballot papers early on the Sunday morning, and he forced a vote on the matter. He narrowly lost but, even though he couldn't cast a vote, thousands of others did and all three were duly elected.

Their political careers didn't last long, however, because meetings were held on a Monday, their only day off. Unwilling to swap their weekly bonding day of barbecues and beer for yet another stint at the Parque São Jorge, they were ousted after missing three consecutive meetings. Sócrates didn't really care, and had unsuccessfully tried to remove his name from the ballot on discovering it was not a direct election. More importantly, though, Pires was easily re-elected, polling 5,138 votes to Matheus' 2,336. The revolution marched shakily on.[4]

The Leão stunt notwithstanding, Sócrates believed in player power more than ever, and he was genuinely baffled that other teams didn't try to copy their experiment. Only one or two players publicly supported their cause and, although Carlos Alberto Torres promised more openness at Flamengo and players at Cruzeiro, Fluminense and Ponte Preta discussed having more control over decisions, no team came close to replicating their own version of Corinthians Democracy. Several top players, particularly those at rivals São Paulo, dismissed it as a fad and told their team-mates to concentrate on the football and forget about everything else.

Sócrates was dispirited by his colleagues' lack of awareness, but as the year went on he was forced to worry about democracy at his own club as Leão made his influence felt. Leão was a consummate professional who was the first to arrive in the morning and last to leave at night. But he thought the whole idea of footballers as agents of political change was a big joke and he worked openly to undermine it. A respected professional and articulate speaker, he successfully lobbied the reserves and younger players for their support, and won them over to his side by convincing them that the movement's leaders got more money than they did because they were friends with the directors. Adilson and Sócrates met with Leão to discuss his stance, but he laughed in their faces and told them that if they thought he was a problem after only a month, they should give him a couple more and he'd have the support to vote the entire scheme into oblivion.[5]

His overt hostility infuriated Sócrates, who watched with dismay as his own influence waned and the atmosphere in the dressing room grew more and more fraught. The split simmered throughout the season and developed into outright confrontation ahead of the Paulista semi-final against Palmeiras in December. Sócrates and Adilson were tired of Leão's attempts to discredit the movement and they rounded on him in the hotel before the game. Tempers flared and voices were raised and Adilson snarled, 'If you lose a goal and Corinthians get knocked out then we're going to the press to tell them you did it deliberately.'

Leão turned in a masterclass of goalkeeping as Corinthians won 1-0, but the constant clashes had made his position untenable. When the tournament was over, he returned to Palmeiras after spending less than a year with their rivals.

Sócrates never forgave Leão for trying to destroy his project and the two men spent the rest of their lives at odds. Leão refused point-blank to talk about his nemesis, but Sócrates was not so restrained, once saying, 'If God made man, then the Devil made Émerson Leão.' His resentment was all the more notable given that he rarely made enemies. When Sócrates didn't like someone, he simply cut them out of his life, as simply and as cleanly as possible, often by just ignoring them altogether. He frequently made snap decisions if he sensed someone was out to take advantage of him or his celebrity. He usually had no problem with people who thought differently and happily debated ideas with anyone holding an opposing viewpoint, which made his bitter relationship with Leão so unusual.[6]

The dressing-room conflicts had an adverse effect, but it turned out to be more on the backroom staff than on results. Sócrates began the season in blistering form, scoring four goals in a 10-1 win over Tiradentes and helping the team to a fine start in the Brasileiro. They lost just two of their opening 16 games, but they were hit with a bombshell in late March when Travaglini unexpectedly resigned.

The popular coach said he was 'tired, dispirited and worn out', but there were also reports he was sick of the 'four-man democracy' and wanted nothing more to do with it. He admitted that Casagrande's disciplinary problems, players' public protestations at being subbed or dropped, and the angry debates over Leão's arrival had all contributed to his departure, but he claimed to still believe in Corinthians Democracy and said his resignation was not an indictment of it.[7]

Travaglini had warned Adilson of his intentions a few days before Corinthians beat Bahia 2-0 and the director of football summoned Sócrates, Wladimir, Uruguayan defender Daniel González and club doctor Luis Carlos Campos to discuss their next move after the game. Adilson suggested Zé Maria as a possible replacement and, eager to keep Corinthians Democracy alive, they agreed that appointing an insider would provide the movement with continuity.

When word got out that Travaglini might be leaving the club, Sócrates' name appeared as a potential successor and he expressed an interest in the opportunity. Sócrates said managing Corinthians would be a 'wholly viable' option and, with his casual self-confidence, declared it would be just another job for someone who was keen to put his revolutionary ideas into practice.

Adilson, though, needed Sócrates on the pitch and his teammates, when consulted about appointing Zé Maria, all agreed that the popular full back would be the best replacement. Super Zé was on the verge of retirement from the game and so, when Travaglini made his resignation official, the club was ready to effect a swift transition.

Zé Maria took over the day after Sócrates picked up his Player of the Year award for 1982, but Sócrates pointedly avoided calling him coach and instead referred to him as our 'representative'. The big full back, though, was as mild-mannered as he was popular, and operating as the team 'representative' was perhaps not the ideal approach for dealing with such a strong-willed band of men, especially with Sócrates taking every chance possible to stamp his own authority on the club. His time in charge was not a complete disaster – they won three, drew three and lost just two of his eight games in charge – but it was not enough to take them into the knockout stages of the Brasileiro and he stood down on 3 May, just five weeks after taking the job.[8]

Zé Maria's period at the helm became known as *auto-gestão*, or self-management, and it gave opponents a whole new opportunity to attack Corinthians Democracy. It was, in Sócrates' words, 'our biggest victory so far', but the sight of players running their own football club was a wake-up call not just to the conservative elements who ran football, but also to the politicians, business leaders and media barons who feared it could serve as a model for the working classes they had controlled for so long. Attitudes hardened, especially in the media, and Corinthians Democracy, so cool and cute in 1982, was slowly turning into something to be feared and challenged.[9]

'We suffered at times,' said Zenon. 'We got threats from outside, from the government, telling us to quieten down, not to be so forthright. The military sent us messages. That increased our responsibility on the pitch to get results so we could have the tranquillity to speak about what we wanted to happen in the country.'[10]

Sócrates later admitted that they had perhaps tried to do too much in too short a time, and Zé Maria's lack of success forced them to take a step back and spend the rest of the year 'consolidating rather than advancing', in Adilson's disappointed and diplomatic words.

Part of that involved appointing a more conventional figure as coach and Jorge Vieira returned to team up with Sócrates for a fourth time. The famously authoritarian coach was given the task of wresting back control of the club. The players had over-stepped the mark, and it wasn't just the discussions over the signing of Leão or the appointment of Zé Maria as coach. Casagrande and Wladimir both acted in low-budget comedies, which brought them condemnation from the usual conservative opponents, and Casagrande, still reeling from his drug arrest, was struggling to cope with the pressure and scored just one goal in the first six months of the year.

Around the same time, Hélio Maffia had walked into his office after a training session to find Sócrates, Casagrande and Ataliba with their feet on his desk and beers in their hands. The outraged trainer kicked them out and complained they were getting way too familiar. Sócrates claimed they were drinking to rehydrate and cool down, but the explanation was dubious and heightened the sense that the lunatics had taken over the asylum.

Sócrates' star power was by this time incandescent and not only in Brazil. His World Cup performances had brought him to the attention of clubs all over the world and, as the gates to free movement in Europe swung slowly open, clubs in Spain and particularly Italy made their interest apparent.

Sócrates had long known that foreign sides wanted to lure him away from Corinthians. He turned down an offer from the New York Cosmos that included a guaranteed medical residency after his three-year playing contract was over, and he rejected a ridiculously lucrative deal from Dubai with the explanation that 'money can't buy happiness'.

Barcelona wanted him to replace Bernd Schuster when the German playmaker was injured in December 1981, but he worried that moving to Europe might jeopardise his place in the World Cup finals and rebuffed their advances. The closest he came to a move was in 1983 when Roma tried to make him their second foreigner alongside Paulo Roberto Falcão. He discussed terms with the capital club and Adilson flew to Switzerland to meet their directors and discuss a transfer fee. However, talks broke down when the Italians refused to free him from the *concentração*. The idea of playing in Italy and learning a new culture and language was an enticing prospect – as was the money – but it wasn't worth giving up his personal freedom for. To Sócrates, that had no price.[11]

Sócrates was happy in Brazil, where he knew how to use his power and influence, as the incident in Maffia's office showed. Given an inch, Sócrates would take a mile, and his fame and his charm could get him out of the tightest corners. His football, though, was starting to suffer, and even his team-mates were beginning to wonder whether he was spending too much time talking about politics and not enough time thinking about football.

Those fears grew as the troubled year wore on. Vieira tried to reinstate the *concentração* but Sócrates refused to go, saying he was contractually allowed to turn up only on the day of the game. The football authorities – who were still run by the military – were feeling similarly threatened and they forced Corinthians to remove the inscription 'Corinthians Democracy' from their shirts because they felt it was too political.

Sócrates couldn't get a break at home, as robbers entered his flat when he and his family were away and made off with a briefcase containing $20,000. The thieves had a key and knew exactly where he kept the money, and the thought that friends or family were behind the assault was truly frightening.[12]

Nor was there respite at his usual sanctuary, the seleção. New boss Carlos Alberto Parreira kept him as captain for a four-game tour of Europe in June and an unsuccessful Copa América later in the year, but they didn't see eye to eye and Parreira's demands for a more pragmatic style offended the sensibilities of a player

207

who believed Brazil should never try to copy the Europeans.

'He shut himself off more in 1983,' Casagrande recalled. 'He wasn't as happy. We were much more free and easy in 1982; in 1983 things got more serious. We did a whole lot of things different from the year before. When you win it's all normal, when you lose it's not. That whole first half of the year was a mess.'[13]

Sócrates found some solace away from football and politics and he continued to blaze his own trail. His affair with Rosemary was still going strong and he was by now a regular at Gallery, the hottest club in São Paulo and a place where he would turn up in old jeans and trainers just to prove that the dress code applied to everyone but him.

He made friends with a host of celebrities, including singers and songwriters Fagner, Chico Buarque and Toquinho, author Marcelo Rubens Paiva and the publishers of the *Estado de São Paulo* newspaper. He enjoyed the company of creative minds and he dug into his savings to produce a play called *The Scent of Camélia* , a romance that turned into a drama and then ended as a comedy.

Always a fan of the theatre, Sócrates played an active role in choosing the director and cast and he took part as often as he could during its four months of rehearsals. It was hardly a success, selling out only on the last night of its 30-day run, but Sócrates wasn't discouraged. He was doing something different and creative and he didn't care what anyone else thought. He discussed adapting another story for the stage and Wladimir, Casagrande, Juninho and Eduardo all agreed to play parts. He wanted street theatre, where people could see it, and even mulled the possibility of putting on a play at Corinthians. But with demands on his time already stretched, the idea died a death.

*

The only time Sócrates felt truly afraid at a football match was at a game involving Botafogo and Corinthians in 1974. With an hour gone in the match, Sócrates set up Geraldão to score and give Botafogo a 1-0 lead. Corinthians players thought the goal was offside and they charged at the linesman. Rivellino kicked him in the shin and his team-mates piled in. The terraces at the Parque São Jorge were just inches from the touchline, and baying fans furiously tried to tear down the flimsy wire fence and invade the pitch. Bottles, sticks and bits of concrete rained down and the referee was forced to abandon the match. The Botafogo players couldn't make it to the dressing room without being attacked and were forced to take refuge in the centre circle, where for half an hour they cowered under the shields of 100 riot police.[14]

'The Corinthians fans were roaring, it was like a lion trying to break out of its cage,' Sócrates recalled. 'I thought, "We're not going to get out of here alive." It was the most scared I have ever been on a football field. I was terrified.'[15]

It is sometimes hard to describe just how crazy it used to be at Brazilian football grounds. Violence grew exponentially in the 1970s and 80s, and although fans were segregated they still fought, sometimes even with guns. Beer was still available inside the ground and everything from peanuts to *cachaça* to skewers of meat were sold on the streets around about. Inside, the atmosphere was electric, with fans hanging banners, waving enormous flags and letting off rockets and flares when the teams came out. Toilet rolls were thrown from the top decks and ticker tape was tossed into the air. Fans then gathered the paper together and set it alight, and by the second half whole sections of the terraces were ablaze with bonfires. Toilet facilities were so rudimentary that fans would relieve themselves into bags or cups and then throw them away, or they would simply go right where they stood. Seven fans were killed in Salvador in 2007 when they fell through an upper terrace that had been weakened by years of beer and urine.

It was in that kind of charged atmosphere that the Corinthians bus edged through the crowds towards the Morumbi for the second leg of the Paulista semi-final against Palmeiras in December 1983.

Jorge Vieira had steered the side back to form after Zé Maria's ill-advised tenure and they had come good again in the Paulista. With Leão outstanding in goal, and new signings Juninho Fonseca, Luis Fernando (hyped by Sócrates as his future replacement) and striker Vidotti all playing a role, Corinthians recovered from their early-season slump. By November, after playing 38 games in just six months, they had powered towards a date with their archrivals.

The coach left the team hotel later than scheduled after the dressing-room bust-up with Leão over his opposition to Corinthians Democracy. They should have been at the Morumbi an hour before the 9.15 p.m. kick-off, but the traffic was atrocious and the coach's engine coughed and spluttered before eventually giving out just a few hundred yards from the stadium. The players were high on adrenaline, but they put down their tambourines and stopped singing and looked at their watches. It was already past nine and Sócrates took charge. 'Let's get out of here,' he said, and seconds later he was leading the players down the coach steps and on to the leafy residential streets that surround the stadium. Almost 96,000 people were at the game and the late arrivals couldn't believe their eyes as the Corinthians players jogged from the bus to the stadium, their kit bags slung over their shoulders. Fans tried to grab them and wish them luck, but the players fought them off and tried to keep moving as fast as possible through the mêlée. There were screams and chants and fireworks going off all around them, but they managed to get to the stadium with nine minutes to spare and avoid the travesty of losing on a technicality.

When the match kicked off 20 minutes late there was no let-up in the drama. The first leg had ended 1-1, with Sócrates getting Corinthians' goal from the penalty spot, but his attacking threat had been snuffed out by a 21-year-old defender called Márcio Alcântara. Alcântara was given the task of man-marking Sócrates and he followed his instructions to the letter, at one point in the match following Sócrates off the field as he went to pick up a ball that had gone out for a throw-in. Sócrates was not used to being so thoroughly annulled by someone else's brilliance and he was furious with himself. Within minutes of the final whistle, he was telling his team-mates it would be a different story in the second leg four days later.

The return was once again memorable for the duel between the young defender and the experienced forward. From the moment the game got under way, Alcântara never gave his rival a moment's peace, but Sócrates knew what to expect and he countered the close attention with the most cunning – and hilarious – of strategies. As soon as the whistle went Sócrates casually trotted from one side of the field to the other, Alcântara just a foot or two behind him. Sócrates meandered this way and that, even when the ball was at the other end of the field. Alcântara followed faithfully, from touchline to touchline, never giving him a moment's respite. At corners, Sócrates cheekily pointed at Alcântara behind his back, laughing at him with an evil grin that the fans couldn't help but notice. He then seized the moment when the ball was out of play and sprinted towards the corner flag as if chasing an invisible long ball. Alcântara instinctively gave chase and the crowd erupted in hoots of laughter as Sócrates drew up with a big smile on his face. The persecution was comical and fans started to laugh at the Palmeiras defender. Alcântara realised how stupid he looked and he dropped off his opponent. It was exactly what Sócrates had planned and, all of a sudden, he was free again. Just a few moments later, with 21 minutes on the clock, he took a pass with his back to goal. He was about 30 yards from the target and his marker was a good few yards behind him. There was enough daylight between the two of them for Sócrates to spin round to the left and leave his man for dead. He strode forward, took one more touch to set up a shot, and then fired home an angled drive from 20 yards out for what was the winning goal.[16]

'It was the best move he ever made on a football pitch,' said Luis Fernando of the strategy that embarrassed Alcântara, 'and yet the ball was nowhere near him.'[17]

The win took them into the final against São Paulo, the team that topped the overall table for the season. São Paulo were favourites not only because Leão and Casagrande were going to miss the first leg through suspension, but also because they were coached by Mário Travaglini, who knew every bit as much about the Corinthians players as Jorge Vieira did.

Entirely unruffled by the criticism that followed his *feijoada* the day before the decisive fixture with São Paulo the year previously, Sócrates stubbornly decided to repeat the gesture, sitting down for pizza and beers with Juninho and friends the night before the final.

He got home well after midnight but it made no difference. Sócrates was the outstanding player in Corinthians' 1–0 win and he himself scored the winning goal after 33 minutes to take his total to three in three games. He then marshalled the team for the remaining hour through rain that started slowly before half-time and then developed into a biblical downpour that made passing the ball along the ground all but impossible.

The result meant that Corinthians only needed a draw on 14 December to lift the Paulista title for the second consecutive year. The match was a big one both for Sócrates and for Corinthians Democracy. The movement had been under fire since the start of the season and they were not playing with the same panache as the year before. They needed a victory and a statement, and as they sat around the lobby of the Hilton Hotel on the morning of the match they discussed how best to go about it. Adilson considered sending the team out in shirts with the Corinthians Democracy logo on them, but the political climate was still sensitive and they shelved the idea for fear of reprisals by the military.

'How about we take to the field with a banner about Christmas and Democracy, both things together?' Casagrande suggested.

'Christmas is a bit too elitist, Casa,' said Adilson.

'Then how about a banner saying: "Triumph or Defeat, But Always with Democracy"?' suggested journalist Luiz Fernando Rodrigues, who was sitting in on the discussion.

'That's it!' Casagrande and Adilson agreed.[18]

They got Waldemar Pires' blessing over lunch and a banner was quickly made up.

A few hours later, shortly after 9 p.m., Corinthians walked out at the Morumbi with a huge banner that had been tweaked slightly from the original idea to read: 'Win or Lose, But Always with Democracy'.

Corinthians fans had long boasted that their club was bigger than the mere act of winning or losing, and Sócrates whole-heartedly agreed with that sentiment. But putting it into words was one of the most iconic moments of Corinthians Democracy. No one actually believed that winning the match wasn't important, no matter what their political position was, and even though they only needed a draw to take the title they were not there to play for a point.

It was a scrappy game that turned in Corinthians' favour 15 minutes from the end when Darío Pereyra was sent off for a professional foul on Casagrande. The scoreline was stuck at 0–0 but if there were any lingering doubts, Sócrates, inevitably, was there to dispel them. With the match in injury time and delirious Corinthians fans getting ready to invade the field, he ran on to a delicious back-heel from Zenon and side-footed the ball home from just inside the box. He was mobbed by fans and reporters who ran on to the pitch, and the referee struggled to get them all off again. No matter that São Paulo ran up the field and grabbed an equaliser with the last touch of the game. A draw was enough and Corinthians were champions for the second year in a row – the first time they had won back-to-back titles in more than 30 years.

Ironically, Leão's arrival, and the dubious way it was handled, had important consequences for Corinthians and Sócrates both on and off the field. Leão made his debut against Fluminense in March and his error cost them the game's only goal. But rather than admitting he was at fault or resorting to the group defence of 'we win as a team and we lose as a team', Leão blamed his defence. His attitude unsettled Sócrates and, after a night on the tiles in Rio, he woke Casagrande at 3 a.m. to admit that the younger man had been right. Casagrande, only half-awake but still angry, told him to go fuck himself and slammed the door in his face.[19]

Sócrates' reaction was to up his game and do all he could to show that, although he had been responsible for Leão's arrival, he would not allow him to drag the team down. As Leão made his influence felt and Corinthians Democracy teetered on the brink, Sócrates pulled out all the stops. His superb performances during the second half of the season were a response to his screw-up.

'Sócrates was bothered by the decision to sign Leão,' Casagrande said. 'They thought they were more powerful that the rest and in that tiny moment he lost it, he was taken in. He didn't usually think like that. What he did was an assault on the essence of who he was.

'So I think he got it in his head, "Shit, I supported Leão coming here and look at the mess I made. Look what I did." I think he regretted it as the season went on and decided, "Fuck, the atmosphere here is not good, and this is my fault. The team isn't playing well and people aren't happy and part of that is my responsibility." I think he got it into his head, we have to win the title no matter what. So it was like, "Shit, I brought Leão here but at least I made us win."'[20]

Sócrates looked back on 1983 as one of the toughest seasons of his life, but those final four games stood out. Sócrates had a particular definition of what football was about. To him, the perfect game was not about scoring goals, or even winning, although those things were important. His vision was more holistic and the perfect game was when players, fans, performance and result all combined harmoniously. The 1983 team did not have the same swagger as the one that had won the title a year previously – and it was certainly not as united. But when he recalled the highlights of his playing career, he rated those 11 days in December 1983 as close to the pinnacle.

'I always had one objective when I played football – perfection; and when I came close to it I felt extremely satisfied,' he told Juca Kfouri. 'That was the big emotion for me when I played football, so when I took to the field I looked not to misplace even one pass, to support my team-mates, to perceive every nuance of the game, every psychological aspect, and get our fans to both get behind the team and neutralise the opposing fans. That to me was perfection. That didn't include scoring a goal, nothing specific is included. Obviously, when you play a game with four or five goals and all the other stuff is there or thereabouts then it's better than not having it, but that wasn't important to me. When you are wrapped up in a mass movement, such as winning a title with Corinthians, then it is really something impressive. In those four title-deciding games where I scored a goal in every one of them, what I really felt was that I was part of the process and that is obviously what's important.'[21]

The title win brought down the curtain on a stressful year in the greatest way possible. The challenges to Corinthians Democracy could easily have affected his performance, but instead Sócrates thrived on the adversity. In love with Rosemary, brimming with confidence, and mostly free from injuries, he played in 55 of Corinthians' 72 games, scoring 37 goals in the process. When he was in the team, Corinthians scored almost two goals a game. Without him, they barely scored more than one. His role and his importance had grown bigger than ever before.

But there was more to come. In 1984, on the eve of his 30th birthday, he would transcend football by taking centre stage in one of the most important political campaigns Brazil had ever seen. The message he transmitted was as exemplary as it was unexpected. And it would have serious repercussions for his future.

13

'He contributed with his charisma and force of personality at a time when he was an undisputed sports star. He was unquestionably vital to Brazil. His participation in the politics that ended up leading to the end of the dictatorship is undeniable.'

Flávio Gikovate, Corinthians' psychotherapist during
Corinthians Democracy

Portuguese mariners touched land on Brazil's northeastern coast on 22 April 1500 and for three hundred years they edged up and down the palm-lined coast and inland through the lush Atlantic Forest, killing and coopting indigenous people and rebuffing attempts by the French and the Dutch to move in on their new territory. This land they called Brazil served as a vital source of cash for the Portuguese royal family, who ruled the colony from 4,000 miles away in Lisbon.

The Portuguese crown was happy to offer Brazilian fiefdoms to their friends and reap the rewards in gold, silver, timber, coffee, sugar cane and exotic fruits. But when Napoleon Bonaparte marched south through Europe in the early 19th century, allying with Spain and then turning west towards Lisbon, the Portuguese royal family feared for their lives and looked for a quick escape. Brazil offered a safe haven and so, just days before Napoleon's troops crossed the border into Portugal, the royals, their families and hundreds of courtiers boarded ships and fled southwest across the Atlantic.

King João VI loved his new home in Rio de Janeiro and even after Napoleon was defeated at Waterloo in 1815 – a defeat that signalled respite for the Portuguese – he didn't exactly rush home. It took the regent six years to finally agree to return and, when he did, he left his 22-year-old son Prince Pedro I in charge.

A year after the king arrived back in Lisbon, he ordered his son to follow him home and return Brazil to colonial status. The young prince responded with one of the most memorable statements in Brazilian history. On 9 January 1822, he took a stand, rebuking his father with the words, 'Tell the people I stay!' and thus setting Brazil on the road to independence.

His exact words in Portuguese were *'Digam ao povo que fico!'* and the day became forever known as the Dia do Fico.

Sócrates' Dia do Fico was 16 April 1984 and was no less dramatic.

It was one of the most emotional days in an exhilarating period that began in March 1983, when a few people gathered in a small town in Brazil's northeast to demand direct elections for president. The generals had finally agreed to hand over power, but they wanted to control the transition. They decided that the first civilian leader would be chosen not through a general election but by an electoral college packed with pro-military lawmakers.

Millions of Brazilians objected to what was yet another abuse and a little-known congressman named Dante de Oliveira decided to risk action. Oliveira presented parliament with a constitutional amendment demanding a direct ballot for president, and support for the proposal grew slowly but surely throughout 1983 and into the New Year. More than 30,000 people turned out to back the idea in Curitiba in January; 250,000 appeared in São Paulo a fortnight later; and a month after that, 300,000 took to the streets in Belo Horizonte. One million people attended a rally in Rio de Janeiro on 10 April and, almost every day in between, tens of thousands appeared in one city or another to express their support. The *Diretas Já* (Direct Elections Now) campaign caught the imagination of the people, and polls showed that almost 80 per cent of Brazilians supported their demands. Newly enfranchised after years without a say, Brazilians wanted to choose their own leader.[1]

Having spent 1982 and 1983 extolling the virtues of democracy, the campaign could have been tailor-made for Sócrates and he wasted no time in throwing his weight behind it. The man who in 1979 said Brazilians weren't ready to vote for their president quickly emerged as one of the most visible and vocal proponents of suffrage for all. He used his privileged position to speak out long, loud and often about the need for direct elections, and he encouraged his team-mates to do the same.[2]

Casagrande, Juninho and Wladimir were the most willing participants and although the majority of the squad did not get too involved they did make some efforts, unlike players at most clubs. The campaign had urged people to wear yellow to show their support, and Sócrates helped convince his Corinthians team-mates to sport something yellow on match days. He used yellow ankle protection over his socks, Wladimir sported a yellow armband, others wrapped simple strips of yellow cotton around their wrists. Serendipity played a part, too. Before the campaign had taken off, a few Corinthians players bought new boots while on tour in Japan. The boots had a yellow stripe along the side and when the players came home, reporters asked them if the symbolism was deliberate. 'Of course,' they all answered.[3]

Congress agreed to rule on Oliveira's amendment and, when the final rally of the campaign took place in São Paulo on 16 April, more than a million people turned up to show the generals just how much they wanted to vote for their next president. It was the biggest public gathering since the military coup 20 years previously and a carnival atmosphere took hold of the city, with a Chinese dragon snaking in and out of the crowds, children flying kites overhead, and a symphony orchestra and samba bands providing musical accompaniment.

Sócrates had agreed to lead a group of Corinthians players who would take part, and they met up at the club before heading to the city centre. The afternoon was warm and humid and the huge crowds made driving impossible, so Sócrates dumped his car at the metro and took a train into town with Casagrande, Wladimir and Regina. Supporters did double takes as the jovial Brazil captain, laughing and joking with his friends, jumped on and off public transport and walked towards the plaza in front of the Anhangabaú metro station. As he strolled the few hundred yards from the station to the stage where the dignitaries were to address the crowd, throngs of people greeted him with shouts and hugs and there were even serenades in his honour from balconies high above the city centre's narrow streets.[4]

Sócrates loved the attention and he loved fronting a cause, but most of all he loved that people were engaged. It was the best of Brazil and he felt the country's potential more acutely than ever. Speculation that he would sign for an Italian club had been rife for weeks – during carnival he had hosted directors of Internazionale in Ribeirão Preto – but as he climbed the steps to the stage the talk of Europe suddenly seemed silly.

This was what he lived for and no amount of lira could change it. By the time he reached the microphone, he had come to a decision. He confided his secret to the evening's MC Osmar Santos and Santos quickly dragged him out front to share the news.

'Sócrates made the following suggestion,' Santos coyly told the multitude in front of him. 'Say it again, Doctor. Are you going to Italy or aren't you? Say it again . . .'

Sócrates grinned and the crowd shouted, 'Noooooooo!'

'So tell us, Sócrates,' Santos repeated. 'Pay attention Brazil!'

Sócrates smiled and scratched his head, drawing out the suspense.

'You won't go to Italy if what happens, Sócrates?'

Sócrates took a step forward and bent his gangly frame down to reach the microphone.

'If the Dante de Oliveira amendment passes in the Chamber of Deputies and the Senate, then I won't leave my country,' he said jubilantly.

The crowd erupted in a roar and Sócrates took a step back from the mike and beamed.

Santos grabbed the microphone again and milked the moment.

'Say it again, Doctor, say it again. If the amendment is approved, you won't . . .'

'I won't leave OUR country!' Sócrates boomed.

The crowd cheered raucously and broke out into a chant.

'He's staying here! He's staying here! He's staying here!'

Sócrates had put democracy for Brazil ahead of financial security for himself. He had very publicly declared that staying in Brazil to help with a transition to a true democracy was more important than guaranteeing his own future.

'It was at that rally that I realised what it must be like to go to war to die,' he said years later. 'Because you don't go with your body, you go with your soul.'[5]

His team-mates teased him by calling him Prince Pedro and he exploited the publicity a few days later by appearing on the cover of *Placar* dressed as a 19th-century Portuguese royal. Sócrates was always game for a laugh, especially if there was a greater cause behind it, and he was willing to do almost anything to boost support ahead of the 25 April vote in Congress. His players thought he looked ridiculous, but they were also inspired and they weren't the only ones. On the morning of the ballot, the *Folha de S.Paulo* newspaper published a tribute to his actions under the headline: 'We Don't Want Sócrates To Leave'. Beside a picture of both him and the team of sports journalists at the paper, they lauded personalities like Zico, Emerson Fittipaldi and Pelé, all of whom backed the *Diretas Já* campaign. But they singled out Sócrates for going one step further and betting on a principle. He was a 'genius, a star and a citizen', they wrote. 'We can't afford the luxury of losing him.'[6]

The tribute was another attempt to put pressure on the deputies who were voting on the Dante de Oliveira amendment that night and Sócrates was flattered by it. He, like many of his 130 million countrymen and women, was convinced the amendment would pass, such was the support shown throughout the country in the weeks and months preceding the debate.

But Sócrates underestimated the government's resolve. The military were determined the measure must fail and they launched all sorts of intimidatory tactics in the days and hours leading up to the vote. State and local politicians were banned from entering parliament lest they make their influence felt, and the media in Brasília – where members of Congress were hunkered down – were forbidden from publishing any stories relating to the proposal. Hundreds of soldiers cordoned off the parliament to prevent pro-democracy protesters from getting too close, and troops took over the nearby University of Brasília to stop students getting too militant. The military did not want people telling lawmakers how most Brazilians really felt.

Millions of citizens responded with a 'night of noise' on the evening before the debate, with motorists peeping their car horns and others letting off fireworks in the streets or beating pots and pans at their open windows. Sócrates led Regina and their boys out on to their balcony where they banged away until their hands hurt.

Sócrates stayed at home the night of the vote, an injury preventing him from going to the Morumbi, where Corinthians beat Atlético Paranaense 2-0 to ensure their passage into the quarter-finals of the Brasileiro. He was too antsy to watch football anyway, and he spent the night glued to the radio and the telephone trying to follow the votes as they were counted.

The amendment needed a two-thirds majority to pass the lower chamber and at around 2.30 a.m., when the last vote was cast, the count read 298 votes for, and 65 against. It was 22 votes short of the necessary majority, a defeat caused by the 113 congressmen who under duress from the military had failed to show up for the most important vote of their lives.

If democracy was Sócrates' public reason for offering to stay, then love was his private one. When he announced he would remain in Brazil if the *Diretas Já* campaign was successful, Sócrates may already have made a quick calculation in his mind. If I go to Italy, I have financial security for the rest of my life, I get to play with the greatest players in the world, and I can try to save my marriage. If I stay in Brazil, I can play a part in the transition to democracy, I remain at the football club I love, and I still have Rosemary. It was a gamble, but all his cards were aces.

Sócrates' affair with Rosemary was still going strong a year and a half after it began and the relationship had been crucial in helping him through the last year of ups and downs. Sócrates had changed since falling in love again and it was sometimes hard not to notice. He had never paid much attention to money matters but he stopped giving his finances even a cursory look, telling Marinho, his former pal at the juniors who now helped manage his daily affairs, 'You deal with it, I can't think about anything else.'[7]

He showered Rosemary with jewellery and presents and even abandoned the old T-shirts and torn jeans in favour of blazers and shirts after the always elegant singer convinced him he was a global star now and needed to smarten up. This was around the time he almost signed for Roma, and Sócrates laughed off the inevitable comments by telling people he was getting used to dressing like an Italian.

Friends told him he was crazy and appealed to him to think twice about what he was doing, if only for the sake of Regina and the boys. But he was so head over heels that nothing else mattered.

'We had an office on Rua Henrique Schaumann and one day he gave me a bracelet and said, "Marinho, deliver this bracelet for me,"' Marinho recalled. 'I didn't know who it was for. When I got there I saw this woman. She was so gorgeous. And as soon as I saw her I twigged. I thought, "What has Magrão done?"

'She said, "Come in, Marinho. I know why Sócrates called." And she started to chat, saying, "I know Sócrates' marriage isn't going too well." And she started to tell me what he had told her. And so when I saw Sócrates I said, "Have you thought this through?" And he said, "I am in love with this woman."'[8]

Rosemary was just as in love as he was, at one point even going to Ribeirão Preto to try to meet Sócrates' mother. She brought a gift and called Marinho to ask him to introduce them, but he tactfully convinced her it wasn't a good idea and instead promised to hand the gift over on her behalf. Marinho quietly stuck it in a drawer and neither Sócrates nor Dona Guiomar ever found out, thus narrowly averting disaster.

When it came, Sócrates' decision to leave Brazil was backed by his father, who wanted him to secure his financial future and save his marriage. Sócrates had told his dad about the affair and asked his advice. Knowing his father would tell him to stay with his wife rather than start afresh with his lover, he sat down with Seu Raimundo and explained all the reasons he didn't think his marriage would survive. Seu Raimundo had an answer to each and every one of them. In the end, an exasperated Sócrates said, 'Dad, it just doesn't feel right.'

'Son,' his father said earnestly. 'What marriage ever feels right?'

Just as he imagined, Seu Raimundo advised him to get as far away from Rosemary as possible and try to work things out with Regina. It wasn't what Sócrates wanted to hear but he felt cornered. He had already told the entire country he was going to leave. There was no turning back.

His passionate promise to stay in Brazil if direct elections were approved was one of the most memorable statements Sócrates ever made. But there was another even more unforgettable quote that outlived him. When Sócrates passed away in December 2011, the internet was agog with reference to the prediction he reputedly first made in 1983: 'I want to die on a Sunday, the day Corinthians win a title.'

The supposed premonition of his dying day was repeated and reprinted the world over and brought him a posthumous reputation as a footballing sage. Predicting his own death was exactly the kind of thing that his most passionate devotees, especially Corinthians fans and leftists who agreed with his cause and already thought of him as the game's coolest and most spiritual footballer, wanted to believe he was capable of. However, no one has ever produced a tape of the recording or any written record of him saying it. After he died, his elderly mother claimed he made the prediction shortly before passing away, and friends agree it was exactly the kind of thing he might say after a few drinks. Whether he said it or not, it has now gone down in footballing folklore.

Even as a child Sócrates liked to make bold statements to provoke people. At home with his father and brothers, he would start an argument, wait and see what side they took, and then deliberately take the opposing view. His innate contrariness enabled him to assimilate different points of view and prepared him for a life of debate. Sócrates ended up being many things to many people – maybe even a sage – but of all the roles he took on, none suited him more than that of devil's advocate.[9]

'If someone says, "It's like this" my first reaction is to say, "No it's not!"' he once said. 'I go looking for other answers and that was always in me. It's not easy to live with me, I know that. Because I can't give it up. I am ten different people in the one day. All those people in one, it's complicated.'[10]

He perfected the art of friendly antagonism as he got older and he took particular pleasure in being different. If everyone was going to an event in a suit, he made a point of turning up in a T-shirt and jeans. While most players promised not to celebrate scoring against their former clubs, he said it gave him 'a different kind of pleasure'. When Brazil held a constitutional referendum in 1993, the ardent backer of Fidel Castro supported a return to the monarchy.

Sócrates rejected conventional wisdom as a matter of principle and he loved to wind people up. He got away with it because he was Sócrates, and because even when his comebacks were cutting or aggressive they were accompanied with a smile and a wink. He conditioned people to expect something unusual and he brushed off criticism of his incoherence by quoting a famous line from Brazilian rock icon Raul Seixas: 'I'd rather be this walking metamorphosis than have that old formed opinion about everything.' There were few things he hated more than being dull or predictable. Just as he couldn't stand the physical constraints of the *concentração*, he couldn't stand the mental cage of consistency.

'I'm radical even when I change my mind,' he said. 'Then I am a radical for the other side. I don't want to commit myself to being coherent.'[11]

Having told a million people he would stay in Brazil if parliament agreed to direct elections, he felt obliged to leave now they had turned the proposal down. But even as a move to Italy became more and more real, Sócrates still had business to deal with at Corinthians. The club were just 90 minutes from the league play-offs and what would be the perfect farewell of a first national title. And yet even at this vital juncture, his lack of professionalism – or his commitment to friends and partying – were to play a role. On the eve of the final league game against Atlético Paranaense, Sócrates went to Ribeirão Preto to take part in a charity face-off between the Vieira and the Garcia families. Thousands of locals gathered to watch two of the city's best-known families play one half of basketball and then another of football, but disaster struck in the dying minutes of the football match when Sócrates pulled a thigh muscle.[12]

The injury was yet another blow to the under-fire Corinthians Democracy. Opponents and fans wanted to know why the club's most important player was risking his fitness at such a crucial stage of the season. A backlash was inevitable and some at the club suggested Sócrates avoid controversy by sneaking home and pretending to pick up the injury in a training session the next day. Sócrates and Adilson refused to lie and went public with the real story, even though they knew they would be slated for it. The response was sharp and their honesty was merely further ammunition to those gunning for an end to the movement.

The injury kept him out of the 2-0 win over Atlético Paranaense that took them into the quarter-finals of the Brasileiro and it prevented him from going to Brasília to witness the vote on the Dante de Oliveira amendment. But his loss was felt more acutely four days later when Flamengo outclassed them in a 2-0 win at the Maracanã. The initial prognosis was that Sócrates would be out for three weeks, but he felt guilty for picking up such a silly injury and disobeyed the doctor's orders, forcing himself to play in the return leg a week later. He was unfit – and maybe even risking permanent damage – but he was inspirational in the 4-1 win. He helped set up three of Corinthians' four goals in what was their best performance of the season and they sailed into a semi-final date with Fluminense.

Sócrates could pull off heroics now and then but miracles were beyond him, and he couldn't stop Corinthians going down 2-0 at home in the first leg of the semi-final. He insisted the tie was not yet over, but a deal with Fiorentina had already been done and his mind was elsewhere. He was fit enough to start the second leg a week later at the Maracanã but he was ineffective as Corinthians stuttered to a 0-0 draw. They were out, their dreams of a league title and a coveted spot in the Copa Libertadores was gone for yet another year.

Sócrates was disconsolate at how things turned out, more because of *Diretas Já* than losing to Fluminense. The political defeat left him adrift, and just as he would have stayed in Brazil had they won, he now felt obliged to leave, not only because he had made such a public promise, but also because he felt let down and couldn't bear to watch such a half-hearted transition to democracy. Within hours of the amendment failing, he told reporters it was all over, that he would be taking the Italians up on their offer and leaving Brazil the first chance he got.[13]

There is no question that his promise was sincere and that if the amendment had passed he would have stayed in São Paulo. For a few gloriously happy weeks of his life football was secondary, to the point where he swore that he would perform any role required of him to help build a new democracy, as a doctor, a footballer or even a bin man. The collective sense of purpose had intoxicated him like never before – or after.

'We can define it as a period when the country learned to smile again, tried to pick itself up, tried to reconstruct itself, to find its way,' he said in the documentary *Democracia em Preto e Branco*. 'A smile was back on our faces. A smile replaced a lot of tears. It was without doubt the richest period in my life, the period that gave me almost everything I am today. As a human being, a person, as an activist for whatever, I learned there.'[14]

The defeat for *Diretas Já* was also a defeat for Corinthians Democracy. Sócrates' imminent departure would deal the movement a fatal blow. Without him as its figurehead, its momentum slowed and when Adilson lost his bid to replace Waldemar Pires as club president in April 1985 the movement died.

It was a sad finale for something that left such an indelible mark on both club and country. As the dictatorship limped to a predictably pathetic end, opposition grew more and more vociferous, with the Church, unions and leftist political parties among those demanding a return to civilian rule. Few of these groups, however, were as important as Corinthians Democracy. They were run by politicians or unionists or social activists and their efforts were unquestionably vital in forcing the military to return to their barracks. But only the musicians who used their melodic poetry to evade censorship and get their veiled message across had any real connection to the masses. Few Brazilians felt much love for politics or politicians. Many millions – and the majority still lived in rural poverty – never even knew who they were.

Football, though, was different. No one cared what the president said before a summit in Washington but everyone listened to what Sócrates said before the World Cup. Sócrates seized the opportunity to talk not just about football, but about everything else as well, and by doing so he helped introduce the concept of democracy to almost two generations of Brazilians who had never experienced anything other than repression, censorship and brutality.

At the precise moment when the military decided to relinquish power, Sócrates was there to give almost daily tutorials on the alternative – what democracy was, how it worked and why it was desirable. He explained what voting was and what it meant, and how it could be used to make life better for those who had never before had a say. He talked about respect for people who thought differently, the need for a living wage and a safety net for the poor, and he hammered home the need for education.

'Discussing these themes in an environment such as football considerably amplifies the range of the debate,' Sócrates said. 'It reaches people who don't have as much information, who are less educated, because it is a working-class environment. I think that was the principal benefit of the movement, it allowed more people to discuss politics. Everyone in Brazil understands football. Not everyone understands politics because the majority aren't educated enough. But if you put both things together you can educate lots of people and provoke transformations in society.'[15]

Sócrates often said that everyone involved in the movement, including himself, could look back on their lives and measure it in two stages: before Corinthians Democracy and after. It was that important. It changed people forever.

Unfortunately for him, the after arrived at a pivotal moment in his career. In the second half of April 1984 Sócrates' luck ran out. After years of everything falling into place, both professionally and personally, the Rosemary dilemma, failing once again to win the Brasileiro, and the defeat in Congress were the first signs that his charmed life was over and that his fortunes were changing. Sócrates would become richer and more famous in the years to come but he would never again reach the same heights. It would be downhill from here on in.

14

'I got there and my head was going a thousand miles an hour. It was like going from carnival in Salvador to a Benedictine convent.'

Sócrates

Fiorentina president Ranieri Pontello watched the 1982 World Cup with undisguised delight, and when it was over he drew up a shortlist of players he wanted for the Tuscan club. The first was Daniel Passarella and he wasted no time in signing the Argentine captain to join his countryman Daniel Bertoni as Fiorentina's second foreigner for the 1982/83 season. The second player to impress him was Karl-Heinz Rummenigge and Pontello tried to sign the German striker in the summer of 1984. When Rummenigge went to Internazionale, Pontello turned his attentions to the third name on his list – Sócrates.

Italian clubs had been made aware of Sócrates' availability at the start of the year when a former airline pilot by the name of Marcello Placidi convinced Sócrates to let him represent him. The São Paulo-based businessman had good connections in Serie A, and Internazionale, Verona, Sampdoria, Napoli, AC

Milan and Fiorentina were among those clubs who called to express an interest.

Fiorentina moved into pole position for his signature in May and the club's director general Tito Corsi flew to São Paulo to open negotiations. Sócrates was still smarting from the failure of the *Diretas Já* campaign and it took him just 20 minutes to agree personal terms on a two-year deal.

Corinthians, however, were not nearly so accommodating. Waldemar Pires met Fiorentina officials in his office on the Avenida Paulista and pushed for a transfer fee of $4.6 million, while Fiorentina put his valuation at closer to $1.8 million. Pires met Corsi at a party later that night, by which time he had dropped the fee to $3.5 million, and the gap narrowed further the following day when they convened at Pires' house and Fiorentina upped their offer to $2.5 million.[1]

Sócrates made it plain he wanted to leave and the meetings continued on a daily basis. A deal looked imminent but Corinthians were out to squeeze as much as they could from the lira-laden Italians. On the third night, Pires and Corsi met with Sócrates and his lawyers once more and things turned desperate. With midnight approaching and both sides arguing over his worth, Sócrates exploded with a mixture of frustration and sadness.

'I am a human being,' he shouted, banging his fist on the table. 'Have some respect. I am not a piece of merchandise.' He jumped up, tears flowing down his face, and stormed out of the room.[2]

Sócrates rarely showed such emotion and his fragile state jolted both sides into action. Pires finally understood how much the move meant to him and the next day he lowered the club's asking price to $3.2 million. Corsi agreed to pay, although after more negotiations the official price was set at $2.7 million. The Italians shelled out several hundred thousand more to cover

Sócrates' personal slice from the deal, and the player waived part of his percentage to ensure an agreement was reached.[3]

At the start of the 1980s you could count almost on two hands the number of Brazilians who had won titles at one of Europe's top clubs.

Evaristo de Macedo shone during a brilliant five years at Barcelona from 1957 to 1962, scoring 178 goals in 226 matches and winning two league titles and two Fairs Cups. After scoring the goal that knocked Real Madrid out of the European Cup in 1960 and ended their run of five successive titles, he crossed the divide and moved to Madrid, where he won two more league titles with the capital giants.

Didi won two European Cups with Real Madrid in 1959 and 1960. Mazzola and Dino Sani won the trophy with AC Milan in 1963; Mazzola did the double with Juventus in 1973 and 1975, and Jair da Costa won titles galore at Internazionale and Roma during a decade-long spell in Italy.

Fiorentina, too, had notable Brazilians. Julinho Botelho is still considered one of the greatest players in the club's history thanks to a glorious three-year spell in the mid-1950s, during which he helped them secure their first ever Italian league crown. Amarildo, the striker who replaced Pelé at the 1962 World Cup and whose goals won them the title and him the nickname 'the Possessed', also won a Scudetto for the Tuscan team in 1969.

With their only two titles coming thanks to goals from Brazilian forwards, it was perhaps no surprise that the directors of Fiorentina saw Sócrates as the man to help them win a third.

Italian football was on a high after winning the 1982 World Cup and the cash-rich clubs were splashing out on the biggest names in world football. Glamorous, sultry and successful, Italy was the place to be and Europe's crème de la crème pocketed all the lira they could and headed to the peninsula.

It was one of the biggest transfer summers ever seen and, within six weeks of Sócrates putting pen to paper for Fiorentina, Júnior had signed for Torino, Graeme Souness had joined Sampdoria and, in the biggest deal of them all, Diego Maradona left Barcelona for a history-making spell at Napoli.

Elsewhere, Juventus had Frenchman Michel Platini and Pole Zbigniew Boniek; Hans-Peter Briegel and Preben Elkjaer joined dark horses Verona; while English pair Mark Hateley and Ray Wilkins brought some old-fashioned English grit to AC Milan.

Fiorentina had finished third in the league the previous season and they were optimistic that their new Brazilian would be the man to lift them higher. More than 5,000 fans turned up to see them head off to their pre-season training camp and Sócrates did nothing to lower their expectations, telling them he had come to the club 'to win the Coppa Italia, the UEFA Cup and the Scudetto'. It was exactly the kind of thing that fans loved to hear.

On the first official day at his new club Sócrates joined his team-mates for a thorough pre-season medical. As he waited to step on the treadmill for respiratory and cardiology tests, he calmly lit up a cigarette and started puffing away. The team doctor walked in and could hardly believe his eyes.

'What are you doing smoking? We're about to test your breathing!' he cried.

'But, Doctor, I'm warming up my lungs for the exam,' Sócrates deadpanned.

His team-mates fell about laughing and the doctor stormed out in disgust.[4]

The incident was meant as a joke but it was also intended as a message, and it perfectly captured his time at Fiorentina. From day one, Sócrates made it abundantly clear he was going to be his own man and make no compromises to his new surroundings. It was to be his way or no way.

Like many Italian teams, Fiorentina did their pre-season training in the Dolomites, where the fresh air, the high altitude and the steep slopes were the ideal conditions for the new team and their marquee signing to ready themselves for the year ahead. The area around their base in Madonna di Campiglio boasted some of the most beautiful scenery in Europe but Sócrates saw only punishment. He was not used to altitude training or extended periods of brutal pre-season preparations. He collapsed and fainted after one run and 10 minutes into another he simply gave up. His team-mates completed the half-hour jog and arrived back to find the unhappy Brazilian waiting for them with a typically Sócratic question.

'Why do I have to run up hills?' he asked. 'I want to run with the ball.'[5]

The Fiorentina players were quickly getting used to his unorthodox antics, and they shrugged it off as the usual struggles with pre-season training. Trainer Armando Onesti was notoriously tough and not everyone could handle his methods, especially in the rarefied mountain air. They also knew of Sócrates' reputation as a borderline eccentric, a renown he soon confirmed. On the coach to one game, he lay down on the back seat rather than sit beside a team-mate. Against Napoli in the Coppa Italia, he played in training shoes because the ground was so hard. And he chafed against Onesti's rigid time-table, which gave players little time to themselves.

'Onesti paid attention to details like when we were eating,' said goalkeeper Giovanni Galli, Sócrates' roommate and one of his few friends at the club. 'He didn't think it was necessary to spend a lot of time eating and so we got just 20 minutes for lunch. Then he used to make us walk around the pitch to digest our food and Sócrates one day got up from the table with his plate in his hand and walked round the pitch with it, eating as he went.'[6]

He ruffled a few more feathers during his first few weeks by turning up to official events in T-shirt and jeans, and there was disappointment when, after appearing in the team's first pre-season friendly – a 7-1 win over Pinzolo – he missed not just the next friendly but the opening two Coppa Italia games with a mysterious injury. He had also refused to perform the ceremonial kick-off in a charity match and a furious Placidi denounced him to the local press, who lapped up the controversy.

Sócrates brushed off the complaints, matter-of-factly telling journalists that what he did in his own time was his own business. When they pushed him about his drinking and what they called his controversial positions, he bristled even further, curtly telling one reporter, 'I smoke, I drink and I think', and that locals better get used to it.

The incidents were all signs that Sócrates was intent on challenging the established order. Personal freedom remained paramount even in a foreign land, and after two years of Corinthians Democracy he had become used to doing what he wanted. In Brazil, when he disagreed with something he simply ignored it or took action to change it. He thought he could bring that same force of personality to bear in his new home, but the Italian structure had been in place for a long time and they were not about to change their habits because of one disapproving foreigner.

It was easy to overlook his idiosyncrasies as the season got off to a decent start. Fiorentina had a strong squad and the makings of a team that could challenge for the league. They won two and drew two of their first four league games and qualified for the last 16 of the Coppa Italia with three wins and two draws from their five group games. They also reached the second round of the UEFA Cup with two wins against Fenerbahçe. Sócrates was on the field for all but 10 minutes of those first six games and turned in man-of-the-match performances in two of their biggest fixtures, the opening-day victory away at Lazio and in the 1-0 win in Turkey. A delightful chipped goal in the 5-0 drubbing of Atalanta in their fourth league match took them into second place in the table and appeared to confirm the pre-season optimism.

A couple of narrow defeats to Sampdoria and Verona in late October were hardly disastrous, but they dented the club's early hopes and things got worse a few days later against Anderlecht. The first leg of their UEFA Cup tie had ended 1-1 in Florence, with Sócrates getting Fiorentina's goal. The return leg, however, turned into a massacre. Sócrates grabbed an equaliser from the penalty spot after Anderlecht had taken an early lead, but the Belgians turned on the style in the second half to demolish their visitors 6-2.[7]

It was Fiorentina's heaviest ever European defeat and Sócrates was one of those singled out for blame. It wasn't just that he had played poorly. He had been signed precisely to add international experience to the squad in the hope of securing their first European trophy since they lifted the Cup Winners' Cup in 1961. Instead, he had gone AWOL in the biggest match of the season.

The loss marked the start of a nine-game winless run that extended all the way into 1985 and laid bare the divisions in the side. They locked themselves in the dressing room for three hours after the 2-1 defeat at Roma 11 days later and harsh words flew on the coach home as they picked over the reasons for the freefall. An irate Sócrates harangued his team-mates all the way up the autostrada, telling them they should be 'fucking ashamed of themselves' and demanding changes. He had long suspected something was up but couldn't quite put his finger on it, and it was only after the debacle in Rome that he finally realised what was going on.[8]

The Fiorentina dressing room was split between two factions, one side led by Daniel Passarella and the other by captain Eraldo Pecci. Coach Giancarlo De Sisti managed to keep a lid on the fissure, but when he was hospitalised with a brain abscess in late August a destructive power vacuum developed. Interim coach Onesti was unable to impose himself and the resentments that had only simmered while they were winning suddenly boiled over.

Sócrates initially felt no particular sympathies for Passarella or Pecci and was reluctant to choose sides, not only because he knew the team could never win if it was divided but also because to do so would be tacitly accepting a subordinate role to either man. But several players did choose sides and Sócrates was stuck in the middle. He was convinced that some of his team-mates were deliberately avoiding him and he felt victimised as both a foreigner and a progressive.

He was vulnerable without the backing of the coach who signed him and, having no allies, he became the scapegoat. Many of his team-mates felt he wasn't pulling his weight and several objected to what they saw as his unprofessional attitude and lack of effort. He had never been a runner but his team-mates didn't know that, and they were angry at what they saw as his selfishness, as well as suspicious at the already abundant rumours of his carousing.

At Corinthians, Sócrates had Biro-Biro, Paulinho and a host of others who would run their hearts out for him in midfield. His team-mates looked up to him, not just as a player, but almost as a more enlightened being, and they were prepared to go the extra mile for him and their cause.

Ironically, his team-mates at Fiorentina were much more egalitarian. Men like Passarella, Pecci and Claudio Gentile didn't play football for fun. They were established internationals and big personalities who were not used to playing second fiddle to anyone, much less doing their work for them. They wanted to win and they were not impressed by Sócrates' easy-going attitude.

'These guys were professional both on the pitch and off it and they didn't understand why Sócrates, who could be great on the pitch, wasn't great off it,' Galli said of his Italian team-mates. 'He lacked professionalism and he didn't want to make sacrifices. He wanted other players to run for him and the other players said, "I run for Sócrates, he needs to run for me." In his head he thought that the other players needed to be more like him, not that he should be more like them. They felt he needed to get used to our world. That was Sócrates' big mistake. He refused to compromise.'[9]

Sócrates was also hampered by the decision to play him in a role where he had little room for manoeuvre. His position, just off a more traditional target man, was similar to the *ponto-de-lança* role he fulfilled at Botafogo, but Italian defenders played further up the field and were always on his shoulder. The strikers – or more often striker – wanted the ball in front of them to run on to, but Sócrates was more used to passing the ball to feet and he was flummoxed by a system that required him to pass the ball to a player with his back to him.

There was also the issue of money. Players arriving on big salaries need to prove their worth early on, either by standing head and shoulders above the rest or by mucking in and showing they are team players. Sócrates did neither, and some players clearly felt he had a cheek expecting them to do the hard work while he picked up the biggest pay cheque.

He lost their respect further by turning up late to training or by heading to the treatment table for a massage and a rest instead of sweating it out with the rest of them. When he did train, he would register his disdain a little too blatantly.

'He did everything that was asked of him, but when he didn't want to do it he did it half-heartedly,' said defender Celeste Pin.

'There would be a sprint and everyone would do it in seven seconds and he'd do it in ten. That was his way of saying no to professionalism. He was being obliged to do something he didn't want to do. Football was fun to him. We thought it was strange. Maybe it's like that when you're a kid, but it's not like that when you're a professional.'[10]

His unrest was exacerbated by the difficulties of adapting to Italian life off the field. Florence is an ancient city crisscrossed by narrow streets that unexpectedly open up into spectacular piazzas crowned with even more spectacular churches, monasteries and libraries. The streets are lined with old stone buildings coloured by centuries of smoke and soot. Because only churches can be built higher than five storeys, distinctive steeples and domes dominate a skyline that has the rolling Tuscan hills behind it.

Sócrates, however, saw very little of it. He moved the family into a mansion in Grassina, a hilltop village about six miles from the Stadio Comunale. The two-storey villa had a big fireplace, a wine cellar and surrounding orchards that produced chianti and olive oil.[11]

Giancarlo Antognoni and Gentile were among those invited to his house for dinner, but Antognoni would miss the entire season through injury and, although Sócrates teased the Libya-born Gentile by christening him 'Gaddafi', the two were never close. He invited a handful of players to a barbecue one day and only one of them turned up, much to his disgust.

The Italians' reluctance to socialise was a serious issue for a man who made friendship and camaraderie a priority, and their iciness toward him deepened his sense of solitude. With no friends on the team and few real acquaintances in his new city, he turned to Brazilians for comfort.

Sócrates and Regina had struck up a friendship with José

Trajano, a journalist they knew from São Paulo who was taking a year out with his girlfriend. Trajano, a former sports editor of the *Folha de S.Paulo*, was taking advantage of his sabbatical to write about Italian football. The two couples became close and one night, after yet another drunken evening ended with Trajano and his girlfriend crashing in Sócrates' spare room, they were invited to leave their city centre pensione and move in more permanently. Sócrates' and Trajano's mutual isolation and longing for home brought them close, like, in Sócrates' words, two hapless drunks who leaned on each other to survive.

Jointly, they put together a ragtag group of friends that included a hairdresser, a travel agent, a gaucho shoe salesman and a businessman who bought and sold marble. They would gather at Sócrates' mansion every night to cook big dinners or play cards or simply just to hang out and drink. Often they would drive him home from away matches – always stopping at the first petrol station to load up on beer – sometimes meeting their wives for dinner halfway home.[12]

The pair would go into the city to buy records, eat at the local trattoria, or just hang out at home drinking and chatting. But even when his circle of friends grew, Sócrates still found Italian life intolerable. He had gone to Italy in part to sample its cultural delights, but it took him months before he got round to seeing Michalengelo's *David* or the Caravaggios, Botticellis and da Vincis at the Uffizi Gallery, as the double training sessions, coupled with his family and social life, kept him fully occupied.

The most brutal winter in a century didn't help matters. Sócrates hated the cold and temperatures of 23 degrees below zero were bitter enough for him to impress visiting friends by buying crates of beer and chilling them outside the front door. But they also caused hypoxia in his feet and all 10 of his toenails fell off. He found passing and running on the muddy surfaces almost impossible and his notorious lack of conditioning meant he was exhausted long before the final whistle blew.

The dressing-room split was becoming more and more evident as the club slipped and stuttered its way through December and into the New Year. Sócrates believed that certain players were only passing to their friends and allies and he was not alone. On the eve of their 19 January match against Lazio, and after nine games without a win, Passarella left the field in the middle of a routine training session and limped back to the dressing room. Reporters fretted he would miss the match and his team-mates worried about the loss of their defensive stalwart. Passarella didn't say what the problem was, but the next morning he called the players to his hotel room for an impromptu meeting.

'I'm completely fine,' the furious Argentine stopper told them. 'I'm not injured and I never was. The reason I left the field yesterday is that there were players in midfield who were not passing the ball to their team-mate.'

Passarella was one of the hardest men in football and he pointed menacingly at Pecci.

'I am going to play today,' he went on, 'and if anything like that happens again I am coming off. And if I do, I'll be waiting for you at the side of the pitch when the final whistle goes.'[13]

The threat had the desired effect and Fiorentina won 3-0, sparking a mini revival that took them to the safety of mid-table. More notably, however, the incident brought Passarella and Sócrates closer together. The media in both Brazil and Italy tried to create a schism between them and there were plenty of superficial reasons to believe they might clash. One was a playful Brazil leader looking to establish himself as a dominant presence in his new team, the other a morose Argentine captain who had been at the club for two years and had already carved out his space.

But Sócrates liked Passarella and saw his gesture as one of solidarity, coming as it did two days after the Argentine had publicly appealed to media and fans to give him more time to adapt. Sócrates believed the South Americans were victims of prejudice, and even suggested their treatment could have had Fascist overtones. In a controversial interview with *France Football* in 2007, he went even further and accused Pecci of trying to fix a match by telling his team-mates they had to draw a game 0-0.

He repeated the allegation in other interviews, but several of the players denied the incident ever happened and Sócrates' recollections did not tally with other details he cited. Pecci also denied it and vowed to sue him for slander, but he never followed through with the threat. Pecci, contrary to all other reports, even claimed the squad was not split. But he admitted the Italians did not welcome the foreigners and pointed out that Sócrates got very little time to acclimatise to his new surroundings.

'Sócrates spent just one year in Italy and those of us who were here didn't help him,' Pecci said. 'Platini needed six months to understand the Italian league, so did Falcão. The only one who played well from the very start was Zico. A bedding-in period is very important.'[14]

Pecci rather ridiculously claimed to be friends with a man he called 'Magron', Italian for Magrão, but he acknowledged that Sócrates was not to blame for the most disappointing of seasons. 'Several players didn't meet expectations. When things are not going well people look to women or nightlife to find excuses. The truth was that several players didn't play well and we didn't get results.'

And then there was politics.

Within hours of arriving at the club, Sócrates was introduced to fans at an impromptu ceremony at the Stadio Comunale.

Thousands of supporters gathered outside the ground to catch a glimpse of their new star, and they went wild when Sócrates greeted them from a balcony above with his arm aloft and his fist clenched. Unbeknown to Sócrates, the clenched fist salute was that used by the Italian Communist Party (PCI) and it immediately raised the hackles of the club's owners, all of whom were prominent supporters of the right-wing Christian Democrats, the biggest political party in Italy. When the event was over, they ate lunch together and club officials quietly took him aside and asked him not to do it again. Sócrates was perplexed at the controversy but he was not about to hide his affiliations.

'Why did you make that gesture?' the club's president Ranieri Pontello asked him.

'Because that's me, it's the symbol of my life,' Sócrates replied.

'Where does it come from?' Pontello wanted to know.

'I don't know exactly but it reminds me of the black-power movement of the Mexico City Olympics in 1968. It has to do with a bunch of things; it's a symbol of, I don't know, a communication with the public, whatever that communication is.'

'Did you know it's the symbol of the Italian Communist Party?' Pontello asked.

'No,' said Sócrates. 'But I love it.'[15]

Pontello blanched but after they had eaten he extended an olive branch by inviting Sócrates to a party he was organising for his daughter. The celebration was to be held at Pontello's mansion the following month and Sócrates' appearance would add some edge to what was sure to be a formal event. Sócrates, however, was not interested in compromise. He was delighted at having dealt a serendipitous blow to the right and, even though the Pontellos were discreet and friendly, he thought they were using him for political ends and to boost their own popularity.

'Thanks for the invite but I don't want to go,' he told his boss. 'That kind of life isn't me and I'd rather not go. I like freedom, I like to be with the people.'[16]

His refusal to play ball was a slap in the face for the club president but, as if that weren't enough, Sócrates inadvertently added insult to injury. On the very same day the Pontellos held a party for their daughter, Sócrates went to a debate organised by the Communist Party at the Casa del Popolo, one of the left-wing community centres common in many Italian cities. The debate was about football and politics, and thousands of people turned up to hear Sócrates proudly speak Italian for the first time. His diction and vocabulary were not perfect, but there was no mistaking his message as he came down hard on the Pontellos and the Christian Democrats.[17]

His uncompromising stance opened an unnecessary rift with the men who ran the club, a rift that deepened with rumours that he was having an affair with a married member of the Pontello clan. Years later, the Pontellos looked back on Sócrates' Italian sojourn with something akin to resignation. Niccolò Pontello, a cousin of Ranieri and a club director at the time, said the problem was never Sócrates' politics. Pontello pointed out that Fiorentina had nothing to gain by censoring their star or by making him feel unwanted. They knew his history before they signed him and, while they might not have been happy about his dalliances with the Communists, they kept their opposition private. The problem, Pontello said, came on the field where he failed to do the business.

'Everyone knew his history with Corinthians Democracy,' said the dapper former director. 'We were prepared for him and we knew what he was all about. Remember, Fiorentina is a left-leaning city and most of his fans were too. It wasn't a problem for us. We were more interested in him being a good player.

'But he was so different and particular that the other players just thought he was weird. If you are different and make the team win then all the problems disappear. But if the results don't go your way then everything becomes more difficult. He was a good player but that wasn't enough. The reasons he didn't do well were not tactical or technical; he just didn't adapt to Italian life. He never integrated.

'We tried to talk to his friends and see what the problems were to try and help, but it didn't really make any difference and very little happened. We had several meetings but at the root of things he was very particular. He didn't have a balance in his life. He wasn't happy. A player needs to feel valued and have a good relationship with the others and he never had that.'[18]

Sócrates' leftist beliefs did not come as a surprise to his colleagues but Italian footballers knew better than to get involved in politics, especially when it meant contradicting their boss. Sócrates came to Italy harbouring quiet hopes of introducing some kind of Corinthians Democracy-style movement at Fiorentina, but he underestimated just how disapproving and uninterested his new team-mates would be.

He tried to talk to them about the issues of the day and he peppered the knowledgeable De Sisti with questions about everything from Italy's transfer law to the club's insistence on blazer and slacks for away trips.

'We meet here at 2 p.m. tomorrow to travel and I want you all here in the official dress,' De Sisti told the players ahead of their first away trip.

'Is that really necessary?' Sócrates asked Corsi.

'That's the way we travel to games in Italy,' he replied.

Sócrates asked if he could talk to the captain about it and approached Eraldo Pecci to get his opinion.

'This is how we represent Fiorentina,' Pecci told him, and

Sócrates wondered out loud if the other players were comfortable with the arrangement. Pecci agreed to take a poll and stood up in the dressing room before the next game.

'Sócrates wants to know if everyone is happy going to matches all dressed up in blazer and slacks?' Pecci asked.

Everyone agreed and the next day Sócrates dutifully turned up in official attire. He never mentioned the subject again.[19]

Sócrates' involvement in the local political scene was not good for his relations inside the club, but it energised him at a time when he was still trying to settle in the city and make friends. He couldn't help but affirm his positions as clearly as possible and befriending leftist politicians and activists helped him feel more at home. Florence was one of the most militant cities in Italy, with a leftist city council and a socialist mayor, and his involvement gave the movement there cachet. In meetings, he lit up the room with his insights and outsider perspectives on inequality, globalisation and workers' rights.

The meetings were also a way to get the fans on his side. In Brazil, where high illiteracy rates meant radio was more important than newspapers or even TV, Sócrates tirelessly repeated the same unfiltered messages into microphones and television cameras. In Italy, the media was dominated by the written press and the big dailies supported the Christian Democrats.

Sócrates – with some justification – felt they were against him and he eventually tried bypassing them as much as possible. Gatherings at places like the Casa del Popolo were one way and another was making direct contact with fans. He thought the Italians were more fanatical about football than Brazilians, but they were also more respectful and they thought twice before daring to approach their idols. He missed that human connection and it took him until the end of the season to really do something about it.

With just three games left in the season, Fiorentina were playing Udinese at home and the injured Sócrates went to watch the match in shorts and flip-flops. He arrived late and, rather than head to the directors' box, he grabbed a beer and stood behind the fence to watch the game just yards from the touch-line. The directors shouted at him to join them, but he ignored their calls and instead dealt them yet another snub. A local comedian friend appeared alongside him and, when half-time arrived, Sócrates suggested the pair watch the second half from the Curva Fiesole, the terrace behind the goals where the team's ultras gathered.

They were greeted as heroes when they got there and the experience of spending 45 minutes up close and personal with the real fans was one of his most enduring memories of his entire time in the city. Inevitably, however, the escapade only served to aggravate matters with the directors and team-mates. The Pontellos were upset at being snubbed and the players thought he was mad. The gulf between them was too big to be closed.

One of the few sunny moments during that bitterly cold winter happened in January when Sócrates went to Rome to meet Tancredo Neves, the man whom Congress had chosen as Brazil's first civilian president in 21 years. Sócrates loved meeting Neves, the president-elect who would tragically die before taking office, and he felt more homesick than ever at the thought of such a profound change taking place in his homeland without him being there to witness it. But the meeting at Rome's Excelsior Hotel did have one happy outcome.

The Brazilian players who were invited to the meeting all complained about how bored they were by Italy's staid social life, and they agreed to do something about it at carnival time. Sócrates loved carnival and he saw the celebrations as an opportunity not just to get the Brazilian players together again, but also to try to show his team-mates how to really have a party. He spent weeks making mix tapes of his favourite samba songs and bought 200 litres of Alla Spina beer, enough antipasto to feed a packed stadium and an entire suckling pig for barbecuing outside in the sub-zero temperatures.[20]

Sócrates split the event over two days, with the Brazilians arriving on the Monday and the Italians dominating the guest list on the Tuesday, which also happened to be his 31st birthday. The party kicked off timidly on the Sunday night when he returned from Atalanta after scoring in a 2-2 draw, but things really got going the next morning when the Brazilians arrived for phase one. Zico pulled up in his BMW with Catania's Pedrinho. Cerezo came from Rome and Júnior arrived with his entire family and a heavily bandaged foot. Edinho turned up in his Maserati turbo.

The tradition in Brazil was for revellers to inhale ethyl chloride in the form of poppers, something Brazilians called *lança-perfume*. But Sócrates was not to be beaten by the lack of a drug that was as much part of the 1980s carnival scene as sex and samba. He got Regina's hairdresser to bring him hairspray, which had the same intoxicating effect, and when the guests walked through the door he good-naturedly convinced them to partake.

'Sócrates said carnival without a *lança-perfume* is no carnival at all,' recalled Trajano, now a well-respected TV pundit. 'So he bought a box of hair lacquer from Regina's hairdresser friend and he put a lacquer-soaked tissue over the mouth of everyone who arrived at the party. The thing was that the lacquers had a different colour. So everyone ended up walking around with coloured noses; one was green, another red, another was pink.'[21]

The welcome for his Fiorentina team-mates the next day was equally unexpected. They turned up in suits and ties, displaying typical Italian elegance, and Sócrates, in his usual uniform of crumpled clothes and ratty trainers, wasted no time in making the party more Brazilian. He had commandeered a pair of garden shears to cut the formality and, when his guests walked through the door, he giggled with delight as they realised their Armanis and Dolce & Gabbana ties were about to be pruned.[22]

Oriali, Massaro, Galli and Gentile were among his victims, who had no choice but to surrender to his good-natured antics. Passarella got down on his knees and begged him to spare his expensive neckwear. Antognoni claimed his tie was a present from his mamma and almost cried. Sócrates loved it and, with his typical playfulness, laughingly ignored their pleas and then grabbed them and gave them a big hug, half a tie in his hand. He was overjoyed they had come and for a brief moment thought his rare feat of getting Italian players to socialise together might give them a boost.[23]

'Now we're a real football team,' he said. 'Now we can really let the spirit of Corinthians Democracy take a hold.'[24]

His optimism lasted just five days. The following Sunday, Fiorentina played Sampdoria at home with the aim of building on the four-game unbeaten run that had started against Lazio. Instead, Trevor Francis took them to pieces, scoring two of the three goals in a demoralising 3-0 rout. Two more defeats in their next three games left them just three points above the relegation zone and the team remained divided.

Sócrates was also torn over what to do about Rosemary. Much of his time in Italy was spent pining for her and fretting over whether or not to leave his wife for the woman he loved.

Sócrates had been married to Regina for 11 years and while he had changed beyond recognition, she was still the unassuming young lass he walked to school every morning. Sócrates had outgrown his wife but deep down he was a traditional boy from the provinces who valued marriage and family. His heart told him to dump her and take up with the famous singer, and his head told him to stay loyal to his childhood sweetheart and mother of his four boys.

Sócrates got 18 return flights to Brazil as part of his contract and he would use them to nip home for the weekend, drinking all the way to São Paulo, spending the weekend with friends or family or Rosemary, and then drinking all the way back to Rome. He had affairs in Italy but he missed Rosemary and he would call her from hotel rooms the world over to sing the year's big hit, 'I Just Called to Say I Love You'.[25]

In the end, the decision to end their affair and try to make his marriage work was a costly one, and not just because his marriage wouldn't last much longer. Almost from the moment he arrived in Italy he regretted taking the easy option, and his resentment manifested itself in what Flávio Gikovate called 'increasingly self-destructive behaviour'.

'When he went to Florence it was almost as if he was running away from the Rosemary situation,' said Gikovate, the psychotherapist who knew Sócrates from his time working with Corinthians and who spent time with him in Italy. 'The impression I got is that he went there totally self-destructive. Self-destructive as in punishing yourself for making the wrong choice. He didn't have the guts to take the decision he wanted to take.

'He ran away from a bigger relationship than the one he had with Regina. That relationship was cosy but it wasn't exciting, and he was a man who liked excitement. So he ran away from what he really wanted and I don't think he ever recovered.

'No matter how extravagant, how eccentric, how much of an outsider he was, when it came to the crunch he didn't have the courage to leave his wife to marry the singer who was more exuberant, more beautiful and more independent. He had a fear of happiness and he didn't think he was worthy of a woman like that, and he was weakened and started to behave like a destructive outsider. It was one own goal after another. He became more bitter, more destructive and more unhappy.'[26]

De Sisti had not recovered fully from his brain operation and was replaced by Ferruccio Valcareggi, the respected coach who had led Italy at the 1970 World Cup finals. But the atmosphere was so corrosive that Sócrates called an urgent meeting and the players were invited to meet at Pontello's palatial home. Sócrates was sure he had discovered the reason for the dressing-room split and he wanted to do something about it.

'Why have you called this meeting?' Pontello asked from one end of his enormous office table.

The players shifted nervously in their seats and mumbled a few inconclusive platitudes while looking to Sócrates at the far end of the room.

'I've got something to say,' said Sócrates, and he began with customary Brazilian cordiality before launching into his controversial accusation.

'If I may explain,' he said, 'what's happened is this. One guy is shagging another guy's wife and so went and formed his own clique. Now these guys aren't talking to these guys and this group won't pass the ball to the others. The only solution is to get rid of the captain.'

'No way,' said Pontello. 'I'm not doing that. No one is leaving.'

'Fine,' said Sócrates. 'Then please excuse me.'

And he got up and walked out.[27]

Sócrates' disinterest was by now plain and a mix of resentment, unhappiness and apathy set in. Relations between him and the other members of the squad were increasingly strained and defender Stefano Carobbi said that in one particularly nasty prank, someone may have urinated in his water bottle as the team drove home from an away game. He knew he had no chance of being happy outside Brazil and he was literally counting the days until his nightmare was over.[28]

'When Sócrates walked into the dressing room he would say hello to everyone with the announcement, "Good morning, today there are 200 days to go" or, "Good morning, today there are 150 days to go,"' recalled centre half Pin. 'It was a running calendar, as if he was counting down the days until he could leave. It was his way of showing his dissatisfaction.'[29]

He just wanted it all to end and he was helped by a young striker named Luca Cecconi. With four games of the season remaining, injury forced Sócrates out of the trip to Juventus and the 21-year-old Cecconi took his place for just his fourth appearance of the season. He scored in a 2-1 win against their hated rivals and Sócrates' fate was sealed. The fans found a new hero and Sócrates never wore a Fiorentina shirt again.

'Football to him was all about happiness,' Carobbi, who now coaches Colligiana, said thoughtfully. 'He was always happy. In Italy, we have a different mentality. Here you need to have your head focused on the game. It's not possible to be smiling before you play and that made him suffer. According to him, the team has to transmit joy. But we transmitted the opposite. Now I am a manager I can see he was right. It's not a case of life and death. We go to a performance to enjoy it. He was the only one who understood that.'[30]

Sócrates had another year left on his contract but he knew where to find that joy and it wasn't in Europe. He was desperate to go home. Maybe a little too desperate.

15

'It was mental. He was a guy who would wake up and say, "Do you want a beer?" And I'd say, "I want breakfast.""

Juca Kfouri

Sócrates wasn't the only Brazilian player who had a year to forget in Italy. Zico, Falcão and Cerezo all missed large parts of the season through injury; Edinho didn't reproduce the form he showed the year before at Udinese, and even Dirceu's consistency at Ascoli couldn't help them avoid the drop. Batista's Lazio and Juary's Cremonese also went down, while in the division below them Luvanor and Pedrinho fought to keep Catania from dropping to the third tier.

The only one to enhance his reputation was Júnior, who had a brilliant year at Torino, helping them to runners-up spot in the league and finishing the season as the club's second top goalscorer behind Aldo Serena. Italian sportswriters voted him second only to Maradona as foreign player of the year, ahead of stars such as Michel Platini, Karl-Heinz Rummenigge and Liam Brady.

The Brazilians' failure to make an impact, and the success of more robust but less technically gifted players such as Mark Hateley, Hans-Peter Briegel and Preben Elkjaer, was used as evidence that the Brazilians did not have the stamina or conditioning, and perhaps also the necessary mental toughness, to cope with heavy pitches, cold weather and no-nonsense Italian defenders.

Sócrates repeatedly dismissed that notion and tried hard to convince both himself and everyone else that his year in Florence was not a total failure.

'I never managed to turn it on in winter, but in autumn and spring I was fucking brilliant,' he said. 'But the team was shit; there was a bastard of a war going on, that kind of situation that you never imagined possible. The team was divided and there were five guys on one side, four on the other, the keeper and me. These guys didn't pass to each other, they didn't even look at each other, they didn't even acknowledge each other. It was a mess. That was the team I ended up at. There was no way to take it forward.'[1]

'The only mistake I would say I made was to speak a new language too clearly and too honestly. And, principally, new and different for the world of Italian football.'[2]

He insisted he would do nothing differently and that what he really missed was the human warmth and interaction that was such a part of his life in Brazil. Sócrates had the skills to succeed – Giovanni Galli, a man who played with Ruud Gullit, Marco van Basten and Roberto Baggio, said he had never seen anyone who could pass like he could – but he had been indulged so long that he didn't understand the need to compromise. Fiorentina, too, could have been more savvy and let him do his own thing. At Botafogo and Corinthians, Sócrates always did the business when he was left to his own devices. But the bottom line was that he was unsuited to Italian football, which demanded running and commitment, and to Italian life, which was formal and structured.

He was the wrong man in the wrong place at the wrong time and the only solution was to come home.

By the start of August, with the Italian season fast approaching, he was so desperate to end his exile that he was prepared to entertain any offers. There were lots of rumours about clubs in for him, but the first solid proposal came from Ponte Preta, the Campinas-based side that proudly claims to be the oldest football club in Brazil.

Ponte had never won a major title but they were enjoying their most successful spell ever. They finished runners-up in the Paulista state championship in 1977, 1979 and 1981, with internationalists Oscar, Carlos and Juninho Fonseca in their ranks, and then stepped up a level to finish third in the 1981 Brasileiro. They had gone off the boil slightly in the years since but they were still bringing through lots of good youngsters, as shown by their 1981 and 1982 triumphs in the Copa São Paulo de Juniores, Brazil's most prestigious youth tournament.

The deal to bring Sócrates back home was anchored by Luciano do Valle, a football commentator who also ran sports-related businesses on the side. Do Valle was as well known in Brazil as John Motson or Brian Moore in Britain, and he knew Sócrates from covering the national team. A fanatical Ponte Preta fan, do Valle was desperate to see the star at his own team and he – with all the fanfare of a garrulous TV reporter – told the world he had put together a deal that would see local companies pay Sócrates' salary and bonuses through innovative sponsorship deals.

On 11 August 1985, Sócrates left Italy for Campinas and within hours of arriving had appeared in front of ecstatic fans wearing the club jersey. Six buses filled with supporters went to greet him at the airport, where they chanted, 'You can't fool me, Doctor, your heart is with Ponte Preta.' A smiling Sócrates told them, 'I am back to the place that is mine.'[3]

Ponte had big plans for their new star and Campinas, a modern, new city just 60 miles from São Paulo, bubbled with excitement. The club quickly put season tickets on sale and thousands were snapped up. They asked Boca Juniors to provide the opposition for his debut on 23 August and planned to parade their new signing through the city in an open-topped limousine. One of the region's best-known bars even hired the barman from his favourite haunt in Ribeirão Preto so that he would have a friendly face serving him ice-cold lager exactly the way he liked.[4]

But Sócrates hadn't signed a contract yet and less than a week after appearing in a Ponte shirt he was back in Italy with his tail between his legs. The deal he said was 95 per cent certain to go through was now almost dead. Do Valle talked a good game in front of the cameras and he promised Sócrates his signing-on fee was waiting for him in a Campinas bank vault. The cash, however, never existed and when Sócrates got wind of the deception he was furious. Do Valle pleaded with him to wait but he hadn't lined up enough companies to help finance the deal, and with the deadline for registrations approaching he didn't have time to get others on board.

The CBF, eager to have one of their stars playing regularly in the run-up to the 1986 World Cup, offered to take the Brazil team to Florence for a lucrative friendly and use the proceeds to fund Sócrates' return to Brazil. The monies would cover some of the outstanding $400,000 he was owed by Fiorentina and he was happy to take a pay cut to free him from his Tuscan purgatory. But the deal fell apart and his future remained uncertain.[5]

Throughout all this, Sócrates made one mistake that cost him dearly. While negotiations with Ponte were still ongoing, he signed a document waiving all rights to monies still owed him by Fiorentina. He claimed the document contained a clause stating it would only be valid if the Ponte deal went through, but Fiorentina rubbished that interpretation and used it as a way to get rid of someone who had become an embarrassment to them. When the Ponte deal cooled and he returned to Italy, Sócrates was treated as an ex-player. He tried to carry on as normal but Pontello wanted nothing more to do with him.

The Fiorentina fans were angry, too, partly because he had advised Falcão not to join the club and partly because a local newspaper maliciously reported uncomplimentary remarks they said he'd made about Italians. When he read about the invented quotes, he was so angry that he got in his car and drove 60 miles to Viareggio to tell his side of the story. He arrived for Fiorentina's friendly against Monza after the match had kicked off and climbed straight into the stands to try to convince supporters he had not given any interviews the previous day, much less insulted them. But they were desperate to see the back of him to free up one of their two foreign spots and he seriously misjudged the mood. Instead of being fêted, he was almost lynched.

'There were only two foreigners per team in those days and so the main issue was that if he didn't leave then Falcão couldn't come,' remembered Alberto Polverosi, a local journalist who knew Sócrates and was in Monza. 'The fans were furious and were physically trying to get at him. They were shouting at him and insulting him, and when he realised how bad things were he had to get out. So he ended up fleeing. And that was when things became very complicated for him.'[6]

Sócrates turned up for training the next day but was denied access on the grounds that he was no longer a Fiorentina player.

The final insult came when officials would not let him appear in the traditional pre-season squad photo 24 hours later. 'You're a Ponte Preta player now,' Pontello told him.[7]

Sócrates was livid at the way he was treated and vowed to do everything within his power to get the money he was still owed, even aiming vague threats at the Fiorentina president.

'I don't mind not getting the $850,000 for next season. But I will insist on getting paid the $400,000 for the work I have done and I will take this to the final consequences. I will get the Italian Communist Party involved too so [Pontello] doesn't get a moment's peace.'[8]

It was an idle threat but it showed how rattled he was. Sócrates never played football for money but he hated to think he had been duped. Even worse, he felt taken advantage of and disrespected. The treatment meted out to him by both the club and some of its fans during those final days of summer disgusted him. He said it showed him 'the coldest, nastiest side of man' and it was the final confirmation, as if it were needed, that he did not fit in.

The answer to his problems came from Rio de Janeiro, the most passionate of football cities, a Third World resort of laid-back lawlessness that was home to the Maracanã stadium; to Zico, Garrincha and Jairzinho; and to Botafogo, Flamengo, Fluminense and Vasco da Gama.

The registration deadline was still open in Rio and when Flamengo got wind of his availability, the 33-year-old marketing whizz kid who brought Zico back from Udinese just a few weeks previously made his move. Rogério Steinberg wanted the midfield maestros together at the city's biggest club and he lined up enough sponsors to pay their wages.

It was a major coup and it was perfect for Sócrates. Rio was beautiful and glamorous and known the world over not just for its football, but also for its beaches, its anything-goes carnival, and a steamy climate that compounded a culture that sweated sensuality. Cariocas are world famous for their warmth, their sociability and their informal and extrovert nature. Sócrates was desperate for love and affection after a year in the frigid wastelands of northern Italy, and he knew that moving to Rio would be a good fit.

Rio was, and still is, the city of the eternal adolescent, where people speak, dress and act like teenagers. The unofficial uniform for males is shorts, T-shirt and flip-flops; the unofficial drink is ice-cold lager, downed at any hour of the day or night; and planning ahead is reserved for the dull and the uptight. It was tailor-made for someone who joked that he couldn't plan more than 10 seconds ahead.

'Sócrates was born in Pará and brought up in Ribeirão Preto but his soul was Carioca,' said Paulo Sérgio, the reserve keeper at the 1982 World Cup and himself Rio born and bred. 'I considered him a Carioca. He was laid-back and knew how to take advantage of what life had to offer.'[9]

Sócrates touched down in Rio early on the morning of Friday, 13 September and hundreds of Flamengo fans, including percussionists with the Mangueira samba school, turned out to greet him, making the most almighty racket. Zico was there with Steinberg to welcome his old pal home.

Sócrates gave a quick press conference at the airport, headed to Flamengo's Gávea HQ to train and then returned to the club at night for a welcome home party that in true Carioca style finally wrapped up at 11 the next morning.

His first comments on arriving home were limited to praising Rio and celebrating Brazil's democratic advances, but he tried hard to focus attention on football rather than any off-the-field activities. He was now 31 and he knew that for the first time in his career there were doubts about his ability and whether the skills he had failed to show in Italy were gone forever or just dormant. Some critics suggested he could be a bad example for other players, that he was a poor professional who cared more about politics than football, but Sócrates refused to be drawn and was admirably honest in his response.

'I need to do a rethink and adopt a different attitude from now on,' he said. 'I've had enough of sticking my head above the parapet.'

When pushed on whether he would angle for more democracy inside his new club or lobby for an end to the *concentração*, he asked for more time to draw conclusions.

'I have just arrived, I don't know what will happen. I'll tell you later. When Corinthians Democracy was implanted people got it all wrong. It was a democracy because people exchanged ideas and that is healthy. Nothing was decided without all the different parties being heard. I am and always will be against authoritarianism. First I need to get to know the club before taking any positions. If the majority is in favour of the *concentração* then I will be the first to adopt the position.'[10]

Flamengo's president, with typical Brazilian hyperbole, said his signing gave Flamengo 'not just the best squad in Brazil, but in the world', and manager Joubert virtually excused him from chasing back by declaring, 'Sócrates isn't a player that marks. He is a player who is marked.'

It was exactly what he wanted to hear, and he was in high spirits when he headed off to Ribeirão Preto the following night to spend the weekend visiting family and friends.

However, it wasn't long before things started to go off script. Although Sócrates hadn't trained in weeks, Flamengo hoped he would make his debut against Fluminense a week after arriving. But just two days before the game, he fell awkwardly on his left ankle after going up for a header in training. The initial diagnosis was a bad sprain, but it soon became clear the damage was more serious and further tests revealed that he had fractured his tibia and would be out for up to four months.

It was a crushing blow for both the player and his team, especially coming so soon after Zico had been diagnosed with a knee injury that would keep him out until the New Year. Sócrates wanted game time to show the fans he hadn't lost his skills while in Europe. Brazilians rarely saw Italian football but they knew he had struggled and there was a sense that he was past his best. He also needed to prove he was worth a place in the squad that would go to Mexico. Now, instead of showcasing his talents at the Maracanã every week, he spent the rest of the year on crutches and in physiotherapy.

When he made his debut early the next year, it was in the unlikely surroundings of the Arabian desert. Starting in the 1950s, Brazilian teams regularly toured the world in the close season, with the glorious Santos and Botafogo teams of Pelé and Garrincha visiting not just Europe but Africa, Asia and North America on months-long trips that brought them much-needed cash. By the 1980s, those tours had moved to the Middle East, where Arab nations were buying up Brazilian players and coaches in a bid to learn from their knowledge and expertise.

After recovering from his fractured tibia, Sócrates was ready to play again in January and a crowd of 12,000 people turned out in Bahrain to see him excel alongside Zico, who was making his first appearance since undergoing an operation on his left knee in October. They won 3-1 against West Raff, with Sócrates not just playing well but appearing in decent physical shape.[11]

Flamengo had originally hoped to play two other games in the region, but a fixture in South Yemen was cancelled at the last minute because of a military coup and a second game in Saudi Arabia also never materialised. They ended their tour in

Baghdad, where they won 2-0 against Iraq – where Zico's brother Edu was coach – but before that they headed to Italy to face Fiorentina in the friendly arranged as part of his transfer deal. Sócrates was to get the gate receipts from the match and in return he agreed not to sue the club for money he was owed.[12]

Sócrates unwisely reopened old wounds before the match by criticising Pontello for exploitation, and he thought the Italians sabotaged the game by deliberately not publicising it. To make matters worse, Italy were playing Germany in a friendly in Avellino two days later and several of the home side were missing. Passarella made a point of turning out, even though he had injured a thigh in his previous game five days before, but Fiorentina had only four regulars in the line-up. To cap it all, the night was cold and wet. Only 4,100 people turned up.

Sócrates threw a bouquet of yellow flowers to the *tifosi* on the Curva Fiesole but there were few other highlights. Flamengo were poor and lost three goals in an eight-minute spell midway through the first half. They staged a mini fightback in the second period and got a couple back through Bebeto, but they couldn't get an equaliser. The low turnout meant that Sócrates walked away with just $6,000 once the overheads had been discounted, a far cry from the $400,000 he had lost in the contractual arm wrestling. He was unrepentant, if consistent, in the post-match interview, declaring that life was not about money.

'Happiness comes from people not from dollars,' he said. 'It's not important how many fans came. I am happy that they came. The few that did come are extremely loyal.'

Ranieri Pontello, who watched the game from the stands, said he regretted 'the crazy decision' to sign Sócrates and in one last twist of the knife he sarcastically told Italian newspapers, 'Given how he played here [last season] tonight he did quite well.'[13]

Sócrates said he had a great time and promised to come back to Italy the next time he got any holidays.

When asked if he would consider returning to play, he was straight and to the point.

'No,' he answered.

Two weeks later, Flamengo kicked off their Rio state championship campaign against Fluminense at the Maracanã. Their city rivals had won the tournament the previous three years and were hoping to become the first team in the competition's 80-year history to win it four times in a row.

Fluminense's dressing room was adorned with a banner saying: 'Thank you, Triple-champions! Happy 1986, Year of the Four in a Row', and their fans goaded Zico with homophobic chants, which served only to spur him on. He ran the show, scoring a hat-trick – the third goal being his 700th in first-class football – in the 4-1 win.[14]

At Flamengo, Zico wasn't just the star, he was a myth, a kid who had supported the club and then gone on to become the greatest player in their history. Sócrates would play second fiddle to the number 10 both on and off the field, but that was fine by him. He realised that he not only had to prove himself again, but also that he had to adjust his game to suit the club's undisputed star.

For Sócrates, that meant playing a little deeper than before but he was comfortable with the change. He could still see the game in front of him and he was happy to cede a little control They knew each other well from the seleção and Sebastião Lazaroni, who had replaced Joubert as boss, thought Zico would make hay from Sócrates' passes.

Sócrates was a little off the pace against Fluminense, but with Adílio and Andrade making up the four-man midfield – the pair played alongside Zico when Flamengo destroyed Liverpool in the Intercontinental Cup four years previously – they were looking good for what promised to be a long, hard season.

Neither of them, though, would play much part in it. Luckily for Sócrates, Telê Santana had been installed as Brazil coach again after Al-Ahli reluctantly agreed to release him from his contract. Telê's Arabian exile meant he was not as up on Brazilian football as he might have been, so when he named his first squad in February he turned to the men who had served him so well four years before. Zico, Falcão, Cerezo, Éder, Júnior and Leandro were all among those chosen and Sócrates joined them, even though the Fluminense game was his first competitive match in seven months.

The opening game of the World Cup was still three and a half months away, but Telê was leaving nothing to chance. The day after the Fluminense game, Sócrates and 24 other home-based players (four Italian-based players would meet them later) underwent medical tests in Rio and then headed to Belo Horizonte where Telê had arranged for them to stay at Cruzeiro's Toca da Raposa training centre, the same place where they had prepared for Spain four years previously. Sócrates vowed to stop smoking and drinking, saying the seleção 'is going to need full capacity from all the players for the World Cup', and he promised he would be in even better condition than in 1982.[15]

That promise was optimistic as there was still a big question mark over whether he would even be in Mexico. His lack of playing time was a real worry and, while he was still popular with the fans – in a postal vote, 32,000 readers of *Placar* chose him for their favoured World Cup team – his selection was far from unanimous among those in the know. Telê didn't say anything but privately he had reservations, and the coaches who knew Sócrates best had passed on their concerns.

The exact nature of that risk was over both his fitness and his behaviour, and it was the second issue that quickly came to the

fore as Sócrates seemed to go out of his way to damage his reputation. A week before he joined the Brazil squad, he was a
judge at the 1986 carnival celebrations in Rio de Janeiro. Rio's
carnival parade was an annual mega-production that dominated
the nation for the first month or two of every year. The main
event took place on the Sunday and Monday before Ash
Wednesday, along the Sambadrome parade ground in the centre
of the city. Starting at around eight each night and finishing
around six, 15 different schools paraded for almost a kilometre
in front of 90,000 fans and a panel of judges. It was billed as the
world's greatest party and it was certainly one of the most flamboyant. Tens of thousands of people, dressed up in costumes
laden with sequins, feathers and spangles, sambaed their way
along the route while smiling, singing and waving to the crowds
packed in the stands along both sides.

Sócrates was asked to be one of the celebrity judges because
he was considered 'incorruptible', but that reputation was
tempered somewhat by his lack of judging experience – and
his decision to get hammered before the parade even began.
Judges were designated a category, such as outfits, floats or
songs, and their task was to give each school marks out of 10.
Sócrates was one of two people chosen to rate the *bateria*, the
thunderous percussion section that anchored the beat of each
song.

The judges sat in the stands to better watch the schools as they
passed by in front of them, but a well-oiled Sócrates wanted to
participate as well as watch. He skipped down the stairs to the
parade ground, stripped off his top and started dancing along in
a pair of tight white shorts. Officials objected and he was reluctantly coaxed back to the judging station. But that wasn't the
end of his travails. Lacking any technical expertise, Sócrates
used his own judging criteria. If the crowd were on their feet
and singing when a school passed by, he gave them 10 out of 10.

If they were on their feet but not singing, he gave them nine. If they were neither on their feet nor singing, he gave them eight. It was hardly sophisticated and he ended up awarding eight of the 15 schools top marks. Another four got nine, and the remaining three got eight.[16]

Supporters of the Portela samba school who had gathered to hear the results being announced were furious with Sócrates for docking their school a point, even though it had no bearing on the final result. Before the votes were even counted, the president of the Salgueiro school accused him of being so drunk he was 'in no condition to judge anything'. He wanted to annul Sócrates' votes and friends had to talk him out of what would have been a hugely embarrassing decision. Salgueiro, who ironically were given 10 out of 10 by Sócrates, finished in sixth place behind winners Mangueira (coincidentally a school traditionally popular with Flamengo fans).

Pictures of Sócrates staggering around with a can of beer in his hand brought him exactly the kind of headlines he didn't need on the eve of a Brazil game, but true to form he didn't mind and he didn't care who knew it. It might have been laughed off had he been playing well, or even just playing. But the derby against Fluminense was his first competitive match since June and he should have been preparing himself physically and mentally for what was his most important season in years. Some fans, including old foes who still saw his outspoken liberalism as a threat, seized on the incident to decry what they saw not just as a lack of professionalism, but the greater crime of a lack of commitment to the seleção.

Placar had always been supportive of the player, and its editor Juca Kfouri was still a friend and admirer. But even *Placar* couldn't pretend his reputation hadn't taken a knock. Since returning from Europe, Sócrates had done nothing on the football field and hit the headlines only for his drinking. Summing up his current plight, an editorial said: 'newspapers, magazines, radio and television news all treat Sócrates as an inveterate smoker and drunkard more interested in political rhetoric than his main task: simply playing admirable football.' Sócrates, true to form, did not even attempt to make excuses for his behaviour.

'We drink more *cachaça* here than in any other country in the world and yet it's like I am the only one,' he said. 'Or I'm the only one to get drunk. I've been attacked so often because of my positions. There is a tendency to destroy anything worthwhile – they want to destroy me. It didn't get to me but it gets to the people around me and that is really upsetting. They don't want me to drink or smoke or think? Well, I drink and I smoke and I think. I went to have a good time and I drank all night. I don't hide what I do.'[17]

Asked if he wasn't damaging his reputation ahead of the World Cup, he replied: 'My reputation is that of someone who is authentic. I am no false moralist. My image is one of sincerity – and the public gets that. There are people who sit at their typewriters and mould public opinion. Conservatives, relics from the old regime. I am here, called up by Telê – and I don't see him worried about my image.'[18]

The scandal made headlines not simply because of the timing, or even his lack of playing time. With no political causes to rally around, ostentatiously throwing back the booze became Sócrates' way of challenging society, a new way of showing his detractors that, in spite of all their finger-wagging, he could still act like a teenager and play football at World Cup level. But he was 32 years old, with a body that was recovering from serious injuries and months of inactivity. Like any other sportsman limping into his fourth decade, he couldn't do what he did five years before and get away with it. Time was sending a message but Sócrates didn't want to listen, and the raucous sounds of Rio de Janeiro made it even harder to hear.

Rio's party atmosphere was seductive and friends could see he was slowly slipping his moorings. His marriage was in trouble and, although his affair with Rosemary had cooled, there were plenty of other flings and one-night stands to keep him busy. At Flamengo, he would sometimes board a private yacht the day after games with a bunch of players and friends. They loaded up on beer, meat and girls and sped off to the island of Jurubaiba to spend the day far from the paparazzi. The players laughingly rechristened the island Surubaiba, from the word *suruba*, which meant orgy in Portuguese.

Sócrates loved Rio but the press and fans there never truly understood Corinthians Democracy, and the natural antipathy towards Paulistas didn't help. The media stopped treating him as a darling and there were more questions than ever about his football, his politics and even the way he spoke. He stopped rolling his 'r's as they did in São Paulo and started pronouncing the 's' more as a 'sh' sound like Cariocas did. Whether or not it was an intentional attempt to fit in, it was noticeable and his friends found it hilarious. 'You've got no personality at all; you change who you are depending on the circumstances,' one friend told him, only half-joking.

Sócrates was loath to admit it but he was frustrated, by his faltering marriage and the loss of Rosemary, by the Fiorentina debacle, and by the injuries that had prevented him from playing alongside Zico at a packed and pulsating Maracanã. Typically, though, he refused to dwell on the past, especially when the present was so alluring, and he dedicated himself to enjoying the attractions his new hometown had to offer. He stood on hustings in both Rio and São Paulo to support his candidates for mayor. He got involved in health education campaigns to help educate Brazilians on the spread of AIDS. And he made his first forays into Rio's famous favelas, drinking beer, listening to live samba music and eating skewers of meat from pavement grills as the sun came up. The simple act of buzzing a carload of poor black musicians past the disbelieving security guards at his upscale gated community brought him pleasure. He was doing exactly what people didn't want him to do and it made him feel alive.[19]

Telê, meanwhile, was worried but he was too clever to show it. He had spent most of the last year in Saudi Arabia and hadn't seen all the players he wanted to see, much less decided what his ideal team might be in Mexico. He knew that football had become more physical since the last World Cup and he warned his midfielders they would have to work harder and mark more than in Spain. His return gave the seleção some much-needed hope after three years and three managers, none of whom had come close to reproducing the magic of 1982.

Carlos Alberto Parreira took over in early 1983, but his attempts to blood young players were unsuccessful and he was fired after winning only five of his 14 matches in charge. Sócrates played in three of them and was never on the losing side, but seven draws did for Parreira, who was replaced by Zico's brother Edu. His reign got off to the worst possible start when a team that included five debutants was beaten by goals from Mark Hateley and John Barnes at the Maracanã. Sócrates missed that game and the next two, a draw and a win, but it was underwhelming stuff and Edu was out after just three games in the hot seat.

Evaristo de Macedo replaced him in the dugout in April 1985 but his decision not to pick any of the foreign-based stars did not endear him either to Sócrates or to most fans. Six games and one month later he too was gone, leaving Brazil adrift just 12 months before the World Cup kicked off in Mexico.

Telê was still fiercely loyal to the class of 1982 but he could not avoid the fact that there were younger and fitter guys staking their claims for a place, and nowhere was that more evident than in midfield. One of the surprise packages of the previous year was Elzo, the midfield dynamo at Atlético Mineiro. Silas and Alemão were in great form for São Paulo and Botafogo respectively. Júnior had excelled in the middle of the park with Torino, and both Falcão and Zico were getting back to their best now that they were back in Brazil and free of injury.

Telê called up 29 players in February with the intention of cutting seven on the eve of the tournament. The decision was criticised for creating heated (and sometimes overheated) rivalries as the players battled each other for a place in the final squad. But with so many of them still recovering from injuries, Telê wanted to cover all his bases by including both his preferred starters and their possible replacements.

The 25 Brazil-based players met in Rio and after undergoing routine medical tests they moved to Belo Horizonte, where they would be joined at the end of the Serie A season by the four Italy-based players Cerezo, Júnior, Dirceu and Edinho.

Sócrates' vow to get in shape was exactly what the coach wanted to hear, and Gilberto Tim worked him and the rest of the squad so hard in those early weeks that they christened him 'Mengele', after the sadistic Nazi doctor. Sócrates, however, came down with a thigh complaint that stopped him from fully extending himself. It started as a niggle and then developed into something more serious, but the medical team couldn't identify the problem to treat it. It was uncomfortable rather than sore, but as the weeks went on it became more and more irritating and prevented him from cementing his place in the side.

It was just one of the many problems that autumn as the black clouds that hung over his early months at Flamengo followed him to the national side and expanded their sphere of malignant influence. The biggest scandal came just a week after the players met up. Telê gave them a night off but told them to take it easy and be back by midnight. Leandro and Renato Gaúcho went wild and were caught sneaking back into the camp at 4 a.m. Telê was livid and wanted to send them home there and then, but he reluctantly agreed to give them a second chance after Sócrates and a few other senior players appealed for leniency.[20]

On 4 March, Zico twisted his knee seriously during training – the same left knee that was operated on five months before – and was sidelined for at least a month. Three days later Leandro sprained his left ankle. Both men were ruled out of friendlies later that month against West Germany and Hungary.

The game in Frankfurt on 12 March highlighted the lack of seriousness surrounding Brazil's preparations. The temperature was a frigid 3°C and the Brazilians didn't fancy spending a minute longer in the cold than was absolutely necessary. While the Germans braved the weather to limber up in front of their fans, the Brazilians did their warming up in their centrally heated dressing room deep inside the Waldstadion. Not surprisingly, the Germans caught their visitors cold, with Hans-Peter Briegel scoring from a corner after just 90 seconds. Klaus Allofs added a second in the penultimate minute of the match to give the Germans a comfortable 2-0 win. The watching England manager Bobby Robson witheringly declared that 'Brazil were using the same tactics they did in 1958.'[21]

Sócrates was one of the better performers, but more thigh problems caused him to miss the Hungary match in Budapest four days later. Again, it was a terrible showing from Brazil. Telê included debutants Elzo and Silas in the side – two more newcomers to add to the four who made their debuts against West Germany – and both started in an untested midfield alongside Alemão. The experiment failed miserably as Brazil went down 3-0.

The players were starting to get worried at the lack of communication between them and the coaching staff, and Casagrande called on Sócrates to assume more of a leadership role to help bridge the gap that was forming. But having not played regularly and with criticism still ringing in his ears, Sócrates did not feel like the leader he once was and he was loath to pretend, especially as Brazil already had a perfectly good captain in Oscar.

Sócrates had in truth grown tired of trying to lead Brazilian football players, who, he now concluded, could not or did not want to be led. He had been at the training camp less than a month but he was already going stir-crazy, and the thought of three more months cooped up without his family depressed him. He had come face to face with the realisation that, even after years of Corinthians Democracy and challenging the system, nothing had changed. The players were in exactly the same place as they were four years ago and living under the same restrictive rules. The game was still run by the same conservative politicians as ever – one of them being José Maria Marin, the future CBF head who would be arrested in the FIFA corruption scandal almost 30 years later.[22]

'Nobody has the guts to change anything,' Sócrates said in March in his only major interview before the tournament. 'I've tried a thousand times to shake things up but I've given up. Enough is enough. I'm going to look after myself a little bit. I've taken enough of a pounding; there comes a time when you have to give it a rest.'[23]

Any chance he might be pressured into stepping up disappeared after he and Branco were accused of getting drunk on the flight home from central Europe. When asked if he thought he was in danger of being cut from the final squad, he gave the less than encouraging answer: 'Not yet.'

*

Brazil had to wait just two more weeks to get back on their feet, as the CBF organised a month of friendlies designed to give Telê maximum opportunity to find his best side. But the problems leading up to Mexico were as much off the field as on it. The head of the CBF went to Brasília in early April to beg for money because they didn't have the cash to fund the whole trip. By the end of the month they still didn't know where they would train in Mexico, as no one had gone to visit possible training camps or hotels. The CBF warned the players that they had enough money to get them there and back but not enough to pay win bonuses in case of victory. Marcio Braga, the Rio de Janeiro congressman who was to head the delegation to Mexico, resigned in early April, saying football was rotten, 'filled with pederasts, *bicheiros* [the shady characters who run popular, but illegal, numbers games] and Paulistas'. Things were so grim that the 46-year-old Pelé offered to come out of retirement to boost the side.[24, 25]

Matters were no better on the field either. Sócrates' thigh failed to improve and Zico was unable to regain full fitness after his knee injury. Brazil beat a Peruvian youth side 4-0 and then overcame East Germany and Finland by the same 3-0 scoreline. But Telê chopped and changed the side and they failed to convince, with Sócrates playing an hour of the first, missing the second and being subbed again after a poor performance in the third. The very next day, Telê relegated him to the reserves in training and said it was clear he 'wasn't yet in peak physical or technical form'.[26]

Telê's uncertainty over his best side was underlined by the statistic showing he gave debuts to 10 players in his first five games back in charge. He wanted to allow Sócrates every chance to prove himself but time was running out, and the experiments came to an end in April when Brazil beat Yugoslavia 4-2 in Recife. Zico made his comeback and scored three goals, and for the first time in months there was a glimmer of hope. Sócrates was left out of the side again but he survived the next round of cuts that saw five players wave goodbye to a summer in Mexico, including Renato Gaúcho, who reacted by telling Telê he wanted to run him over.

There was just one last full international friendly before the squad flew to Mexico, and the team that began the game against Chile in Curitiba was thought to be the one that Telê wanted to see line up against Spain three weeks hence. Once again, Sócrates was left out of the starting line-up and once again Telê pointedly told him he wasn't fit. He got a game but in the worst possible circumstances, after Zico twisted his knee and was forced to come off at half-time. Fans were so angry after the 1-1 draw that they pelted the team bus with stones.

The players got a half-day off before flying to Mexico and several of them gathered at Sócrates' house in Rio for a final barbecue. No one was happy with the CBF and no one believed the bookies' prediction that Brazil were favourites. They tried to enjoy their last meal before heading off, but as they loosened their official ties and stretched out on the charter flight to Mexico news filtered through of the biggest bombshell yet. Leandro had decided to abandon the national team. The defender had his bags packed and got to the door of his apartment, where he turned to the friend who was driving him to the airport and said simply, 'I'm not going.' After unsuccessfully pleading with him to change his mind, the friend roared out to the airport to pass on the news, and Zico and Júnior piled in a car and raced back to try to talk some sense into him. Leandro, though, was adamant. After almost an hour of fruitless appeals, the two Flamengo stars headed back to the airport and Telê was forced to leave for Mexico without his first choice right back.[27]

Leandro said the problem was his knee. He claimed it would not hold up over another month of bombing up and down the wing and that he wanted to play in the centre of defence, where he started for Flamengo. Telê already had three capable centre halves in Oscar, Edinho and Júlio César, and Leandro's characteristic reserve and Telê's increasing isolation meant the two men never even discussed the issue. Malicious rumours swirled over the close relationship between Leandro and Renato Gaúcho and many people believed that Leandro was striking back at Telê for dropping his best friend.

Sócrates would later call Leandro's decision 'maybe the most beautiful public gesture I've ever seen in these 50 years' and he seriously considered joining the boycott, more out of sympathy for his pal than because he disagreed with Telê's decision. But he didn't want to miss the tournament or upset the coach he still admired, and he had his own issues to deal with.

Off the field, Sócrates had taken a conscious decision to keep a low profile. He was acutely aware he had to prove himself again and he could only do that by playing and putting in performances that mattered. He gave fewer interviews and shied away from expressing opinions on controversial topics. In one of his few public comments before jetting out, he tried to put a positive spin on the chaos by saying, 'If we did everything right last time and lost, maybe this time we're doing everything wrong and we'll win.'[28]

Things eventually started to look up for both Brazil and Sócrates within days of arriving in Mexico. Doctors finally discovered the cause of his thigh injury and set about treating it with intensive sessions of physio. In a matter of days, he was strutting around with a poise and confidence he hadn't shown for months. He replaced Elzo at half-time in a friendly against Atlante and the team immediately improved thanks to his midfield promptings. He got the decider in a 2–1 win when he turned in a low cross from Müller, and there was some optimism it might be the performance that would give him and the team a springboard to success.[29]

That was reinforced three days later when he was equally decisive in a friendly against América. Again, he came on in the second half and lifted a team that had been leading 1-0 to a 4-0 victory. He started a third warm-up against the Universidad de Guadalajara on 25 May and played well in the 3-1 win, even if he tired visibly at the end of 90 minutes. It was enough to guarantee his place in the starting line-up versus the UdeG junior team on 29 May. Brazil won 9-1. Sócrates had done just enough. He was named as a starter against Spain.

16

'It's great when you play well. But when you can't manage that then you have to play to win. And that's exactly what we are going to do.'

Sócrates

When Casagrande got married in October 1985 he asked Sócrates to be his best man and Sócrates was happy to oblige. But when the big day came, it wasn't the bride who kept everyone waiting. An hour and a half after the ceremony was supposed to have started, Sócrates still hadn't arrived. The priest got impatient, then angry, and then told the groom that he had other appointments and that if he wanted to get married he'd better choose another best man and get on with it. Oscar stepped up, the bride kissed the groom and they were declared man and wife. Well after 1p.m., more than two hours late, Sócrates burst in, clearly the worse for wear. If the intention was to steal the show then he succeeded, even before the groom and several of the guests were pushed fully clothed into the swimming pool.[1]

One of the consequences of living for the moment is that

other people's moments don't matter. Sócrates did what he wanted when he wanted and the people around him were expected to join in or suffer in silence. And the older he got, the less time he had for moderation or restraint.

It was easy to get away with such behaviour when he was one of the best-known faces in the nation. It was harder now that his star was fading. The principled stances he took as a footballer and activist were too often replaced by immaturity and it drove a wedge between him and some of his oldest friends.

Sócrates was like an elder brother to Casagrande during his first two years at the club, but the tables turned as they got older and Casagrande's patience gradually wore thin. The younger man became frustrated by Sócrates' semi-alcoholic drift through life and the pair fell out in the early 2000s after Sócrates called his old partner a sell-out for working on TV Globo, the country's biggest (and right-leaning) media empire. Sócrates had asked Casagrande to get him a screen test at the channel just a few days before, but when they turned him down he rounded on his pal with the barbed critique and they remained estranged for years. When a mutual friend finally got them together at a public debate a few years later, Sócrates once again turned up more than an hour late, infuriating everyone involved and deepening a rift that was only repaired in the final weeks of Sócrates' life.[2]

Casagrande always considered Sócrates one of the most important figures of his generation, not to mention his own life. He was famously forthright and didn't shy away from telling Sócrates the home truths that others preferred to avoid.

'Magrão was so fucking selfish,' Casagrande said. 'He didn't think of anyone else but himself. He wasn't selfish to fuck you over. He wasn't a bad person. He was emotionally selfish; he harmed other people.'[3]

Self-indulgence had always been one of Sócrates' most

dominant traits, but the people around him just couldn't see it through the haze of greatness and celebrity. Casagrande's analysis came after Sócrates passed away but it was astute and especially pertinent to those tumultuous months leading up to the 1986 World Cup. Sócrates could treat women and friends poorly, and he wasn't always the best of fathers to his boys. But when matters were professional and collective rather than personal and individual, he was more than capable of harnessing his demons.

In the run-up to Mexico, Sócrates couldn't shake off his mysterious thigh injury and his place in midfield was given to a series of uncapped youngsters. But even as his dream of taking a final tilt at football's greatest prize ebbed away, he never nagged or sniped. He worked hard to get back in the side while magnanimously doing all he could to help the new boys fit in.

'You can tell when a player is bitter, when he's in a bad mood, even if he doesn't say anything,' said full back Édson Boaro, his team-mate both at the seleção and at Corinthians. 'But Sócrates was never like that, he was always professional. Most players are selfish, they see only their own side of things, but he saw the big picture and it was never about just him. It was always about the group. He always helped and participated with the whole squad.'[4]

The 1986 World Cup was originally planned for Colombia but it was moved to Mexico in 1983 after financial and political problems forced the Colombians to withdraw. However, in the early hours of 19 September 1985 the tournament's future was thrown into jeopardy once more when a massive earthquake rocked Mexico City. At least 10,000 people died and large parts of the city were destroyed, and even though the Mexican government insisted the tournament would go ahead as planned, there was widespread concern over whether it was right to spend money on football while hundreds of thousands of homeless and hungry people were still trying to put their lives back together.

Brazil arrived in Mexico City eight months later but the damage was still extensive, and as he drove in from the airport Sócrates could not have missed the flattened buildings, the rubble-strewn lots and the pavements that rose and fell like waves. Sócrates felt an instant solidarity with the Mexican people and he wanted to make some sort of statement. He tossed ideas over in his head but couldn't quite work out what to do. Then one night, as he lay on his bed flicking through the Mexican TV channels, a little girl in a tiara appeared on the screen in front of him. It was a eureka moment and he scribbled a few words on a sock and wrapped it around his head to see what it looked like. The prototype was good enough and the next day he went in search of someone who could make a proper headband with his message on it.

The slogan he chose for the opening match against Spain was: *'México, Sigue en Pie'*, or 'Mexico, Stand Tall', and the Mexicans appreciated his gesture of solidarity. His team-mates, however, were none the wiser. He hadn't told anyone what he planned to do, not Zico, not captain Edinho, not even best mate Casagrande, and he slipped the headband on as he was walking up the tunnel.

The photographs of Sócrates with the headband below his unkempt mane of hair would become one of the most iconic images in World Cup history. The picture of his face, scowling slightly through his trademark beard, was reminiscent of the famous photo of Che Guevara and it became one of the enduring images of an already photogenic career.

The scowl was down to the screw-up that almost delayed the start of their opener and threatened to ruin the impact he wanted to make. Sócrates knew that the cameras would be focused on him while the national anthem played and that his statement would make headlines. But after a long wait for the music to begin, organisers played the wrong tune, the 'Anthem to the Brazilian Flag', a song that almost none of the players recognised. Sócrates quickly realised what was happening and he was furious. Hearing the national anthem before every game inspired him and, robbed of that pleasure, he shook his head with irritation and didn't even wait for the recording to finish. The Brazil players broke off prematurely and ran to warm up as the martial strains crackled away through the Tannoys overhead. It was an inauspicious start to his last World Cup.

Luckily for both him and Brazil, it was the only thing that didn't go their way. Spain had a perfectly good goal disallowed when the referee failed to see that Míchel's volley had crossed the line after bouncing down from the crossbar, and then Sócrates himself nipped in to head home the winner after a shot from Careca hit the woodwork and fell nicely for him in front of an open goal.

In a nod to his premonition in 1982, he vowed to score Brazil's first and last goal in the competition, and then made a much bigger splash in the days after the win by suggesting that the World Cup was rigged in favour of the big sides. He called Míchel's disallowed goal 'totally legitimate' and was scathing of the Australian referee who missed it. His contention that hosts Mexico and big countries such as Brazil got special treatment caused a huge scandal and forced both the CBF and FIFA to launch investigations. Sócrates stood his ground, saying, not at all unreasonably, that the big teams usually always get the breaks.

'When I spoke about the Spain–Brazil game I said that the referee and linesmen were well positioned and could have given the goal. Then I said that teams like Corinthians, Flamengo, Juventus and others are not just champions because they have the best teams: they also have more fans, more political weight, more representation. In relation to the World Cup, it's obvious that it is in the interest of the competition for certain teams to continue. That's why they have seeds. After the first phase it's more random, you can't control it; all the games are knockout.'[5]

The controversy dragged on for days and the CBF eventually banned players from making political comments on pain of being sent home. João Havelange, the Brazilian then heading FIFA, reportedly called the CBF and told them to keep Sócrates under control, as if that was a viable option. Sócrates didn't give any more interviews after the incident but it wasn't until September that Brazil's Superior Court of Sporting Justice unanimously absolved him of disobeying internal team regulations prohibiting political statements.[6]

That scandal aside, one of the most notable things about Sócrates this time around was how quiet he was. He gave no major interviews in the two months leading up to the competition and even after the football began he avoided talking with the reporters who hung around after training. He never once went into details about why he wore the headbands or what his declarations were about, and he was clearly not as comfortable as he was in Spain four years before.

Part of it was down to the thigh injury and his insecurity about game time. The months spent fretting over whether or not he would start had shaken his confidence. Another reason was the disunity within the squad and his inability to do anything about it. Reserve keeper Leão was his usual arrogant self, Casagrande complained long and loud about being dropped after the first two games, and Edinho, who was made captain at the last minute, alienated a lot of people by revealing that Serginho and Éder took money four years earlier for celebrating their goals in front of certain pitch-side adverts. Captain Oscar was dropped after leading a delegation to complain about the lack of preparations, and the entire squad was angry that the CBF had refused to discuss prize money, preferring to tell the players they'd work something out later.[7]

In one telling example of just how unprepared they were, Leandro's replacement Josimar hadn't played a competitive match since early March when he got the call from Telê. The Botafogo defender forgot to bring his own training shoes and played his first practice matches in footwear borrowed from the team's cardiologist.[8]

Having been abroad or injured for most of the previous two years, Sócrates barely knew some of the young players in the squad, and there was a clear division between the old guard who were past their best and the inexperienced newcomers who were looking to make their mark. They were all fighting for their lives and the tensions created an ultra-competitive atmosphere on the training ground. Passions boiled over on an almost daily basis, prompting a headline in the *Folha de S.Paulo* one day that read: 'The Seleção Managed To Train Without Any Fights'.

In years gone by, Sócrates would have stepped in to appeal to or cajole his team-mates into playing for each other, but the disunity this time around was not something he could change with a few inspiring words and he didn't feel as though he commanded the same respect. He had enough to worry about getting fit and ready, and being handed the number 18 jersey was a fair indication of how far his stock had dropped.

When the games kicked off, he became more relaxed and he happily assumed a role of mentor to the younger players, many of whom had no idea just what it meant to represent Brazil at the World Cup finals. Eight of the 11 that started against Spain were making their World Cup debuts and he knew exactly the kind of pressure they were under. Sócrates made a point of talking them through the opening stages, in the hope that a calm and reassuring voice would help ease them into the competition.

'He was very concerned about telling us not to make mistakes,' said Elzo, the 25-year-old midfielder who was making his debut. 'He came up to us, when we had the ball at our feet, and he told us what to do and he gave us confidence, especially at the start of the game. He always said, "Let's not make mistakes." He wanted us to start well, make the first few passes and keep it simple at first, and only then start to make the longer passes. He was like a protective father. It was a great help.'[9]

They managed to keep it together, labouring to overcome Algeria 1-0 and then effortlessly beating Northern Ireland 3-0 in a game notable for Josimar's 30-yard goal and Zico's first appearance in the competition, as a replacement for the outstanding Sócrates midway through the second half.

But the tensions inside the squad spread rather than abated after their wobbly first two games. Casagrande and Alemão were photographed shirtless and on the town after one match, and the former was dropped to make way for Müller after the Algeria game. He wasn't happy and neither was Zico, who wanted to play from the start. Brazil's inability to dominate the opening games raised all sorts of questions about tactics and Telê almost came to blows with Gilberto Tim, who sided with the players in their view that the coach was being too conservative. Sócrates and Falcão were both withdrawn from one training session after deciding to ignore Telê's orders and run things themselves, and their duplicity infuriated the coach. Sócrates immediately backed down but Falcão was dropped from the side and never even made the substitutes' bench for the remaining matches.[10]

With São Paulo pair Müller and Careca starting up front together for the first time against Northern Ireland, Brazil looked more dangerous and they were equally clinical in the first knockout match against Poland. Brazil started poorly and Poland hit the bar twice in the first 25 minutes, but as if to confirm Sócrates' earlier claims about favouritism a refereeing mistake once again helped them on their way to victory. He himself converted a dodgy penalty award after half an hour and then three goals in the second half sealed their most convincing win yet.

The victory, their fourth in four games, meant Brazil stayed in Guadalajara, the city that had long been their home away from home. In the 1970 World Cup, Brazil played all five of their games there before heading south for the final in Mexico City. The quarter-final showdown this time, against France, was at the same Estádio Jalisco where they had never lost a match and on the auspicious date of 21 June, 16 years to the day since they turned on the mother of all World Cup performances to beat Italy 4-1 and lift the Jules Rimet trophy for a record third time.

Sócrates took to the field with a headband declaring: '*Violencia No*', or 'No to Violence', and he was a commanding presence during what was the most thrilling 45 minutes of the cup so far. He forced Joël Bats into a great save after quarter of an hour and watched Müller hit the post after he'd stretched the French defence with a beautiful 50-yard pass. Careca put Brazil in front after 17 minutes, but France were not outclassed and Michel Platini equalised with five minutes to go in the first half when he tapped in a deflected cross from close range.

The second half was just as exciting but neither side could get a goal and it was left to Zico to provide the headlines. The Flamengo star had begged to start the game, but Telê still didn't think his knee would withstand the full 90 minutes. Zico eventually replaced Müller with 18 minutes left, and he made his presence felt just moments later when his inch-perfect pass put Branco through on goal. The big left back tried to go round the keeper but Bats brought him down and the Romanian referee pointed to the spot.

Sócrates had taken Brazil's first penalty in the previous round against Poland, but Zico was the regular taker and he wanted the responsibility for himself. As the Brazilian players celebrated the award like it was already a goal, Sócrates approached his pal and said, 'Go on, Galo. You take it.'[11]

'Leave it to me,' Zico replied.

Zico's kick was struck low and to the right but Bats got down well to parry the ball and the score remained all square. It was end-to-end stuff for the remainder of the game, with neither side able to break the deadlock, and the stalemate continued into extra time as both teams slowly ran out of steam. The match kicked off at noon in the wilting heat and Sócrates was just one of those who tired noticeably as the clock ticked down. He would have been subbed had Júnior not taken a knock and needed replacing in extra time, but he still managed to haul himself up field in the dying seconds and was just inches from glory as he vainly stretched to get a touch on a cross that flashed across goal. The match ended 1-1 but the drama was far from over. Penalties beckoned.

It was a clammy evening in early 1976 and Sócrates was exhausted as he walked towards the penalty box at the Moisés Lucarelli stadium in Campinas. He was the last of Botafogo's five penalty takers and if he scored the final kick then the pre-season Vicente Feola tournament would be theirs. Up in the stands, Sócrates' father was crossing himself and praying.

Seu Raimundo had never seen his son play in a professional final before and the way Sócrates took penalties made him nervous. It wasn't just that he was blasé, meandering up to the penalty spot looking like he was going for a beer. It was also his style, what Brazilians call the *paradinha*, the stop-start strategy that involves a short run-up, followed by a halt or a shuffle, and then a side-foot to one side of the goal once the keeper has committed himself. The strategy works if the goalkeeper moves but can be heart-stopping if he stands still. Sócrates scored that night against Ponte Preta and Botafogo were champions but his father made his feelings plain.

'He takes penalties with a *paradinha*, he doesn't know any other way, and so if the keeper doesn't move you can't hit it hard,' Seu Raimundo said. 'So, he takes it. Carlos chose a side and he put it the other way. After that I said to him, "You're not taking any more penalties."'[12]

With characteristic devilment, Sócrates ignored his old man and kept on taking them. He adopted more of a run-up for a while after, but he was soon back to his old tricks and by the 1980s he was cocky enough to have shortened his run-up to a walk-up. It looked cool, and added to his mystique, but boy did it give his dad palpitations.

When Telê drew up his list of penalty takers at the end of extra time, he looked at Sócrates and told him he was going first. Sócrates had always taken the last penalty and he immediately baulked.

'Let me take the decider,' he said.

'No,' Telê replied. 'I want you to go first.'[13]

Sócrates liked going last for two reasons. On a personal level, it enabled him to study the goalkeeper's reaction to the first four. By watching the keeper he gained a better idea of where and when he dived, and he could tailor his kicks accordingly. The second reason was all about the collective responsibility that he so loved. He fed off the pressure of going last and he liked playing his part in helping the men before him prepare.

'When you are the last to take one you can influence the others because that's your responsibility,' he said. 'If you are first and you score, you're home free, and fuck everyone else. That's the way everyone sees it – so how are you going to participate in the rest of the kicks? Psychologically, you're not going to play a role.

'[When you are last] you can stick close to some guy and encourage them. Some players are more nervous, some are calm, and so you joke with them, take their mind off it, you try and ease the pressure. When you're first, whatever happens, you're done, it's over.'[14]

Sócrates thought Telê was traumatised by Zico's earlier miss and picked him to go first because he was the nearest thing to a guaranteed goalscorer in the Brazil side. He missed just four in four years at Botafogo and only three out of almost 40 during six years at Corinthians.

That excellent record was built on what Sócrates thought was a foolproof way of taking them. His run-up could be as short as two or three steps, with him feinting almost imperceptibly in order to lure the keeper into making a move. When the keeper dived, he simply stuck the ball the other way. Because the keeper had already made a decision, he never had to worry too much about putting it right in the corner or striking it particularly hard. And although he kept his eye on the keeper rather than the ball, that counterintuitive strategy proved less of a problem than it might have been because he was such a clean striker of the ball.[15]

Against France, Sócrates did exactly the same as against Poland in the previous round. He took two steps forward, stopped and swung his right leg to hit the ball high to the keeper's right side. Against Poland, the keeper went the wrong way and the ball flew into the net. But Bats had done his homework. He had watched Sócrates' spot kick a few days before and he refused to commit himself. When the shot came, he sprung to his right and palmed the ball away. Brazil were already behind.[16]

The next six players, including Zico, all scored. And then

Michel Platini, on his 31st birthday, stepped up and the best player in Europe skied it over the bar to let Brazil back into the game. The scores were level and there was one kick left for each side. Centre half Júlio César had been Brazil's outstanding performer so far in the tournament, so it was perhaps inevitable that he smacked their final kick off the post and handed the advantage to their opponents.

French midfielder Luis Fernández had the task of deciding the game and he walked slowly to the penalty area, head bowed all the way. Carlos tried to put him off by stamping on the penalty spot as he walked towards goal but Fernández was unperturbed. He strode up to send the keeper the wrong way and knock Brazil out. For the second time in a row, Brazil's golden generation had failed to go all the way and their last chance at World Cup glory was gone.

The post-mortem focused on the misses by Zico and Sócrates, Brazil's two regular penalty takers and most skilful players. Experts lined up to offer explanations, many of them claiming the Flamengo star wasn't properly warmed up and hadn't caught the tempo of the game. Sócrates thought that was ridiculous and defended his friend for having the guts to take one so soon after coming on.

'You only miss a penalty if you take one,' he said. 'They said Zico was cold. That's bullshit! Do you need to be hot to take a penalty? If I get out of bed and take 100 penalties I'll score 99 of them.'[17]

When it came to his own profligacy, Sócrates was equally unrepentant.

'People are going to say that I was negligent in the way I took the kick, just because I didn't score,' he said after the match. 'No one said that against Poland. I took it like I always did but this time the ball never went in. Against Poland I scored and the rout began and it was a big party. In this game, the French goalkeeper was fortunate or I was unfortunate. All I will say is that we all make mistakes and I don't think I should be crucified for it.'[18]

Sócrates claimed he experienced the same sense of loss as in Spain, but the fact was that none of the senior players felt the same way as four years before, which was also true of the fans, who never took to them the same way and never expected them to win. The team was put together on the fly, with the chopping and changing going on right up to the opening match. Fans didn't connect with them in the way they had four years earlier and the players did not have a chance to show the same passion. The top men, Sócrates, Zico, Falcão, Júnior, were all past their best and the youngsters were not yet household names. Most obviously, the national team did not play with the same joy they had in the previous tournament and the early exit, coming at a time of turmoil at home, was just one more disappointment, a metaphor for unrealised promise. In the end, the 1986 World Cup would go down in history as one to forget, much like those of 1966 and 1974. There were no books written about it, no tales of romance or glorious failure, and many of the players were largely forgotten.

Nevertheless, the exit was in many ways more unjust than the loss to Italy four years previously. Brazil did not lose because of repeated defensive lapses or because they got their tactics wrong, and there was no single Paulo Rossi-like figure whose performance of a lifetime brought about their demise. At no point in the tournament were they behind. They won four and drew one and went out unbeaten. They scored 10 goals and conceded only one. They had a better record than all four semi-finalists and the best defence too, with Carlos going 401 minutes without picking the ball from his net, just short of Gordon Banks' record of 445 minutes. One of the French penalties smacked the post, hit him in the back and then rolled into the net. This time, luck, quite simply, was against them. Brazil in

1986 may not have been the scintillating Brazil of 1982 but it was far from embarrassing.

'That [1982] team was more skilful, more as fans like it,' Sócrates said. 'This side, however, worked harder and was better prepared for the demands made by today's football. And the numbers prove that, even though we were stronger defensively, we weren't a team that was worried about going out to defend. The opposite was true, we always took the initiative and against France we created numerous chances to score.

'It was very different, the [1986] team was more or less put together during the weeks before the competition. So maybe the expectation was a little different. We had a great time with the 1982 team. And in this side we had a lot of worries, fixing this and fixing that. The team was structuring itself during the tournament but, at the same time, the best game we played was the game we lost, right?

'I'm sad but I don't have any regrets and nor do I feel frustrated about what happened in 1982 or in 1986. What happened to us also happened to the Hungarians in 1954, to the Dutch in 1974 and 1978 and even to Brazil in 1950 and 1954. It's not unusual that great players and great managers didn't win the titles they deserved.'[19]

Perhaps nothing illustrated the change in mood better than the players' reaction to the defeat. In 1982, they all agreed they would share the blame and then sat around and got drunk. In 1986, they all went their separate ways.

'Against Italy we drank all the beer in the hotel, there wasn't a can left,' Júnior recalled. 'It was a moment of consolation for us, having spent all that time together. It was a complete and utter cry-fest. When we lost to France, we were married and we went out for dinner with our wives, me and Sócrates and Zico and Edinho. It was a gloomy occasion. The wives did all the talking. We knew that was our last chance.'[20]

Sócrates' penalty miss was his last kick of the ball for Brazil. He knew before the tournament started that this would be his swansong and, while he never really believed the makeshift side would win, he had at least hoped to go out on a high. Instead, his abiding memory was one of suffering. He suffered trying to nail down a place. He suffered from the pain of his thigh injury. He suffered for his friend Zico. He suffered in the penalty shoot-out. And he suffered for Telê, who walked into the dressing room after the France game to be told his father had had a heart attack back in Brazil.

As usual, Sócrates wanted to put the defeat behind him as quickly as possible, and he set himself the challenge of getting fit and motivated for what would inevitably be the slow march towards retirement. He was keen to settle at Flamengo and repay the club for putting their faith in him, but his back was sore and he could feel the years of wear and tear starting to take their toll. On the upside, he could also see limitless potential for all sorts of high jinks in the Marvellous City. More fun and games awaited.

17

'I always thought Magrão had retired too early. He created this utopia in his head about medicine and never realised how difficult it would be to switch off from an activity he had spent so long at. I always knew it and now he's realising it.'

Zico

On 29 July 1986, Sócrates underwent what was supposed to be routine surgery to mend his slipped disc. The operation ended up taking four hours because the damage was more serious than the doctors first thought: when they opened him up and saw inside, they could hardly believe he'd played for so long with such a debilitating injury.

The surgery put him out of action for months and he spent the time reading and drinking and campaigning for candidates in the upcoming elections. It was November before he was fit and ready to play again and when he did, 132 days after missing that fateful penalty against France, he did so against Goiás in typically convincing style.

On a blazing hot day in the arid city of Goiânia, he set up

Kita to score the first goal with a perfect through-pass and then 26 minutes into the second period, as Bebeto prepared to take a free kick, Sócrates told him, 'Leave this to me, this is my last kick.' He curled the ball perfectly into the top corner before walking off to a standing ovation.

Flamengo's results in the lead-up to Christmas were mixed but, this being Brazil, the 1986 league was still going strong in early 1987 and they qualified for the last 16, only to lose to Atlético Mineiro over two legs in February. The defeat was a blow to Sócrates, who harboured dreams of winning his first national title and hoped that this would be the year he could get a series of games under his belt and return to form.

But while Sebastião Lazaroni publicly played up his importance for the upcoming Carioca state championship, Sócrates' lackadaisical attitude in training annoyed the coach, as did his tendency to spend much of the game ambling around the centre circle. The back operation was a success, but the pain never disappeared entirely and neither did the stiffness. He couldn't move as freely as before and Lazaroni started to employ him as an impact sub he could bring on when they needed a creative spark.

Sócrates and Lazaroni didn't see eye to eye and the player started to avoid the club as much as possible. Increasingly, and against Flamengo's wishes, he would fly to São Paulo after the final whistle on a Sunday night and he often didn't return until three or four days later. Lazaroni decided that his notoriously poor stamina had worsened to the point where he couldn't last a whole 90 minutes, and Sócrates didn't get off the bench for more than half an hour in any of the first four games of the 1987 season.

'He was left out because of his physical condition,' Lazaroni said. 'He wanted to spend Monday, Tuesday and Wednesday in São Paulo and then do some light training on Thursday before playing on Saturday or Sunday. That's impossible for a professional athlete. Maybe now and again, when a player has to resolve personal issues, but with him it was constant and that caused conflict between us.

'Maybe I wasn't clear enough in convincing him he needed to change his behaviour, but he had this personal issue that was affecting him and a separation is always difficult. We often argued about it. I said, "Come on, there are two Sócrates and they are conflicting. One is the *craque* on the field and the other not so much of a *craque* off the field." There was a great conflict between the two and I questioned that and wanted him to think about it, even though he was nearing the end of his career. I wanted him to understand that for the great Sócrates, the player who was triumphant on the field, to show his best, he'd have to overcome the Sócrates that existed off the field.'[1]

Sócrates, however, believed his problems stemmed from the injury – 'I can't turn, I feel like a ship,' he told Zico – and he suggested to Lazaroni that a young pair of legs alongside him in the middle of the park would free him to take care of the creative duties. Lazaroni, though, thought Sócrates was just trying to hoodwink him and kept leaving him out. Sócrates felt he was being punished for his honesty. Other players would have kept quiet about their injuries, he thought, and Sócrates still believed he was too good to be left on the bench.

His team-mates shared that view and wanted him in the side. In a repeat of the situation a decade earlier at Botafogo, his team-mates didn't care that he wasn't as fit as they were; they knew he was still capable of moments of magic that could make a win bonus appear out of thin air.

'Sócrates was not a player who you put on the subs' bench,' said Leandro. 'If he's not fit then put him in the reserves or train him till he's fit again. It wasn't that he wouldn't sit on the bench, he did, but seeing it up close I could see that it pained him. It hurt me to see him there on the sidelines.'[2]

After four substitute appearances in February and March, the final straw came in Itaperuna, a small town 200 miles north of Rio where Flamengo went to play minnows Porto Alegre. Sócrates was named as sub and, when Lazaroni finished his team talk in the hotel before the game, Sócrates piped up in true Socratic fashion.

'What does justice mean to you?' he asked a stunned Lazaroni.

'Lazaroni had told him he wouldn't be playing,' recalled Leandro, one of the players who witnessed the scene. 'And he came out with this question and even Lazaroni was a bit taken aback. I can't remember what he said, but he took a while to answer and he mumbled something. But it was so surprising that he went red, gave his answer and Sócrates said, "Thank you."'[3]

And that was that. The minnows ran rings round Flamengo and although they improved when Sócrates came on after going 2-0 down in 56 minutes, his intervention couldn't save the game. Sócrates was not a happy man and, when the team bus stopped at a service station on the way home to Rio, he bought a bottle of whisky. Lazaroni travelled home separately but he found out and challenged him.

'I told him it wasn't to happen again. But he changed the subject. He didn't want to face up to it.'[4]

The relationship between them had become untenable and a few days later, on 16 March 1987, Sócrates decided enough was enough. He took part in a light training session at Flamengo's Gávea training ground and, as he walked to the edge of the park, he pulled off his boots and ostentatiously chucked them in the rubbish bin at the side of the pitch. 'That's it,' he announced. 'I've had enough. I'm retiring.'

Of the 67 matches Flamengo played in 1986, Sócrates appeared in just 13 and scored only two goals. Overall, he played 20 games for the club, scoring five times. He and Zico played together on just three occasions and only once in an official match, the 4-1 win over Fluminense.[5]

Lazaroni was cool about Sócrates' departure, saying he was not physically, technically and psychologically prepared to play top-level football. He was delighted to be rid of a player who had promised much and delivered little. Sócrates, at this point tired of the back and forth and relieved to have come to a decision, opted not to get into a slanging match but tried to explain his decision to bemused fans.

'I know I can be a regular first-team player at Flamengo. He doesn't. What kept me going was playing. I came to the conclusion that with this [management] team in charge I wouldn't play. If I can't play then I can't justify the salary I am getting.'[6]

'I know my standard of life will fall considerably,' he added. 'I will start as a medical resident as soon as possible. I am prepared psychologically for this new start in my life. I don't lack strength to face what lies ahead. To begin with, that means my studies, as I haven't read anything about medicine for a long time. What will help me in these two years of internship is the contract I have with Topper, which was signed with one eye on the day I would swap football for medicine.

'The important thing is to have a clear conscience. I can't keep getting a big salary without deserving it.'[7]

In truth, Sócrates had been thinking about packing it in for some time. He always said he would stop playing when he no longer enjoyed it and that moment had arrived. His back pain was more or less constant and he could no longer keep up with the youngsters who zipped past him on the training ground and on match days.

He hated the *concentração*, where at Flamengo he shared a room with four or five other players and a bathroom with up to 10. He could have put up with those hardships if he really wanted to, but he didn't really want to. He didn't want to train, he felt bored and at a dead end, and being dropped gave him the excuse he was looking for to wrap it up six months before his contract ended.[8]

The sudden nature of his retirement did prevent him from fulfilling one long-standing promise. He had always said that when he called it a day he would halt training by putting a big barrel of beer in the middle of the pitch so everyone could celebrate his departure with a drink.[9]

Instead, he gave his gear to Flamengo's kit men as souvenirs and never looked back.

Paulo Roberto Falcão famously said that footballers die twice, the first time when they are forced to give up playing. The sudden withdrawal of the drug that has kept them so alive for so long is a shock to the system and it can prove lethal for many footballers. Sócrates was slightly less fatalistic and said that players don't abandon football, football abandons them.

Since moving to Rio de Janeiro, Sócrates had to live without more than football. He felt an affinity with the city and its people, and he loved being surrounded by the beach, the mountains and the gorgeous lagoons and rivers that ran past his home. But there was something missing. He lacked a purpose.

'I'll throw it all away for a passion and I don't necessarily mean a woman,' he once said. 'Passion for me is worth more than anything else; it's a sublime moment for me. If you ask me, "Did you do anything by halves?" I don't think so. I went as far as I felt I could go and I did everything possible.'[10]

That lack of passion was more evident than ever in 1987. He had retired from football and was no longer a relevant figure in the world of politics. Even his love life had cooled. He had not seen Rosemary since he first moved to Rio, and although she was the person he ran to after walking out on Flamengo it was for a night spent as friends rather than lovers.

He found a temporary solace in medicine, signing up for a refresher course at the Federal University of Rio de Janeiro within days of leaving Flamengo. The classes were similar to his third year in university, and he enjoyed both the lessons and the endless opportunities for drinking and flirting with the younger students.

But even that came with complications. The university was on the opposite side of the city from his home in Barra da Tijuca and navigating the traffic every day in Rio's searing heat left him drained. More seriously, the university hospital was dilapidated and underfunded and he felt like he was operating in a straitjacket. When Christmas came he decided to transfer to Ribeirão Preto and continue his studies at the Hospital das Clínicas there. He was instantly happier back in his hometown, surrounded by friends and family and at a university he knew well. And just a few months after moving back, his life took another unexpected turn thanks to a chance meeting with a young tennis player.

Silvana Campos was a former world number one at youth level who had long idolised her local hero. A fanatical Corinthians fan, she had followed his career ever since he started out at Botafogo, and just a few years earlier she had agreed to go out with a persistent suitor only after he promised to give her his Fiorentina jersey. The 20-year-old Campos had always wanted to meet Sócrates and her opportunity came one afternoon at the school across the road from her parents' house. Sócrates had returned to the Colégio Marista to take part in a charity match involving former students, and Campos went over to watch. Once inside she bumped into her friend Zé Bernardes, who knew she was a fan and offered to introduce them. Sócrates was standing shirtless behind the goal and Bernardes walked her over and made the introductions.

'Magrão, this is Silvana. Silvana Campos,' Zé Bernardes said.

'Ah, right, the tennis player,' a sweaty Sócrates said, stopping to kiss the young girl.

'Nice to meet you,' Campos said.

'Pleasure,' said Sócrates. 'If you're not doing anything, go and get me a beer, will you?'

Campos was barely out of her teens but she was strong-willed and not used to be taken advantage of.

'I'm an athlete,' she said. 'I don't like people to see me with drink in my hand.'

'Cocky, isn't she?' Sócrates replied, laughing.

Campos blushed and, after chatting for a few moments, she ran home, ecstatic at having met the man of her dreams. She thought Sócrates was handsome and charming and funny, and Sócrates was just as impressed by her cheek. He got her phone number from Zé Bernardes and a few weeks later they spent the first of many afternoons together in a local love motel.[11]

Sócrates had enjoyed many such flings but this felt different. He would later describe the moment as one of the most vulnerable of his life and he was certainly in search of something new. The mad flame he carried for Rosemary had dimmed and his marriage to Regina had changed to the point where they were more like friends than lovers. He needed to fall in love again and the young spitfire filled his life with lust just when he needed it most.

He wavered for a few weeks over whether or not to leave Regina and he finally reached a decision one Friday night at the Ribeirão Preto city chambers. Sócrates was presented with the keys of the city at a special ceremony and Campos was invited along as another of the area's sporting personalities. Sócrates didn't know she was going, and he almost did a double take when he walked on stage and saw her sitting in the front row wearing a mini skirt and a smile.

Sócrates' entire family was there so they didn't speak, but

when the event ended they both, by complete coincidence, had tickets to see a concert by Gonzaguinha, a popular singer who had been friends with Sócrates for years. Sócrates and Regina sat at a big table right next to Silvana's family and, although they managed to keep the glances and provocations to a minimum, as the night drew to a close Sócrates followed her into the women's bathroom for a kiss and a grope.

'I can't go on like this,' he told her. 'I can't keep hiding this.'

'You're crazy,' she told him. 'I'm going to São Paulo to play in a tournament on Sunday and I'll be gone for two weeks. Don't come after me.'[12]

It was an ultimatum dressed up as an invitation and Sócrates got the message. The following day he had planned to take his family to Maurinho Saquy's ranch, where they often enjoyed long boozy afternoons beside the pool and the barbecue. Regina arrived early in the afternoon but Sócrates did one of his disappearing acts and didn't show up until midnight. He spent 15 minutes chatting like nothing was amiss and then dragged Maurinho outside to tell him he was about to dump his wife. He asked his friend to look after her and the kids and warned him they might not see each other for a while. Maurinho knew his pal had the hots for Silvana, but he was taken aback by the suddenness of the decision. He tried to talk him out of it but Sócrates had made up his mind. When they finished chatting, Sócrates calmly walked over to Regina, informed her that their 13-year marriage was over and disappeared out of the door, leaving an unsuspecting and distraught wife in his wake.[13]

The next morning he broke the news to Regina's father and then bundled his boys in the car and headed over to Maurinho's ranch. He rang the bell, left the children at the door and disappeared again. It was the last his friends saw of him for years.

Campos, meanwhile, had decided to break free. She was

lovestruck but uncomfortable with her status as the other woman, and she thought the only way to get over Sócrates was to get out of town and not see him again. But as she waited for the bus to São Paulo that Sunday afternoon, there was an announcement over the loudspeaker asking her to report to the ticket office. When she got there, Sócrates was on the other end of the line. 'Get a taxi to the petrol station on the edge of town. I've left my wife and I want you. Come here and I'll drive you to São Paulo.'[14]

She jumped in a cab and a few hours later they were in São Paulo, ready to start a new life together.

His break-up with Regina – and particularly the cold-hearted way it was done – disgusted many of the people who knew him best. Regina was a saint, his soulmate and his refuge, a woman who had stoically stood by him his entire adult life. She loved Magrão the man, not Sócrates the footballer or Sócrates the celebrity, and many people ominously predicted he would go under without her there to provide the stability he so obviously lacked.

Sócrates went to ground after meeting Silvana. It was the first in a series of disappearing acts he would perform as soon as a new woman appeared in his life. When he met someone new, which would be often, nothing else mattered. Old friends were abandoned and new ones were made. He was always looking for passion, his innate curiosity and intelligence sending him in search of something new to stimulate his heart and his mind. When it came to women, he loved the thrill of the chase and once his prey had been conquered it was often just a matter of time before he was off hunting again.

'I am a restless person and I have no limits for anything,' he said. 'When I go in pursuit of pleasure that's all there is to me, and in large parts of my life that is incompatible with the other needs that I have and responsibilities that there are. That is the eternal battle in my life and always has been, and marriage is in truth a limit for me, a major limit.'[15]

Sócrates believed that the way he acted with women was down to the fact that he never had a strong feminine influence at home. His mother was around and a loving presence his whole life, but with six boys and a husband who was often away for work or studying at night, she was obliged to play a fatherly role too. He admitted he had 'glaring errors in upbringing', simple tasks that he never learned to do, like cook basic meals or wash dishes. Not only did his dad forbid the boys from entering the kitchen, they ran wild elsewhere in the house, throwing clothes and shoes around and leaving their mum to clean up behind them. Sócrates took after his father. Seu Raimundo was an unapologetic, old-fashioned macho man; he wanted his boys to study, not cook or clean.[16]

Those deficiencies were amplified with Silvana, who was assertive and confident. They quickly moved in together but she wasn't an old-fashioned stay-at-home mum and she wasn't used to a submissive role. She was also closer in age to Sócrates' eldest son than to her new partner. There was 12 years between the new couple and when they got together she was barely equipped to be a wife, never mind a stepmother to four young boys. His sons liked her and they got on, but Sócrates was never much interested in dealing with children, and that included his own. The arrival in 1990 of a son, her first and his fifth, named Sócrates Jnr, did nothing to ease the strain.

'I wanted the things that a young woman wants,' Campos said. 'I was young and in perfect physical shape. I was an athlete, full of energy, 1,000 mph, and what did I have around me? I would take the five kids to the mall and I looked like their sister. It was crazy.'[17]

*

Sócrates didn't only get a new love that spring. His relationship with Campos was quickly followed by a rekindling of an old love, his first love.

Encouraged by Campos, who was keen to see her partner back doing what he most loved, Sócrates signed a one-year deal with Santos in October 1988. The two of them wanted to escape the disapproving glances of Ribeirão Preto, where they were both public figures, and the prospect of living by the beach was more attractive than ever. Corinthians were interested and he turned down a million-dollar offer from Mexico, but there was really no contest. He was struggling to get used to life as a doctor and he decided that a year playing football would be just the therapy he needed to help him ponder his future in medicine. He met with a couple of Santos directors and it took them only a few minutes to hash out a deal that included a promise from Flamengo to pay him the fortunes they still owed him with the proceeds of three future friendly matches. Santos offered Sócrates a regular salary and a percentage of image rights but they weren't breaking the bank, for both they and Sócrates knew this wasn't about money.[18]

For Santos, who were floundering near the foot of the table, it was about avoiding relegation and providing the young side with some experience in midfield. For Sócrates, the move was motivated by his desire to play for the club he supported as a boy and he was once again savvy enough to make the return on his own terms, with guarantees that he trained when he wanted, that he didn't have to attend the *concentração*, and that Silvana could accompany him to away matches and on tour. He was 34 and his back pain was still a problem, and before making his debut he practically admitted he was coming back for the fun of it.

'I have no pretensions about being successful here,' he said. 'I just want to do something that makes me happy and that's playing football. I am not worried about what happens after that. It's only now that I'm realising how little I enjoyed myself in my career. The attention of the fans used to bother me. Not now. I've never been so at ease with myself and from now on I want to take advantage of every moment.'[19]

Sócrates made his debut in a friendly match against Uruguayan side Cerro on 29 November. He started in right midfield alongside César Sampaio – the 20-year-old who 10 years later would open the scoring against Scotland in the first match of the 1998 World Cup – and he gave no indications that it was his first proper football match for well over a year. He created Santos' first goal with a perfect pass to Mílton da Cunha Mendonça, scored their second with a spectacular diving header and was just inches from getting one of the best goals of his career when he dribbled from the halfway line past three players only to see his deft chip beat the keeper but sail agonisingly over the bar.

'It was a dream come true and much more,' he said after the game.

Reality, however, was not far away and two days later fans invaded the Santos dressing room after they were lucky to lose just 3-1 to Cruzeiro. A security guard fired his gun in the air to frighten off the protesters and the magnitude of the task at hand quickly became evident.

Nevertheless, he made his presence felt and led them on a mini run of form that was enough to rescue them from the drop. They lost just once in their last five games, and beat Corinthians 2-1 in an emotional night at the Pacaembu, to finish 18th in the 24-team table.

'We had a lot of young players and he took charge of them,' said coach Marinho Peres. 'He was a hero to most of them and they liked to sit in his room on the eve of a match and listen to him. He took part in the team talk the day before the game and he was the one who spoke to the players just before they went out on the pitch. He was brilliant at the psychology. He told the players we were good enough to get out of the bad spot we were in, but he also told them that it was all right if we didn't, that football wasn't life and death. And they took it all in.'[20]

Sócrates had by this point given up any chance of reproducing a Corinthians Democracy-like movement at another club. Brazil now had a civilian president, a new constitution, and voters were electing new mayors, state governors and MPs. The end of the dictatorship in 1985 had robbed the left of a cause to rally behind and, with annual inflation surpassing 700 per cent in October, people were more worried about the economy than politics.

The country had moved on and Sócrates reluctantly did too. He still believed there was a huge amount of work to be done, especially in making players conscious of the power they had, but he knew most of them didn't care and so he concentrated on enjoying himself rather than raising awareness and it paid off.

With expectations scaled back and his private life settling down, Sócrates' year at Santos was his happiest since leaving Corinthians in 1984. He had missed the game and regretted having treated it so shabbily. Football, he finally realised, was not just a hobby after all; it was something more serious than that, something that had an intrinsic value. He belatedly realised it was a game he truly loved. He knew Santos lacked the players to challenge for either the Paulista or the Brazilian championship but he wasn't there to win titles. His sole motivation was to fulfil his dream of playing for the club he supported as a boy. For the first time since he started at Botafogo, he was playing football mainly for fun.

He was helped along by the directors and backroom staff, and the players were mostly in awe of the legend in their midst. He didn't spend much time at the club, but he was friendly and helpful and a pleasure to be around. He had a beer with his team-mates after the game and revelled in the role of elder statesman.

'Once we had a problem, I can't remember if it was a player who was subbed or wasn't picked but there was a conflict,' César Sampaio recalled. 'He got the team together to clear the air and said the important thing is that no matter what happens we had to respect each other and that we all should put our feelings on the table. That for me was new, saying what I thought was right and wrong. He went round everybody asking them what they thought. He asked me if I wanted to speak and I said no. At that point I thought I was too young to have any right to speak my mind. But I remember thinking how great it was that he wanted to hear us all. That helped us. We respected each other more.'[21]

Sócrates returned to Santos after the Christmas and New Year break but the team's performance in the 1989 Paulista state championship campaign was poor, and it was only the ridiculous rules that allowed them to progress to the second stage. They qualified eighth from a group with 11 teams but were predictably outclassed in the next round, winning just one of their four games to bow out of the tournament in June.

Their early exit gave the club two months in which to take advantage of their new star but a depressing round of friendlies was exactly what Sócrates didn't need. He could never get excited about meaningless games and the latest end was nigh. When it came, it was in the Far East, where Santos became the first Brazilian team to play in China for a quarter of a century. The club got a fat fee of $20,000 for each of their eight games there and in Hong Kong, but there was unrest from the get-go, with some of the players unhappy that Sócrates was getting three times the per diem they were.[22]

The trip was long and poorly planned, with some matches added as they went along. Sócrates played in most of the games because the fee would be slashed if he didn't, but he soon got bored of the travelling and wanted out. To make matters worse, just when it looked like the ordeal was coming to an end, the club tacked on two more hastily arranged friendlies in the US. That took the tour length to five weeks and it all got too much. Sócrates' best friend on the team was Juary, a veteran striker he knew from their time together in Italy, and on the eve of departure they sat in a hotel bar in Hong Kong and drowned their sorrows.

'I can't take it any longer,' Sócrates confided.

'Why, Magrão, things are just starting to get good,' Juary said.

'Nah, it's not working for me. I can't take it any longer.'

'There's only a week to go. We're going to the US and then we'll be home. It's almost over,' Juary told him.

'No, I've had enough,' Sócrates said. 'I am going back to Brazil. I want to rest.'

Juary looked at his friend and said no more. He looked like he was going to cry.[23]

Sócrates flew to Brazil via Los Angeles, where he took Silvana to Disneyland before boarding a flight to São Paulo. His departure was an embarrassment to the club, who had arranged the two US friendlies around him. His team-mates were also unhappy that Sócrates, having already been given more money and more privileges – Silvana accompanied him all along – had quit. They had just spent more than 24 hours on three flights from Hong Kong to Tokyo to Los Angeles to Boston, and they were exhausted. Arriving to find Sócrates had abandoned them was the final straw.[24]

Club officials appealed to him to fly back north for the last couple of games and at the same time discuss renewing his current contract, which ended on the last day of September. The Brazilian championship started on 7 September and Santos wanted him to sign a new deal before the season began. But Sócrates never boarded the flight, meekly claiming he got stuck in traffic on the way to the airport. The president was furious at being made to hang around Boston for no reason and, adding insult to injury, newspapers in Santos reported that, instead of returning to the US, Sócrates had met with Corinthians officials to discuss ending his career at the club.[25]

The Corinthians talk came to nothing, in part because directors there didn't want to risk having the head of Corinthians Democracy back at the club to challenge the status quo. Sócrates eventually opened negotiations with Santos over a new deal, but he asked for such an obscene amount that directors thought he was taking the mickey and decided not even to make a counter offer.

His football career, it seemed, was over. Or very nearly over.

The farewell match is to Brazil what the testimonial is in Britain, one last, not altogether serious game designed to pay tribute to a player retiring after great service to club or country. The matches are extravagant celebrations loved by fans, players and media. Almost 60,000 São Paulo supporters paid to see goalkeeper Rogério Ceni play a final game against former and current team-mates in 2015; more than 138,000 people turned out at the Maracanã for Pelé's final match for Brazil in 1971; and the seleção even arranged special friendly games so that fans could say goodbye to stalwarts Ronaldo and Romário.

Sócrates dismissed such occasions as sentimental nonsense and went out the way he wanted, with the minimum of fanfare. He did imagine one unrealised goodbye, but the focus would be friends and beer, not football and certainly not fawning crowds.

'It would bring together all the people I've loved, with

fucking loads of beer and all that,' he said. 'My crowd, that's what I had imagined, not a football match. That's what I'd like to have done, got everyone together, even directors, who played a part in my life and who in some way I had a good relationship with, and I'd invite them for a barbecue and we'd play football. That's how I'd imagined it. But a goodbye? I don't like goodbyes.'[26]

Instead, unable to end his career at Corinthians and rejecting offers from as far away as Japan, Sócrates left Santos and headed home to Botafogo for a short swansong at the place where it all started almost two decades previously. Ribeirão Preto had always been his home and, although he had been gone for 10 years, he had in many senses never left. It wasn't just the home where his heart was. His family were there, his friends were there and both his current and ex-wife – by this time he had divorced Regina – were from there. He still went back every chance he could, often driving through the night to spend a morning with his mother or staying late at Maurinho Saquy's ranch to suck every possible moment from a barbecue and drinking session with his closest pals.

The return to Botafogo was never going to be much more than an excuse to bring some symmetry to a career path that veered off at angles both acute and obtuse. The club had fallen on hard times and were in the second division of the Paulista state championship, and although their manager was none other than Mário Travaglini there was little else to suggest the comeback would be a triumphant one. Even the fans were split, some of them delighted at the return of their hero, others unhappy that the club was shelling out money it couldn't afford on someone so clearly past his best.

Sócrates signed a short-term deal just a week after leaving Santos and he made his debut on 16 September in the 2-1 win over Uberlândia at the Estádio Santa Cruz. He was in almost constant pain from his slipped disc and things got worse when a brutal knee in the side forced him off after just 23 minutes.[27]

The challenge appeared to give him pause for thought and he failed to show up for the next match, away at Goiânia. It was a further three weeks before he made his second appearance, in a 2-1 win over Grêmio Catanduvense, the second of four games he played without ever being on the losing side. That mini run was enough to help guide Botafogo into the second stage of the competition, but the squad was as weak as Sócrates' legs and they were eliminated in their first play-off match, a home and away fixture against São José.[28]

That would have been the end but for one last futile friendly. On 26 November 1989, Sócrates made his final professional appearance in the 1-1 draw against Itumbiara in the state of Goiás. Just over 1,000 people turned up to see him run the midfield before quietly trotting off midway through the second half.

And that was it. There was no fuss and no official announcement that he would be hanging up his boots. The pain was too much, and so was the hassle. After 17 years, more than 700 games and over 300 goals, one of the most inspiring footballers Brazil had ever seen was calling it a day. At least as a player.

18

'He was looking for something that he never found.'

Sócrates' brother Sóstenes

The medical students at the USP's Ribeirão Preto campus had a union with the grand name of the Centro Académico Rocha Lima. The name, however, fooled no one. The centre was in actual fact a building of bars and sporting facilities run by students, who would organise conferences, discos and competitions between both the different faculties within the USP-RP as well as against other universities across the state.

The president of the union was elected by students and, after another drunken night, Sócrates and his friend Aloisio Abud decided it would be a wheeze to run for office. They thought the two main candidates were boring and political, so they decided to form a third-party ticket whose main platform was to promote drinking and partying. The campaign they created with four friends went under the nonsensical name of 'Itch Le Nitch' and their manifesto was all about having a laugh. It was only when the election got close and it looked like they might win that they realised the prank was getting out of hand. With responsibility looming, they frantically backpedalled and begged people not to vote for them lest they get saddled with running one of the university's most visible institutions.[1]

On the night of the election they sat at the student bar to watch the count and take the mickey out of their more earnest rivals. Sócrates paid to send the other candidates fake telegrams from US president Jimmy Carter and Soviet leader Leonid Brezhnev, and when the winner was announced and Sócrates lost by a mere 13 votes he breathed a huge sigh of relief.[2]

That early flirtation with power was Sócrates' first brush with elected office but it was not his last foray into organised politics. In 1991, at a loose end and still not entirely sure what he wanted to do with the rest of his life, he was encouraged by future president Fernando Henrique Cardoso to join the PSDB, a social democratic party that was emerging as one of the most important in the country. Sócrates had long been friendly with Mário Covas, who was close to his father and one of the party's leading lights, and he was selected to run for mayor of Ribeirão Preto against Antonio Palocci, a Botafogo fan and doctor whom he knew from both the university and football.

The Workers' Party (PT) candidate did not fancy going head to head against a man he considered a friend and who, not coincidentally, had the star power to embarrass him at the ballot box. Palocci phoned him up to discuss an alliance – the PT would eventually form a joint ticket with the PSDB – and he was pleasantly surprised when Sócrates told him he didn't want to run after all and that he was withdrawing from the race before it had even begun.[3]

Palocci thanked him profusely and offered him a future role as the city's Sports Secretary, which Sócrates accepted immediately. His reputation for eschewing details, administration and planning – not to mention bailing out on projects long before they were completed – did not bode well, but to Palocci's surprise he stuck at it.

'He really dedicated himself and there were some great results,' Palocci said. 'Every programme that he ran, 1,000, 2,000 kids would turn up. Normally, there would be about 10 or 15. He put his prestige on the line but not just that; he didn't just give us his name, he organised, he turned up, he met with his team every day. I was surprised by the way he dedicated himself to the job five to eight hours a day.'[4]

Small-town politics wasn't without its problems but Sócrates got round his lack of political experience with charm and contacts. One of his biggest coups was convincing the CBF to bring the seleção to Ribeirão Preto to play a friendly match against Poland in March 1993. When they agreed to a date, he called Botafogo to ask if they could use the Estádio Santa Cruz. Botafogo said yes, but when an advance team arrived to prepare the ground they were almost forced to abandon their plans because of beer. The CBF was sponsored by Brahma and the stadium advertising was owned by rival Antarctica. The standoff between two of Brazil's biggest brewers could easily have ended in stalemate or lawsuits. Instead, Sócrates got on the phone and appealed directly to the presidents of both companies, neither of whom wanted to disappoint a legend. They sorted it out amicably and the match went ahead as planned.

'He was very good at resolving problems,' recalled Palocci. 'No one could ever tell him no. He just steamrollered through and got things done.'[5]

After more than a year in the position, Sócrates eventually tired of the job and it was consultations over where to put a new park that provided the final straw. Residents of one lower-class community all wanted the park outside their door instead of coming together to put it where the community most needed it. Sócrates was frustrated by their selfishness and decided that if people weren't going to think collectively then there wasn't much more he could do.[6]

Overall, though, the experience was positive for both him and the PT and they proposed he stand as a candidate for federal Congress the following year. Sócrates agreed but then changed his mind a few weeks later, and despite phone calls and entreaties from Palocci, Lula and other PT bigwigs, he was unshakeable. The party wanted to drag him around the state as a celebrity vote-winner and he realised the enormity of the job ahead. More importantly, he was turned off by the thought of losing his independence and spending half his life in meetings. The prospect of long, sober encounters with men in suits was Sócrates' idea of hell, and he also hated the notion of having to publicly support policies he didn't believe in. 'I love politics but hate political parties,' he said a few years later, and that summed up his view perfectly.

If he was going to be an insider then football was the place and there were few clubs more suitable than Botafogo, where he still had close friends in both the dressing room and the boardroom. He was appointed manager in 1994 and in just his second game in charge he stood in the middle of the dressing room and told the players what he wanted from them.

'I got everyone out of the room [except the players] and I said, "For the first five minutes I don't want to see a football match, I want to see a show,"' he recalled.

The players looked first at each other and then at him, not really knowing what to say.

'What do you mean?' one of them eventually asked.

'I don't want you to play to win, or to score goals,' Sócrates said. 'I want you to dribble, to do nutmegs, don't let them get the ball, all that fancy stuff.'

'Really?' one of them said. 'You want us to do that?'

'Yes,' said Sócrates. 'I want you to do that. After those first five minutes you can play football but for the first five minutes I better see a show; I want you to really get the fans going.'[7]

The game ended 2–2 but that strategy summed up Sócrates' management philosophy and was entirely in keeping with the way he played the game. His job depended on results, but to him pleasure was more important than points. Losing was acceptable as long as his players at least tried to entertain.

Sócrates had returned to the club in 1993. Botafogo was the place where his legacy was still strong and where the directors both adored and indulged him. He accepted an invitation to serve as 'adviser' to then president Laerte Alves, and when coach José Galli Neto was fired after a string of poor results left them languishing ninth in the second division, Sócrates agreed to fill in until a replacement could be found.

He immediately brought his own style to the club, standing at the side of the training ground in Bermuda shorts and flip-flops while his deputies ran drills and refereed bounce games. He abolished the *concentração* and would sometimes be the last to turn up for games, arriving at the ground after spending the day drinking beer and eating barbecue with his friends. He treated the players as equals – a novel and shocking development for most of them – and he rarely bothered with tactics or chalk-boards or what the opposition could or couldn't do.

'He got us together and asked us how we wanted to play, he always wanted to hear our opinion, if we wanted to sit back, or mark high up the field,' said Édson Boaro, the former Brazil and Corinthians full back who was now at Botafogo. 'He wanted to give us freedom to play and he did that to take the pressure off us. It was interesting because we went out and we weren't so worried about scoring goals or losing. As a coach he brought that kind of freedom of expression.'[8]

Typically, Sócrates took it to extremes, one match day dumping the ice that was meant to wrap knocks and bruises into his freezer full of beer. When one of his players came off injured, his assistant had to ask the other team to lend them packs of ice.

The easy-going strategy, though, had a positive effect. His side drew their first match 0-0 against Sãocarlense on 27 February and then shared four goals against city rivals Comercial a week later. Although they failed to grab all the points, the players responded to his appeals for expansive football and their performances were enough to get him the job on a full-time basis. His management was unorthodox but Botafogo picked up maximum points in two of their next three games to move up to joint sixth.

However, an episode in the last of the three games, a home win over Paraguaçuense, soured him and led him – once again – to abandon a project before it had really got going.

Sócrates repeated his demands for a show and told his players the only thing they should do for the first 10 minutes was give the ball to their tricky winger Toninho. They followed his instructions to the letter and Toninho so destroyed the opposing right back that the defender was taken off at half-time and replaced with someone whose sole job was to halt his runs. Sócrates' response was to remove Toninho and shift all their attacks to the other side of the pitch. The fans were furious at him for taking off their best player and he was roundly booed, but the move worked like a charm. They scored three goals and romped home 3-1 victors.

The big problem came with the half-time team talk by assistant Tiri, the same Tiri who was on the backroom staff when he first arrived at the club. The veteran coach lambasted the players for having all the ball and failing to score, and when he left the room Sócrates was forced to go behind his friend's back and tell them to disregard all his criticisms and keep doing what he had told them. Sócrates did not want to challenge Tiri, who was one of his oldest friends in the game and a legend at Botafogo, but he mulled over the incident when he flew to Japan a few days later.

Sócrates had a prior commitment to hold some football clinics in Tokyo and Osaka, and he gave up control of the side while he was away for two weeks. His first game back was a 3-0 win over Olimpia but it was followed by a 4-0 hammering by Araçatuba, and when they couldn't win their next match at home to Catanduva he decided that enough was enough. His record was won three, drawn three and lost just two, and he had taken the side from ninth in the table to joint fourth. But he didn't have the stomach for it. It was too much stress, too much hard work, too much hassle.[9]

'A manager needs to be first in in the morning and last out at night,' said Serginho, his friend and team-mate from the 1982 Brazil side, who himself had a go at management. 'You need to be able to come down hard on players sometimes. You have to shout at them. You can't be their friend. Sócrates just didn't have the personality for management.'[10]

Sócrates' return to Botafogo was a treat for fans but it wasn't such good news for Silvana Campos. For the first few years of the decade, Sócrates had cut back on his drinking and smoking as he enjoyed an extended honeymoon period with the woman he had officially married in a quiet ceremony in May 1990. As an athlete herself, Campos liked to stay in shape and she tried to ensure her husband did likewise. They would walk together first thing in the morning or cycle at weekends, and the arrival of their first child together in September 1990 gave him an added incentive to stay healthy.

He was aided by his long-awaited return to medicine. Sócrates had spent the early 1990s first studying to bring himself up to speed with the latest techniques and developments and then working full time as a doctor for the first time in his life. He loved doing both and they were among the happiest years of his life, even though he was madly busy. In 1990, he was driving 400 miles back and forth to São Paulo three nights a week to attend a course in sports medicine, and he was also travelling all over Brazil to attend meetings and congresses on his chosen subject.

Sócrates had wavered for years about what kind of specialisation to pursue, first imagining orthopaedics and then paediatrics but never seriously seeing himself at home in the world of football. That changed when he realised he did not want to spend all his days cooped up in a hospital, so he signed up for a postgraduate course in sports medicine at the Escola Paulista de Medicina. He believed the subject was still hugely underestimated and he astutely saw that with the rise in diabetes, obesity and hypertension the field was only going to grow.

Sócrates had purchased a property in Ribeirão Preto years before where he intended on setting up a clinic, and he began to hire staff and equip the place to deal with an influx of patients. Running the Medicine Sócrates Centre started out as a dream come true but it soon turned into a nightmare. His biggest challenge was a moral one, dealing with the breaches of professional ethics. He was shocked by the number of misdiagnoses and doctors recommending surgery when none was needed, and he faced constant dilemmas over whether to speak up and criticise colleagues or keep his mouth shut and say nothing. In the end, one of his employees sued him over an administrative claim and spared him the decision. Sócrates had neither the time nor the energy for a protracted court battle and he settled the suit, closed the centre and moved on.[11]

Losing the clinic and the job he had spent all his life working towards was one of his greatest setbacks and he started drinking more heavily again. The process began when he returned to Botafogo, first as an adviser and then as coach. Footballers like to drink and socialising was an integral part of the job, especially in Ribeirão Preto, where the heat made hydration crucial and where so many of his old friends were on hand to share a few beers and talk about old times.

Campos, however, couldn't take it and their relationship soured. The arguments mounted and in May 1994, Sócrates walked out. They almost got back together over Christmas, but even though he had returned to the clinic after his stint in management he was still drinking too much, often calling in sick or cancelling appointments and heading out for a beer. His heart was no longer in either the job or the marriage and he drew a line under them both.

Sócrates proudly boasted that he lived only for today and that the future would take care of itself. But that insistence on living for the moment had a downside. In Sócrates' world, everything was fleeting and he was unable to relax and enjoy the good times. Satisfaction was like a drug and every happy moment was quickly forgotten as he went in search another one.

That was understandable in football, where a title triumph or a superb performance was quickly forgotten in a culture where you were only as good as the next result. But it was more damaging on a personal level as his family and friends struggled to keep up.

'Let's say I score a goal in the World Cup final, that's an enormous fucking pleasure,' he said. 'Then two hours later we're sitting having a great conversation that we never want to end. That kills the goal, the goal is now meaningless, it's over.

'Glory is totally ephemeral,' he went on. 'For any individual it is like that, even more so for a footballer. I never think about what might happen tomorrow, man, never. It drives my wife crazy. She'll say, "Let's plan ahead," and I say, "Forget planning ahead – let's live, let's live!"'[12]

Campos blamed the drink and felt it turned her husband into a caricature of someone he wasn't. Without the booze, Sócrates was quiet and domesticated. At home alone, without a beer in his hand, he would get so lost in a book or a television programme that he'd forget there were other people in the room. But when he had a drink in him, he was restless and mercurial.

'A person who only lives for today is hiding something,' Campos said. 'He's not so much living for today as for himself. He's living for today as the personality he's created, that the drink has created.'[13]

Campos pointed out that when the booze was under control Sócrates dedicated himself to projects that made him happy, first as a young man at university and Botafogo, and then with her at the start of the 1990s, doing his postgrad course and working as Sports Secretary. But once the crutch of football had been taken from him, he flitted from project to project, never sticking at anything and never totally happy. Like a child with a sugar addiction, he openly admitted he required constant stimulation.

'I need to be creating something, what's done is done for me. It needs to be something new. When I do something with any regularity it makes me so fucking anxious, it kills me, that's how I feel, like I am dying, I just can't do it. I need to be inventing something different.

'Of course, there are things that give me pleasure and I manage to keep them close to me in one way or another and they continue to give me pleasure. But it can't be just those things because there is no way I could live like that, not with just one thing.'[14]

*

After leaving Botafogo and closing the clinic Sócrates spent the next couple of years trying his hand at television. He joked that he was never handsome enough to be on TV, but he carried off a series of small-time presenting and guest spots with aplomb. His co-presenters were in awe of the idol alongside them and viewers loved his insights and sincerity. His early attempts at interview shows in Ribeirão Preto served as vital experience for later work on national television as a guest on the football talk shows that dominate Brazilian TV almost every night of the week.

The epic fail came in the commentary box. Sócrates was hired by SporTV in 1995 to provide match analysis but he turned up late for one of his first gigs, a Paulista state final between Corinthians and Palmeiras. He came straight from a barbecue at Maurinho Saquy's house smelling of beer and having done precisely zero advance preparation. To compound matters, he spent half the game cheering for Corinthians.[15]

SporTV executives got dozens of calls from angry Palmeiras fans but when they couldn't find a Palmeiras legend to replace him for the return leg they were obliged to gamble on Sócrates once again. He arrived on time for once but walked on to the pitch to greet the Corinthians fans before kick-off and then screamed with joy when they got the winning goal. Palmeiras fans went mad, executives threw up their hands in despair and his commentating career was over before it had begun.

The separation from Silvana sent him into a downward spiral and when their divorce was finalised in 1996 he went abroad for a fresh start. After his disastrous year in Italy, Sócrates never considered living outside Brazil again. He loved the informal chaos of his homeland too much and he considered Europe too structured and impersonal.

But when the chance arose to go to Ecuador he grabbed it, not quite with both hands, but in the knowledge that it would give him something to focus his energies on. The president of Ecuadoran first division side Liga Deportiva Universitaria had good contacts with Corinthians and he visited São Paulo with the intention of signing some players. Talk turned to Sócrates and before he knew it Darío Ávila was on the plane back to Quito with four out-of-favour Corinthians players and a new manager.[16]

Sócrates once again made no great demands and was happy to be given a half-decent salary and a small apartment to call home. He took his own assistant and trainer but he struggled almost from the moment he touched down. LDU, as they were known, were building a new stadium and wanted a high-profile manager for the inauguration the following year, but it quickly became apparent that Sócrates wouldn't be there that long.

The main issue was the results – just one win in five games and three 1-0 losses, all at home. More surprisingly, Sócrates never managed to connect with the players. He complained that the Ecuadorans lacked technique and, when one of the rein-forcements he brought from Corinthians publicly criticised their lack of professionalism, a split opened up that was impossible to mend.

Off the field, Sócrates never took the time to enjoy Quito, one of the world's most charming capitals. Set at altitude high in the Andes, the city is surrounded by snow-peaked volcanoes and is home to a beautifully preserved colonial centre. He rarely saw anything other than the football pitch and the apartment where he spent his evenings writing poetry and watching VHS tapes of opponents. He found a local girlfriend but even that wasn't enough to cheer him up. Just a fortnight into his Andean sojourn, he told the club's chairman he was thinking of resign-ing. The directors tried to dissuade him and took turns at wining and dining him to make him feel more at home. But their efforts were in vain and less than two months after touching down he quit.[17]

'He complained that the players weren't good enough and after two weeks he said he wanted to leave, as if he realised that this wasn't for him,' said Edwin Andara, LDU's director of football at the time. 'He was a melancholy guy, he had a real deep sadness to him. I never saw him happy when we won or sad when we lost, he was always the same, with the same expression. At the start the players admired him. Who wouldn't admire this monster of the world football? But then they just didn't understand him and eventually they just tried to avoid him. He couldn't motivate the players, he was too sad for that. He couldn't make a team out of them. After the last game, when we lost to El Nacional, he came to us and told us he was leaving and there was no discussion at all, he didn't even want to get paid. It was a relief to us because the team wasn't playing well and the media spotlight had dimmed.'[18]

Sócrates was still trying to find his niche but he was always up for doing the unusual, and in 1996 he accepted an invitation to meet Colonel Gaddafi in Libya, which was then suffering under an economic embargo. He drove through the night from Tunisia in a darkened convoy of 4x4s and they met up first at his desert camp and then at a home where the beleaguered dictator had created a shrine to his adopted daughter killed in US bombing raids a decade previously.[19]

They talked about 'football, politics, history and feelings' and Gaddafi offered Sócrates funding to run for Brazilian president, which he politely declined.[20]

Instead, he returned to more mundane pastimes, spending his days writing newspaper columns and tapping out the first words of what he hoped would be his autobiography. He used to joke that he was a multi-media artist and that the writing and presenting were adding to a CV that already boasted the theatre and music gigs of the 1980s. (He would later act, paint, write poetry and songs and compose and record more albums.)

The writing came easily to him when he put his mind to it but it never seemed like a career, and when he was presented with the chance to get back into football he couldn't say no. The opportunity arose at the end of 1999 when the mayor of Cabo Frio approached his old friend Leandro and asked him if he wanted to run the local team. The Flamengo and Brazil right back was born in Cabo Frio, a seaside resort around 100 miles east of Rio, and he returned there to open a B&B after retiring from the game. The spot was popular with tourists – and especially Flamengo fans – who went there for the wide beaches with their incredibly white sand, and Leandro's trophy cabinet adjacent to a whole wall plastered with pictures from his glory days.

Leandro didn't feel he was management material but he liked the idea of getting involved in the administrative side of the club and he called Sócrates to share the news. He was surprised by his friend's enthusiastic response.

'He said to me, "Leandro, take me with you. I want to get involved, I'll help,"' Leandro recalled. 'And I said, "Are you sure? Do you really want to leave there and come here?" And he said, "Sure I do."'[21]

The idea of running a small football team by the beach was about as perfect a prospect as any for Sócrates, but right from the start he saw it being about much more than football. Even though he had been out the game for years he still believed in the philosophy of Corinthians Democracy, and he was keen to see if he could make it work at a smaller club, with no star players and little media attention. Football was becoming infinitely more commercial but that only served to make the challenge greater, and his excitement grew after his first visit to the crumbling little stadium.

The building had some empty rooms underneath the stand and Sócrates' thoughts immediately turned to education. He had packed boxes of books into his car in Ribeirão Preto – more books than clothes, recalled his friend Bueno – and driven the 550 miles to Cabo Frio with the intention of stimulating his new charges. Now that he had the space, he got his hands on some computers and chalkboards and within a fortnight of arriving at the club, every day before training, Sócrates was leading a group discussion on the topic of the day. Sometimes he would rip a page from a newspaper and pin it on the wall for the players to read. Sometimes he would discuss a book. Sometimes he just chose a subject that interested him. The theme didn't matter and neither did the method. The key thing was to get his young charges talking about something other than football.[22]

The experiment was a success and Sócrates decided to push on and try to emulate another of Corinthians Democracy's core ideas. His dream was to end the *concentração* and he got the club's 41 employees together to vote. Having seen how the players responded to his daily debates, he was optimistic they would have the courage to take more responsibility for their own care off the pitch. Instead, he was dealt a crushing blow that once and for all confirmed the death of the lofty ideals he fought so tirelessly to implant.

'I put democracy on the agenda,' he recalled, with a sheepish smile. '[I said] "Let's vote on the issues that are of common interest." And so we voted on the *concentração*. And I lost 40-1. The only vote against the *concentração* was mine.'[23]

Sócrates was more successful on the playing side, even though they arrived at a club with only 10 players on their books, six of whom were injured. Because they had no youth teams and little in the way of scouts, they relied on old friends to help them out. Leandro's brother suggested players he saw playing in São

Paulo. Sócrates called ex-colleagues and asked for recommendations. Zico lent them some players from the club he had set up in Rio.

The idea was to use the last few months of 1999 to construct a team that could compete in the Rio de Janeiro state championship the following year, and they were good enough to make it out of the second division – although that wasn't hard given that eight of the 10 teams went up. However, they got no money to invest after promotion and the higher standard proved too much for them. After two draws and one defeat in their opening three games, Sócrates was fired.

'We had a team to get us into the first division but we didn't have a team to keep us in the first division,' said Leandro. 'It's all about results and we started losing. The mayor asked me to fire him and I said, "I'm not firing him. You can get someone else to do it but I don't have the guts for that." So someone else did it. Sócrates had no idea. He had just signed a four-month contract with an apartment but he knew that's football, these things happen when you lose. It's normal.'[24]

The six months he spent in Cabo Frio were thoroughly enjoyable on a personal level but were also a tragic confirmation that his democratic ethos was anachronistic. The seeds he planted with such success at Corinthians had failed to take root. No other clubs followed suit and, even today, Brazil's clubs function more like dictatorships than democracies. The country's top sides have become more professional and now boast modern marketing departments, nationwide scouting systems and training centres that are equal to those in Europe.

But the players' participation is limited solely to playing football and they have little or no say in how the club is run. A few teams have temporarily abandoned the *concentração* over the years, but not because the players demanded more freedom or because the clubs considered them mature enough to look after themselves the night before a game. Rather, players at clubs that include Botafogo, Portuguesa and Vasco da Gama refused to turn up in protest at not being paid on time. In some cases, the clubs were so indebted they had to cut costs and slashing hotel bills was an easy option. When the finances were sorted out, the *concentração* was re-established. The players who were suddenly released from their pre-game prison professed delight at the newfound freedom, but none of them ever demanded a definitive end to the system.

Rather than release players, clubs have actually taken more steps to restrain them. Atlético Mineiro, Cruzeiro and, ironically, Corinthians are among those that have built their own hotel-like accommodation inside their training grounds as a way of keeping players isolated before match days.

'In general, players are conservative because the system is conservative,' Sócrates said in 2011, long after it was clear Corinthians Democracy would never be repeated. 'They are born into the system and are unable to break out of it. So they accept being treated as children all their life because it's comfortable for them. That's why they have big problems when their career comes to an end. Because at that point you have to be an adult. You have to do things for yourself.'[25]

His forced exit from Cabo Frio did not bother him in the least, and he was more concerned about having to give up the walks on the sand and the nights out with Leandro than losing his job at the club. He knew that sacking is inevitable in football and his departure was notable mostly for being the first time since he left Fiorentina that he didn't choose the moment to go.

The move, though, turned out to be significant in another respect: it was his last full-time job at a football club. When he left, Sócrates missed the game more than he ever let on, but what affected him more was missing a purpose. The new millennium held other opportunities and he was ready to try them out. But most of them were fleeting. Caught between a past he had no desire to revisit and a future that was always undefined, he concentrated on the present and the thing he loved doing most. For the last decade of his life, his most constant companion was the demon drink.

19

'He was a very tormented man who looked for a reason
to live and never found it. He was disenchanted with life.
There was no motive to keep him here.'

Sócrates' friend Mino Carta, publisher of CartaCapital

In December 1980, *Placar* magazine asked Sócrates to imagine
what his life would be like in 2004 at the grand old age of 50.

The then 26-year-old envisaged retiring after winning the
1982 World Cup and devoting himself to running a children's
orthopaedic clinic in Ribeirão Preto. The clinic would show
little sign he was once a famous footballer, with no photos on
the walls or sports magazines in the waiting room, and he
would have no interest in going to the 200,000-capacity
stadium where Corinthians would now be playing their home
games.

He would take part in bounce games at the weekend with
old student friends and pals from his office, and he might even
go to see Botafogo now and again. But, in this projection,
professional football was behind him and he was happy that
way, or at least that's what he wanted people to believe.

He made up some words for Regina to poignantly sketch out her husband's imaginary new life. Sócrates told the world he wanted nothing to do with football, she would say, but there were moments when even he couldn't resist getting out his scrapbooks and looking back.

'I think,' Regina said in touching quotes, 'that the album is locked away in a drawer and he is the only one who has a key. Sometimes, he'll spend hours in his office and when he comes out his eyes are red as if he's been crying. Sócrates doesn't say anything but I know why. He denies it, but football marked his life.'[1]

Football had a greater effect on Sócrates than he ever admitted and one of the tragedies of his later years was that he never found anything remotely as fulfilling. Sócrates had never imagined doing anything other than practising medicine and when that dream went up in smoke he floundered.

'He put medicine aside to be a footballer and when he finished he was going to be a doctor,' said his brother Sóstenes. 'And when that didn't work out he got lost and didn't know what to do. I think at that point he was in the bohemian phase. He was always falling in love and I don't think that helped either. He was looking for something that he never found. I never saw him get really excited about a project. He never did anything that he really wanted to do. He had ideas but he never put them into practice.'[2]

In truth, Sócrates was now, more than ever before, a philosopher. He was a man of words and concepts and theories, not a man of deeds or action. He was constantly coming up with ideas but he never had the energy or patience to turn them into working projects. He soon lost patience with the real world and its tedious barriers of bureaucracy, administration and funding.

Sócrates' last unfulfilled ambition was to work with young players, preferably at Corinthians. He wanted to coach them on and off the field, teaching them about life and politics and the pitfalls that awaited them. His job description would be to produce great players, but most of all he wanted to produce savvy young men who were ready for the world and aware of how their exalted status could change it. Unfortunately, he never formulated a detailed plan and, even if he had, Brazil's football clubs were as conservative as ever and would have baulked at hiring someone with his track record for independence. In the 21st century, revolutionaries were even less welcome than they were in the time of Corinthians Democracy.

Instead, he wrote newspaper and magazine columns and even an unpublished memoir, and he produced and presented TV talk shows in Ribeirão Preto. He composed and recorded with his musician friend Roberto Bueno, got involved in a cinema-cum-community centre called Cineclub Cauim, and he went round the country teaching sport to underprivileged kids in towns and villages far from Brazil's biggest cities. He occasionally gave talks to corporate clients and he remained a brand ambassador for Topper, whose line of Sócrates merchandise was still one of their most successful 20 years after his peak. In 2004, he went to Paris to receive an award from FIFA as one of the world's greatest living footballers.

He found one purpose, albeit brief, to fire him up in the early part of the millennium when he campaigned for changes inside the CBF. The organisation's leaders, several of whom would be indicted in the FIFA corruption scandal more than a decade later, were named in a wide-ranging congressional enquiry and accused of crimes that included tax evasion, racketeering and money laundering. Sócrates was disgusted by the reports and, while the organisation's oblique statutes meant he stood no chance of being elected president, he set himself up as an alternative candidate so that he could hammer away at the leaders. He never wavered in his criticism of Ricardo Teixeira, the head of the CBF for 23 years and one of those who would be indicted in the US, and he amused and delighted reporters when leaving hospital near the end of his life by shouting, 'Teixeira Out!' when asked how he was feeling.

In November 2004, in one of the more memorable interludes, the 50-year-old Sócrates came out of retirement to play for Garforth Town in the ninth tier of English football. Garforth's owner Simon Clifford was a keen Brazil fan and devotee of *futebol de salão*, or *futsal*, which he had brought to the UK through a chain of 600 soccer schools. Sócrates signed up to play a few games but the bitter cold got to him and his only appearance came during the last 13 minutes of Garforth's 2-2 draw against Tadcaster Albion. The pair travelled around the British Isles giving football clinics every day and drinking every night, and together they plotted a revolution in world football. Inevitably, Sócrates never took it any further, and Clifford's lasting memory of the trip was Sócrates convincing the teetotal Yorkshireman he should start smoking because it was cruel to make him smoke and drink alone.

'We were sitting in the restaurant those first few nights and he said, "If you're not going to drink then you can at least smoke,"' Clifford recalled. 'He said, "You're either my brother or you're not my brother." I had smoked at school but that was a long time before, so I thought, "OK, I'll have a cigarette. I can give it up next week." Well, I was still smoking nine years later.'[3]

Such ventures brought Sócrates into contact with new and interesting people, which he always loved. Ten times the usual crowd turned out to see him play for Garforth and he was fêted everywhere he went, including at Manchester United where manager Alex Ferguson halted training to introduce him to his multimillionaire band of pros, many of whom were too young to remember him. But it was more entertainment than work and there was certainly no future in it. The main aim, like much of his last few years, was simply to keep busy and have a laugh.[4]

'He couldn't find himself professionally and if you don't have that and aren't in a stable relationship then bohemianism takes over,' said Sóstenes. 'His life was all about having a good time.'[5]

Sócrates was coming down Ribeirão Preto's Avenida 9 de Julho when he bumped into former Botafogo director Hamilton Mortari. It was early in the new millennium and Mortari was going to buy a cell phone and Sócrates decided to tag along.

'I'll come and help you choose your number,' Sócrates said.

The aging Mortari was delighted to see his old friend and together they sat down in front of a screen and scrolled down a list of potential numbers.

When the cursor hit 51, a number synonymous with Brazil's bestselling brand of *cachaça*, Sócrates said, 'Stop, that number's for you.'

'Why 51?' asked Mortari.

'Because with 51 you'll remember me for the rest of your life,' he replied with a smile.[6]

Sócrates frequently joked about his lifelong love affair with the booze. He told his longtime pal and drinking buddy Fernando Kaxassa that his wife Barbara was the perfect woman because she had two bars in her name. When he was introduced to Fernando Beer, a sales executive with Topper, he grinned and said, 'I like you already.' At least two bars in Ribeirão Preto had tables reserved especially for him and one of them, the Pinguim, allowed him to drink for free because his presence attracted other customers.[7, 8]

For Sócrates, drinking was synonymous with fun. He never took his drink problem seriously or even admitted he had a problem. Fresh out of hospital just weeks before he died, he still insisted he had no regrets and promised never to change. 'I do what I want and I am going to keep doing what I want. If it gives me pleasure then I'll keep doing it. If I don't want to do it, then I won't. I am not addicted to anything. I am not dependent on alcohol. I don't get withdrawal symptoms. I am not chemically dependent.'[9]

Sócrates chose to live life to the full, but the years of hard drinking were taking their toll and friends started to notice subtle changes in his behaviour. He was never a violent drunk or a falling-down drunk, and because he drank weak lager at a slow pace it was difficult to tell when he was in a bad way. But as he moved into his sixth decade his body found it harder to take the strain. He could no longer drink all day and not feel the effects. The instances when he stumbled or slurred his words were still rare but they were becoming more common.

His first health scare came in 1996 when he coughed up blood in the middle of the night and had to drive himself to hospital. The same thing happened nine years later but both times he ignored the doctor's advice to stop smoking and drinking or at least limit his intake. In fact, Sócrates did the opposite. With no real job to fill up his days, drinking became his one regular pastime and, by the end of the 2000s, he was hitting the bottle with a vengeance.[10]

His friends could see him going downhill and some of them called Sócrates' university buddy Aloisio Abud to ask for his help. After failing to show up for the first appointment with Abud, Sócrates eventually appeared for a blood test, endoscopy and ultrasound. The results were not encouraging but Sócrates didn't even bother picking them up for a full six months. He wasn't listening to reason and Abud, bound by the doctor's code of silence, was prevented from telling his friends and family the full extent of the problem.

The tests showed that Sócrates' liver was damaged to the

point where it was working at less than full capacity, but he refused to admit he had cirrhosis and instead described his condition as the less serious fibrosis. Fibrosis inevitably leads to cirrhosis but Doctor Sócrates was in denial and no one could talk sense into him.

Instead of cutting back, he continued drinking, now having convinced himself that, while beer might be bad for him, wine was just fine, either not knowing or not wanting to know that wine had a higher alcohol content than beer. Some friends were refusing to serve him his favourite tipple and he hated drinking the alcohol-free kind because, he said, 'it tastes like shit'. So they reluctantly drank wine together and Sócrates gulped down his cabernet and merlot with gallons of water because he believed it diluted the wine's alcohol content.[11]

'He was heading for the edge of a cliff but instead of slowing down he speeded up,' said Maria Adriana Cruz, his partner for eight years at the start of the decade. 'Every day was a party. He would get up, have coffee and then go for a walk. By 10 a.m. he had opened a beer and was in front of the computer writing. He had lunch, then took a rest and by four o'clock he had found a friend to go drinking with. He'd be out drinking till late and he did that every single day of the week.'[12]

Kátia Bagnarelli was young, blonde and attractive and in January 2010 she was hired to produce a series of corporate talks that Sócrates was to give to Brazil-based multinationals.

The first time they met the couple discussed the presentations he would give to her clients. The second time they met, he was dropping heavy hints about becoming her husband. The third time they met, Sócrates sang her sambas and they went to bed. They soon moved in together and in November 2010 they were married in a small civil ceremony in her home city of Campinas.[13]

Whenever he found a new girlfriend Sócrates dropped his old pals and devoted himself 100 per cent to his new love, and that was especially true after he broke up with Silvana Campos in 1994. Sócrates hated being alone and the split from Campos prompted him to look to the past. Not for the last time, he realised he had made mistakes when it came to women and, after divorcing Campos, he attempted to get back with Regina, calling her up and lobbying mutual friends to intervene. No matter that his first wife had quickly moved on and remarried a man who Sócrates knew and liked and who was a wonderful stepfather to his four boys. Sócrates had belatedly realised his error and tried to woo her back, at one point driving his car right up to her front gate and turning the CD player up loud so she could hear the old songs that were the soundtrack to their courtship. Regina called her best friend who, knowing how much she still loved him, kept her on the phone and convinced her not to go downstairs and give in to temptation.

After he returned from Ecuador and following a short-lived affair with a teenage model, he met Simone Corrêa, a dental student 16 years his junior. He was instantly besotted with the down-to-earth Corrêa and, after a concerted campaign to charm the understandably hesitant 26-year-old, she became his third wife in May 1997. Corrêa managed to get him to cut down on the drink, pointedly telling him that beer was something you drank at night in bars, not at home over breakfast, and the couple were crushed when she suffered a miscarriage during the 1998 World Cup.[14]

They drifted apart the following year, when Sócrates met Maria Adriana Cruz while playing in a veterans' tournament during the 1999 Copa América. The 45-year-old Sócrates was so head over heels with the 34-year-old divorcee that he would drive 350 miles from Cabo Frio to São Paulo just to see her for a few hours before leaving again at 3 a.m. to drive all the way back. Cruz was a social animal like Sócrates and, although their relationship was one of the most tempestuous of his life, they were a good match.

However, that changed after they had a son in September 2005, another boy they named Fidel, after the Cuban president he so admired. Children made Sócrates feel trapped – 'It was as if he felt a child meant this is forever!' Cruz said – and he treated the new arrival as something to be avoided. He started hitting the pubs and bars again and the inevitable split, when it came, was unlike any that had come before. Sócrates always did his best to ensure the break-ups were amicable but this separation was slow and difficult. Fidel was just three and the bitterness dragged on for years as they fought over child support and access. There were times when he would go months without seeing his youngest son.[15]

There were other girlfriends in between the four wives and he lost touch with many of his closest buddies. When a new woman appeared he threw his heart and soul into the relation-ship – always calling them 'my beauty' so as not to get their names wrong – and friends were forgotten as love blinded him to everything else. By the time he met Kátia, he hadn't seen some of his closest pals, people like Palhinha, Adilson and Casa-grande, for years.

'He would just disappear,' said Regina Saquy. 'When we never saw him for months we knew that things were going well with the new woman. But when the problems started, he came running back.'[16]

That pattern repeated itself when he got together with Kátia, who was every bit as possessive as he was. The pair moved to a new house outside São Paulo in January 2011, two months after tying the knot, and they celebrated with a party at their palatial new home in February. The gated community was designed to keep people out and their isolation was accentuated by the mutual antipathy between Kátia and many of Sócrates' oldest acquaintances. Only one of his sons went to their wedding – none of his five brothers was even invited – and the couple detached themselves from their former friends as they set up their new home together. The 26-year age gap was no obstacle to their love and Kátia adored her new husband, to the point where she believed he could cure ailments just by passing his hands over a stricken patient. (She later went on television and gave teary-eyed interviews alongside the spirit mediums who convinced her Sócrates was sending her messages from the grave.)[17]

Sócrates had years before found Spiritism, a New Age-y 'religion' that originated in France in the 19th century and which grew quickly in Brazil in the 1900s. The doctrine is based on the belief that humans are inhabited by immortal spirits that can communicate with the living and it filled Sócrates with an inner peace he had never felt before. He would often go to spirit centres and participate in services during which dead people 'spoke' to their relatives.[18]

More worryingly, he was still drinking and the cumulative effects were increasingly visible. He turned up at his godson João's wedding in October 2010 with a tie wrapped around his head like a bandana and carrying a painting he had finished just hours before as a present. He was in a sorry state and João's father, Maurinho Saquy, tried to convince him to move in with them for a while. Their ranch was a sanctuary for him all his life, somewhere he could relax in the company of his closest friends. They hoped he might stay with them and dry out, but he was under Kátia's spell and it wasn't long before the inevitable happened. In July 2011, Sócrates woke in the middle of the night with pains in his stomach and before he could even reach the bathroom, he collapsed on the floor vomiting blood all over his stricken partner. Kátia rushed him to hospital, where he spent two days before being allowed home.

The diagnosis was chronic digestive haemorrhaging caused by cirrhosis and it was the loudest warning shot yet. The couple kept the incident secret, hoping it was a one-off that would be resolved through abstinence and healthy living. Kátia successfully tried to keep him away from his old friends, people she thought were a bad influence because they drank together, and Sócrates managed to cut back a bit as he devoted himself to painting and writing his still unfinished autobiography.

He was determined to stay fit enough to enjoy a belated honeymoon in Cuba, where he had agreed to discuss coaching the Cuban national team, as well as go to Venezuela to interview socialist president Hugo Chávez.[19]

Before he could get to the Caribbean, however, he was coughing up blood again, and in August he spent nine days in hospital and another month convalescing at home, too weak to attend his son Marcelo's wedding. This time the vomiting was more serious and more prolonged and he fell into a coma. His doctors managed to save him but it was touch and go, and when they discharged him almost a week later they saw him off with a stark warning. 'This is your last chance,' Dr Bueno Boueri told him. 'Not one drop of alcohol must pass your lips. If you do that then we can think of getting you a transplant.'[20]

He finally made it to Havana in September with Kátia, albeit for a shorter trip than they wished, but the planned interviews with Fidel Castro and Chávez, who was on the island undergoing treatment for cancer, both fell through. Sócrates was so weak that Kátia convinced him to postpone their other dream, that of having IV treatment for the twin girls they dreamt of.

Still there was no let-up. A day after they returned from the Caribbean he was rushed to hospital again with fresh bleeding, perhaps not helped by his insistence on drinking wine when-ever they went out in the old centre of Havana. The Cuban capital was hot and sultry, but Kátia felt chills run down her spine whenever Sócrates picked up a glass of red and she was powerless to make him stop. His condition was worse than ever and although doctors cauterised some veins to stop the haemorrhaging, his stomach started to bleed as well and there were moments when he looked past repair. A team of surgeons once again brought him back from the brink, but it was a close-run thing and he spent another 10 days in a coma. Never one to learn a lesson, much less be told what to do, he insisted on smoking a cigarette on the hospital terrace before being discharged.[21]

He cut back on his commitments and gradually improved as October moved into November, and he was fit enough to start working again, mostly presenting the odd corporate talk and appearing on the football talk show *Cartão Verde* on TV Cultura. But he was still smoking and friends despaired. 'Have you decided just to say fuck it and give up?' an exasperated Juca Kfouri asked him shortly before he died. Sócrates just shrugged.[22]

In 2007, not long after he separated from Cruz, Sócrates looked up an old friend in Rio de Janeiro. More than 20 years after he ended his torrid affair with Rosemary he arranged to see her again.

Sócrates' split from Rosemary in 1986 had been traumatic. He called it quits on his return from Italy because he was afraid of taking a leap into the unknown and fearful of what would happen to his wife and kids if he abandoned them. But he was never quite sure if he'd done the right thing, his lingering doubts stemming from the fact that it was a decision he made with his head rather than his heart. He trusted his heart more and the affection he felt for her had never really gone away. She was not *the* love of his life – she shared that title with Regina – but she was definitely the lust of his life, and his muse during one of the most tumultuous periods of his career.

So when his marriage to Cruz foundered, he looked around for a familiar face and the obvious thing to do was try to fan the embers of an old flame. Rosemary was by now almost 60 and semi-retired from the music business but she was still delighted to hear from him. She too felt there was unresolved business between them and they began an on-off love affair that continued until the final year of his life.

Rosemary had maintained a dignified silence for more than a quarter of a century, refusing until now ever to discuss their affair. But she also felt that their love had never really died. 'We were like a painting that had never been finished,' she said. 'It was difficult for him back then with all the responsibilities that he had. We just weren't able to be together. What I did was put my feelings in a little box and lock them away. But he always knew how I felt about him and I always knew how he felt about me.'[23]

They kept seeing each other at irregular intervals and in early 2011, just weeks after he married Kátia, Sócrates took his son Gustavo to Rio to spend carnival at her house. They sat on her balcony and drank prosecco in the sultry Rio night and he went to see her sing with the Mangueira samba school. It was the last time they met and the trip ended in frustration. Sócrates was never able to fully open up and tell her how he felt, and he did not want to burden her by revealing the full extent of his cirrhosis. Rosemary already suspected the damage was serious and she could see how the drink was taking its toll. In her own subtle way, she pleaded with him to stop drinking and take better care of himself. But even Rosemary's words had no effect. Sócrates was past help.

*

The question of how such an intelligent man could so delude himself was both a contradiction and a mystery. As a trained doctor, Sócrates clearly knew what the drink was doing to his insides, but even after the spitting of blood, the hospitalisations and days spent in a coma, he couldn't or wouldn't do anything to help himself. Even more perplexing was his inability to admit he had a problem. When questioned about whether he considered himself an alcoholic, he almost always hid behind shrugs and pretentious explanations.

'It's all semantics,' he told a SporTV interviewer who asked him point-blank after one stint in hospital. 'People like to put labels on things. If they call me literary because I like to read books then what am I going to do, there's no problem. I don't like dogmas or labels. People should do what makes them happy. I do what I like and I am going to continue doing what I like. I am not dependent on alcohol. I don't need cigarettes, even though I smoke. That's my personal choice.'[24]

Another personal choice was not to push for a liver transplant much earlier. Doctor friend Zé Bernardes had encouraged him to get his name on the transplant list as far back as 2008 because, even though he had to be off the drink for six months before a transplant was possible, he had to first get on the list and let doctors know he was a candidate. Sócrates suspected his friends wanted to help push his name up the list and he refused to even consider an option that made it look like he was jumping the queue. He was amazed at how complete strangers offered to donate their own organs, but he still didn't seem to realise he was in real trouble.[25]

Bernardes, one of Ribeirão's top haematologists, tried to make him understand the severity of his condition but his old pal was impervious to logic and common sense.

'I think he thought it wasn't going to happen to him,' Bernardes said. 'That's often the case with doctors. Doctors are bossy. They tell patients what to do, they tell mothers of children what to do, they tell old people what to do, they tell nurses what to do, they tell social workers what to do. So they get a bit arrogant. University trains you to be like that and so you start to think of yourself as a bit like God: I am immune, I treat diseases, diseases don't happen to me. So I think he thought it wasn't going to happen to him.'[26]

On Wednesday, 30 November 2011, after more than a month of relatively normal life in his spacious home just outside São Paulo, Sócrates gave a speech to documentary filmmakers. He did not look well and had trouble finding his words, but he wanted to eat something afterwards and so he and Kátia went with the 20 or so producers and directors to lunch on beef stroganoff at a nearby hotel.

At night he ate just water biscuits and an ice lolly, and he woke up on Thursday morning with a fever of 39 degrees. He wanted to sweat it out and so Kátia bundled him up like he asked and together they hoped the worst would pass.

But he soon started vomiting again and Kátia called the doctors in a panicked state. Sócrates begged her to let him stay at home, but he looked grey and in trouble and an ambulance was soon whisking them along the side of the Pinheiros river to the same Albert Einstein hospital where he had spent much of the last four months. Sócrates was lucid and joking with the paramedics, but he was clearly ill and the doctors in the intensive care unit diagnosed him with septic shock, likely caused by bacteria in something he ate at lunch.[27]

He awoke on Friday morning with good news – the infectologist told him the drugs were having the desired effect and that he would be out in a few days. He had dialysis, but then his nose started to bleed and because he was having trouble breathing doctors gave him oxygen.

Kátia got worried and she freaked out on Saturday afternoon when a wheezing Sócrates looked at her and said, 'My love, don't think about my body. My soul will always be with you. Don't leave.'

She immediately called the infectologist and the doctors rushed in to intubate him. A few hours later, just after midnight, he took a turn for the worse and the physician pulled her aside.

'Kátia, you need to prepare yourself,' he told her. 'It's almost over and you need to be aware of that. He doesn't have a lot of strength left. We've done all we could.'

Between 2 a.m. and 4.25 a.m., Sócrates' blood pressure was about as low as it could be, 20/20, compared to the normal rate of 120/80. And while a normal resting heartbeat is between 60 and 100 per minute, Sócrates was so weak his heart was beating just once every two seconds. At 4.25 a.m. it stopped completely and the machine went dead.

EPILOGUE

Sócrates was a legend but nothing he did or said was as legendary as his fateful premonition: 'I want to die on a Sunday, the day Corinthians win a title.' It was a wish as morbid as it was romantic and, on 4 December 2011, his wish came true. He was only 57.

When great people die in Brazil their bodies are often laid out in public so that fans can pay their last respects. Actors, singers, athletes and writers are placed in open coffins in the foyer of city chambers or theatres and mourners shuffle by with their heads bowed.

The tributes are even grander for the greatest of the great, people like double World Cup winner Garrincha or three-time Formula 1 world champion Ayrton Senna. Superstars like these, who captured the imagination or the zeitgeist, are placed on the back of open-topped fire engines and driven slowly through their hometowns. Hundreds of thousands of people turn out to bid them farewell, packing avenues, hanging over bridges and balancing precariously from lampposts and trees.

Sócrates was one of those rare players whose appeal went beyond football, but he got no such ceremony and that would have been fine by him. The captain of the greatest Brazil side never to win the World Cup and the leader of Corinthians Democracy, the most extraordinary and progressive movement ever to shake the antiquated corridors of Brazilian football, was averse to idolatry. As he neared the end in that São Paulo hospital, Sócrates just wanted it to be over, to be taken home and buried in the family plot with the minimum of fuss.

As soon as doctors filled out the paperwork, his body was loaded into a hearse to be driven 200 miles to Ribeirão Preto. In one car was his youngest brother Raí, the former Brazil captain who had decided on the quick, private burial. In another was his 90-year-old mother Guiomar. Wladimir, the black-power leader who helped launch their historic movement at Corinthians, was not far behind.

The convoy headed straight to the Bom Pastor cemetery, where a crowd of people had gathered at the gates to welcome him home. Sócrates wasn't just a father to six, a brother to five, and a doting son. He was one of the city's best-known and most-loved characters, a lapsed physician who liked nothing better than to drink, sing and laugh while cursing and teasing those around him with his wicked smile. Everyone in Ribeirão had met him or knew someone who had, and hundreds of mourners turned out to say goodbye. When the cortege drove slowly along the city's Avenue of Tears towards the cemetery gates, the fans, many of them wearing Botafogo or Corinthians shirts, followed behind chanting his name.

The coffin was taken to an air-conditioned room where family and friends could quietly pay their last respects. Guiomar sat quietly in a private room next door, comforted by the presence of her nearest and dearest. Four of his former partners were there, as were his sons and brothers. Regina stood at the head of the coffin, stroking her former husband's hair. Beside her, overseeing it all, was Raí, who had effortlessly assumed the role of family patriarch.

It was late afternoon by the time the simple wooden coffin was loaded back in the hearse and driven slowly to the far side of the cemetery. It was still bright and sunny and hundreds of people were in shorts and T-shirts as they walked past blooming magnolia trees and manicured lawns towards Plot No. 1126. When they got to the Vieira family grave, the paving stones had already been removed and, in typically chaotic fashion, gravediggers and mourners shunted the coffin awkwardly into the void alongside Sócrates' father, who was laid there seven years before.

After a brief ceremony, the crowds packed six deep around the grave recited the Lord's Prayer and sang the national anthem before the stone was replaced and a Corinthians flag was laid on top. Everyone clapped. As workers piled floral tributes around one end of the grave, his friend Bueno got out his guitar and led the last remaining mourners in song.

At exactly the same moment across the state, football fans were making their way to the Pacaembu stadium in São Paulo. Sócrates' former club Corinthians were about to face city rivals Palmeiras in the last game of the season. The home side needed just a point to clinch their fifth Brazilian league title, but as the fans traipsed through the leafy streets surrounding the stadium their expectation was tinged with an almost palpable sense of loss.

Sócrates' death was headline news in Brazil and his passing was the main topic of conversation for many of the 34,000 people who pushed through the turnstiles. More than being simply one of Corinthians' greatest players, Sócrates, with his scraggly beard, lanky gait and unapologetically libertarian views, was indisputably their most iconic. He hadn't played for the club since the mid-1980s but he was a diehard Corinthiano and the fans could not hide their grief. Behind the goals, where the hard-core supporters were shirtless and bouncing in the late afternoon sun, people waved flags and banners. 'Dr Sócrates,

Rest in Peace' read one spray-painted sheet hung from the terraces. 'Sócrates, eternally in our hearts' read another scratched out in hand just minutes before the game began.

Tributes were held at games all across the country, but when the stadium announcer called for a minute's silence grown men cried and a deafening chant of 'Sócrates! Sócrates! Sócrates!' rang round the magnificent art-deco stadium. Fans held up their right arms, their fists clenched in a militant salute, exactly like Sócrates did when he scored a goal. Down below them, the Corinthians players lined up around the centre circle did the same.

The game that followed was unrecognisable from that of Sócrates in his pomp. Football had long ago disowned the sportsmanship and political activism that made Sócrates such a compelling figure. Tactics and tattoos were what mattered now. Corinthians drew 0-0 and got the point they needed to lift the title, but the final moments of wind-ups and brawls, with four men sent off, were exactly the kind of scenes that meant football was no longer a game he loved. He would have been watching, with a cold beer in one hand and a cigarette in the other, but he would have despaired at it all.

Sócrates was perhaps unique in being a brilliant footballer who was more important off the park than on it. His actions helped transform not just a football club but a country. He helped Brazil through those pivotal years that led from dictatorship to democracy, and he put his country before himself with a promise to eschew European riches and remain at home to help his people.

As the sun set on his twin cities of Ribeirão Preto and São Paulo that Sunday night, the most original of men, wherever he was, would have been smirking at having confounded the world one last time. 'I want to die on a Sunday, the day Corinthians win a title,' declared the legend. He did. And they did. And the final chapter of an extraordinary life was complete.

NOTES ON SOURCES

Chapter 1 – Opening quote: Author interview with Sóstenes
1. Author interview with Oscar
2. Author interview with Juca Kfouri
3. *Sócrates & Casagrande: Uma História de Amor*
4. *Folha de S.Paulo*, 3 July 1982
5. Sócrates' unpublished memoir, from Kátia Bagnarelli
6. Author interview with Nené
7. Author interview with Marinho
8. *Placar*, Sócrates special edition, 1979
9. *Jornal da Tarde*, 2 July 1979
10. Author interviews with Sóstenes and Raimundo
11. Interview with Juca Kfouri in 1999
12. Author interview with Raí
13. Interview with Juca Kfouri in 1999
14. Ibid
15. Author interview with Dr Helio Rubens Machado
16. *Caros Amigos*, no. 45, 2000
17. Interview with Juca Kfouri in 1999
18. *Jornal da Tarde*, 2 July 1979
19. Interview with Juca Kfouri in 1999

Chapter 2 – Opening quote: *O Gênio da Bola*
1. *Diário da Manhã*, 7 February 1974
2. Interview with Juca Kfouri in 1999
3. *Folha de S.Paulo*, 14 October 1975
4. Author interview with Alberto Helena Jnr
5. Author interview with Dr Said Miguel

6. Author interview with Ney
7. *Placar*, special edition, September 1979
8. Author interview with João Sebinho
9. *CartaCapital*, 2 June 2010
10. *Recados da Bola*
11. Author interview with Geraldão
12. *Sócrates & Casagrande: Uma História de Amor*
13. Author interview with Sóstenes
14. Author interview with Raí
15. Author interview with Raimundo

Chapter 3 – Opening quote: Author interview with Raimundo
1. Author interview with João Sebinho
2. Author interview with Maritaca
3. Author interview with Ney
4. Author interview with Zé Bernardes
5. Author interview with João Sebinho
6. *Jornal da Tarde*, 22 June 1976
7. Author interview with Zé Bernardes
8. *A Concise History of Brazil*
9. *Compagni di Stadio*
10. Author interview with Dr Said Miguel
11. *Diário da Manhã*, 18 July 1976
12. 1980 census from the Brazilian Institute of Geography and Statistics
13. *Diário da Manhã*, 18 July 1976
14. *Botafogo: Uma História de Amor e Glorias*
15. Ibid
16. Author interview with Atílio Benedini
17. Author interview with Dr Said Miguel
18. Botafogo TV report from 29 October 2013
19. Interview with Juca Kfouri in 1999
20. *Botafogo: Uma História de Amor e Glorias*

Chapter 4 – Opening quote: *CartaCapital*, 16 February 2011
1. Author interview with Alberto Helena Jnr
2. Author interview with Zé Bernardes
3. Hamilton Mortari interview on Radio Jovem Pan, February 2012
4. Author interview with José Teixeira
5. Hamilton Mortari interview on Radio Jovem Pan, February 2012
6. *Placar*, 11 August 1978
7. Ibid
8. Ibid
9. Author interview with Zé Maria
10. Author interview with Palhinha
11. Author interview with Jairo

12. Author interview with João Roberto Basílio
13. Interview with *Playboy*, September 1979
14. Interview with Juca Kfouri in 1999
15. Author interview with Alberto Helena Jnr
16. Author interview with Arlindo

Chapter 5 – Opening quote: Interview with Juca Kfouri in 1999
1. *Placar*, 26 March 1982
2. *Placar*, 20 April 1979
3. *Placar*, 30 March 1979
4. *Placar*, 20 April 1979
5. *Jornal da Tarde*, 22 June 1979
6. *Zico Conta Sua História*
7. *Placar*, 31 August 1979
8. Ibid
9. Author interview with Vaguinho
10. *CartaCapital*, 28 July 2004
11. *Folha de S.Paulo*, 29 September 1979
12. *Placar*, Sócrates special, September 1979
13. Interview with Juca Kfouri in 1999
14. Ibid
15. Passe Livre documentary film
16. *Compagni di Stadio*
17. Sócrates' unpublished memoir, from Kátia Bagnarelli
18. *Placar*, 14 September 1979
19. Ibid
20. *Placar*, 21 September 1979
21. *Folha de S.Paulo*, 20 November 1979
22. *Folha de S.Paulo*, 7 November 1979
23. Author interview with Palhinha
24. *Democracia Corintiana*
25. Author interview with Amaral
26. Ibid
27. *Jornal da Tarde*, 11 February 1980

Chapter 6 – Opening quote: Author interview with Wladimir
1. *III Berro* magazine
2. Author interview with Osmar Zan
3. *Placar*, 26 October 1987
4. Author interview with Jairo
5. Author interview with Amaral
6. *Folha de S.Paulo*, 27 May 1980
7. Author interview with João Roberto Basílio
8. *Recados da Bola*
9. *Placar*, 27 June 1980

10. *O Gênio da Bola*
11. *Folha de S.Paulo*, 20 August 1980
12. *Folha de S.Paulo*, 21 August 1980
13. *Placar*, 1 August 1980
14. *Folha de S.Paulo*, 19 October 1980
15. *Jornal da Tarde*, 22 August 1980

Chapter 7 – Opening quote: *Placar*, 31 December 1981
1. *CartaCapital*, 5 April 2006
2. Ibid
3. *Fio de Esperança*
4. Ibid
5. *Roda Viva* television interview, 22 June 1992
6. Interview with *Isto É Gente*, 2001
7. Sócrates' unpublished memoir, from Kátia Bagnarelli
8. *Placar*, 29 May 1981
9. Ibid
10. *Placar*, 17 April 1981
11. *Compagni di Stadio*
12. Author interview with Sergio Scarpelli
13. Author interview with Leandro
14. Ibid
15. Interview with Juca Kfouri in 1999
16. Author interview with Mauro Beting
17. *CartaCapital*, 11 December 2002
18. *Placar*, 17 April 1981
19. *Placar*, 17 July 1981
20. *Placar*, 13 February 1981

Chapter 8 – Opening quote: *Ser Campeão é Detalhe*
1. Author interview with Marinho
2. Author interview with Jairo
3. Ibid
4. *Placar*, 13 February 1981
5. *Almanaque do Corinthians*
6. *Sócrates Brasileiro*
7. *Placar*, 5 February 1982
8. Wladimir presentation to Núcleo de Estudos do Corinthians
9. *Placar*, 16 April 1982
10. *Placar*, 27 November 1981
11. *Recados da Bola*
12. *Placar*, 27 November 1981
13. *Mario Travaglini: Da Academia à Democracia*
14. Author interview with César
15. Author interview with Raimundo

16. Author interview with Waldemar Pires
17. *Democracia Corintiana*
18. Author interview with Hélio Maffia
19. *O Gênio da Bola*
20. Author interview with Juca Kfouri

Chapter 9 – Opening quote: *Placar*, 17 April 1981

1. *Placar*, 27 June 1980
2. *Placar*, 11 January 1985
3. *Placar*, 25 March 1983
4. *Placar*, 2 April 1982
5. *Placar*, 31 December 1982
6. Author interview with Zico
7. Zico interview with ESPN, 4 December 2011
8. *Folha de S.Paulo*, 26 June 1982
9. *CartaCapital*, 12 June 2002
10. *Folha de S.Paulo*, 18 June 1982
11. Author interview with Zico
12. *Placar*, 25 June 1982
13. Sócrates' unpublished memoir, from Kátia Bagnarelli
14. *Folha de S.Paulo*, 25 June 1982
15. *Placar*, 2 July 1982
16. *Folha de S.Paulo*, 23 June 1982
17. Interview with Juca Kfouri 1999
18. *Placar*, 9 July 1982
19. *Folha de S.Paulo*, 2 July 1982
20. *Folha de S.Paulo*, 1 July 1982
21. *Placar*, 9 July 1982
22. Ibid

Chapter 10 – Opening quote: *Jornal da Tarde*, 22 June 1982

1. Juninho interview with Fundação Getúlio Vargas http://cpdoc.fgv.br/museudofutebol/juninho_fonseca
2. *Folha de S.Paulo*, 30 June 1982
3. Oscar interview with Fundação Getúlio Vargas http://cpdoc.fgv.br/sites/default/files/museu_do_futebol/oscar_bernardi/TranscricaoOscarBernardi.pdf
4. Interview with Juca Kfouri in 1999
5. Interview with Luizinho
6. Edinho interview with Fundação Getúlio Vargas http://cpdoc.fgv.br/sites/default/files/museu_do_futebol/edino_filho/TranscricaoEdinho.pdf
7. Sócrates' unpublished memoir, from Kátia Bagnarelli
8. Author interview with Raí
9. Interview with Luizinho
10. *Placar*, 7 April 1986

11. Sócrates' unpublished memoir, from Kátia Bagnarelli
12. Interview with Juca Kfouri in 1999
13. Ibid
14. *Folha de S.Paulo*, 7 July 1982

Chapter 11 – Opening quote: Author interview with Luiz Inácio Lula da Silva
1. *Democracia Corintiana*
2. *Placar*, 17 September 1982
3. Author interview with Sergio Scarpelli
4. Author interview with Milton Neves
5. *Placar*, 15 October 1982
6. *Placar*, 8 October 1982
7. Author interview with Rosemary
8. Sócrates' unpublished memoir, excerpted in *Sócrates & Casagrande: Uma História de Amor*
9. Author interview with Washington Olivetto
10. Sócrates' unpublished memoir, from Kátia Bagnarelli
11. Author interview with Ataliba
12. Interview with Juca Kfouri in 1999
13. Ibid
14. Author interview with Biro-Biro
15. *Doutor Futebol*
16. Author interview with Biro-Biro
17. Interview with Juca Kfouri in 1999
18. Author interview with Biro-Biro
19. Author interview with Washington Olivetto
20. Author interview with Waldemar Pires
21. *Democracia Corintiana*
22. Author interview with Washington Olivetto

Chapter 12 – Opening quote: Author interview with Casagrande
1. Author interview with Casagrande
2. Author interview with Zenon
3. *Casagrande & Sócrates: Uma História de Amor*
4. *Folha de S.Paulo*, 23 February 1983
5. *Democracia Corintiana*
6. *Isto É Gente*, no. 1622
7. *Folha de S.Paulo*, 30 March 1983
8. *Folha de S.Paulo*, 4 May 1983
9. *Folha de S.Paulo*, 30 March 1983
10. Author interview with Zenon
11. *Placar*, 9 September 1983
12. *Jornal da Tarde*, 26 February 1983
13. Author interview with Casagrande
14. *Folha de S.Paulo*, 13 October 1974

15. Interview with Juca Kfouri in 1999
16. *Placar*, May 1992
17. Author interview with Luis Fernando
18. *Folha de S.Paulo*, 15 December 1983
19. Author interview with Casagrande
20. Ibid
21. Interview with Juca Kfouri in 1999

Chapter 13 – Opening quote: Author interview with Flávio Gikovate

1. *Diretas Já*
2. *Playboy* interview, September 1979
3. Author interview with Luis Fernando
4. *Folha de S.Paulo*, 17 April 1984
5. *Democracia em Preto e Branco*
6. *Folha de S.Paulo*, 25 April 1984
7. Author interview with Marinho
8. Ibid
9. Author interview with Raí
10. Interview with Juca Kfouri in 1999
11. *Placar*, 9 September 1983
12. *Placar*, 4 May 1984
13. *Folha de S.Paulo*, 26 April 1984
14. *Democracia em Preto e Branco*
15. *Recados da Bola*

Chapter 14 – Opening quote: *O Gênio da Bola*

1. *Jornal da Tarde*, 24 May 1984
2. Ibid
3. Ibid
4. Author interview with Stefano Carobbi
5. Author interview with Celeste Pin
6. Author interview with Giovanni Galli
7. http://www.worldfootball.net/player_summary/socrates/2/
8. Interview with Juca Kfouri in 1999
9. Author interview with Giovanni Galli
10. Author interview with Celeste Pin
11. *Placar*, 28 June 1984
12. Author interview with José Trajano
13. Author interview with Stefano Carobbi
14. Interview with Eraldo Pecci
15. *Recados da Bola*
16. Ibid
17. Ibid
18. Author interview with Niccolò Pontello
19. Author interview with Tito Corsi

20. *Placar*, 1 March 1985
21. Author interview with José Trajano
22. Author interview with Júnior
23. Sócrates on his own TV programme, *Brasil + Brasileiro*
24. *Placar*, 1 March 1985
25. Author interview with Rosemary
26. Author interview with Flávio Gikovate
27. Author interviews with Giovanni Galli and Stefano Carobbi; interview with Juca Kfouri in 1999
28. Author interview with Stefano Carobbi
29. Author interview with Celeste Pin
30. Author interview with Stefano Carobbi

Chapter 15 – Opening quote: Author interview with Juca Kfouri
1. *Recados da Bola*
2. *Jornal do Brasil*
3. *Jornal do Brasil*, 12 August 1985
4. *Placar*, 16 August 1985
5. *Placar*, 23 August 1985
6. Author interview with Alberto Polverosi
7. *Placar*, 30 August 1985
8. Ibid
9. Author interview with Paulo Sérgio
10. *Placar*, 20 September 1985
11. *O Globo*, 28 January 1986
12. *Jornal do Brasil*, 6 February 1986
13. *O Globo*, 3 February 1986
14. Flapédia
15. *Folha de S.Paulo*, 19 February 1986
16. *Doutor Futebol*
17. *Placar*, 3 March 1986
18. Ibid
19. Sócrates' unpublished memoir, from Kátia Bagnarelli
20. *Folha de S.Paulo*, 8 March 1986
21. *Placar*, 24 March 1986
22. *Folha de S.Paulo*, 8 March 1986
23. Ibid
24. *Folha de S.Paulo*, 6 April 1986
25. *Folha de S.Paulo*, 9 April 1986
26. *Folha de S.Paulo*, 24 April 1986
27. *Placar*, 19 May 1986
28. *Folha de S.Paulo*, 13 May 1986
29. *Folha de S. Paulo*, 18 May 1986

Chapter 16 – Opening quote: *Jornal da Tarde*, 29 May 1986

1. *Sócrates & Casagrande: Uma História de Amor*
2. Author interview with Casagrande
3. Ibid
4. Author interview with Édson Boaro
5. *Folha de S.Paulo*, 6 June 1986
6. *Folha de S.Paulo*, 6 September 1986
7. Author interview with Oscar
8. *Placar*, 14 July 1986
9. Author interview with Elzo
10. *Placar*, 7 July 1986
11. Author interview with Zico
12. *Jornal da Tarde*, 2 July 1979
13. Interview with Juca Kfouri in 1999
14. Ibid
15. *Recados da Bola*
16. *Folha de S.Paulo*, 23 June 1986
17. *Recados da Bola*
18. *O Globo*, 22 June 1986
19. Interview with Juca Kfouri in 1999
20. Author interview with Júnior

Chapter 17 – Opening quote: *Placar*, 21 October 1988

1. Author interview with Sebastião Lazaroni
2. Author interview with Leandro
3. Ibid
4. Author interview with Sebastião Lazaroni
5. Flapédia
6. *O Globo*, 17 March 1987
7. *Jornal do Brasil*, 17 March 1987
8. *Placar*, 23 March 1987
9. *O Globo*, 3 November 1986
10. Interview with Juca Kfouri in 1999
11. Author interview with Silvana Campos
12. Ibid
13. Author interview with Maurinho Saquy
14. Author interview with Silvana Campos
15. Interview with Juca Kfouri in 1999
16. Ibid
17. Author interview with Silvana Campos
18. *Placar*, 21 October 1988
19. Ibid
20. Author interview with Marinho Peres
21. Author interview with César Sampaio
22. *A Tribuna*, 5 August 1989

23. Author interview with Juary
24. *A Tribuna*, 2 September 1989
25. *A Tribuna*, 2/3 September, 1989
26. Interview with Juca Kfouri in 1999
27. *O Diário*, 17 September 1989
28. *Botafogo: Uma História de Amor e Glorias*

Chapter 18 – Opening quote: Author interview with Sóstenes
1. Author interview with Aloisio Abud
2. Interview with *Playboy*, September 1979
3. Author interview with Antonio Palocci
4. Ibid
5. Ibid
6. Interview with Juca Kfouri in 1999
7. Ibid
8. Author interview with Édson Boaro
9. *Botafogo: Uma História de Amor e Glorias*
10. Author interview with Serginho
11. Interview with Juca Kfouri in 1999
12. Ibid
13. Author interview with Silvana Campos
14. Interview with Juca Kfouri in 1999
15. Author interview with Mauro Beting
16. Interview with Mario Naranjo
17. Ibid
18. Ibid
19. *Caros Amigos*, no. 45, 2000
20. *Sócrates Brasileiro*
21. Author interview with Leandro
22. Ibid
23. Interview with Marília Gabriela, 27 October 2011
24. Author interview with Leandro
25. Interview with Marília Gabriela, 27 October 2011

Chapter 19 – Opening quote: Author interview with Mino Carta
1. *Placar*, 26 December 1980
2. Author interview with Sóstenes
3. Author interview with Simon Clifford
4. *O Globo*, 27 November 2004
5. Author interview with Sóstenes
6. Radio interview with Jovem Pan, broadcast 26 December 2012
7. Author interview with Fernando Beer
8. Author interview with Fernando Kaxassa
9. Interview with SporTV, September 2011 (aired after his death) https://www.youtube.com/watch?v=JF37oweELRY

10. Author interview with Silvana Campos
11. Author interview with Maurinho Saquy
12. Author interview with Maria Adriana Cruz
13. *Sócrates Brasileiro*
14. Author interview with Simone Corrêa
15. Author interview with Maria Adriana Cruz
16. Author interview with Regina Saquy
17. Author interview with Kátia Bagnarelli
18. Author interview with Bueno
19. *Sócrates Brasileiro*
20. Author interview with Dr Bueno Boueri
21. *Sócrates Brasileiro*
22. Author interview with Juca Kfouri
23. Author interview with Rosemary
24. Interview with SporTV, September 2011 (aired after his death) https://www.youtube.com/watch?v=JF37oweELRY
25. *Sócrates Brasileiro*
26. Author interview with Zé Bernardes
27. *Sócrates Brasileiro*

SELECT BIBLIOGRAPHY

A Concise History of Brazil, Boris Fausto
A História de um Campeão, Rafael Cammarota
Além do Divã, Flávio Gikovate
Botafogo: Uma História de Amor e Glorias, Igor Ramos
Casagrande e Seus Demônios, Casagrande and Gilvan Ribeiro
Como Gostar de Esporte, Raí
Compagni di Stadio, Solange Cavalcante
Corinthians é Preto no Branco, Washington Olivetto and Nirlando
    Beirão
Corintiano Graças a Deus!, Dom Paulo Evaristo Arns
De Sócrates a Sócrates, Wilson Roveri
Democracia Corintiana, Sócrates and Ricardo Gozzi
Diretas Já, Alberto Tosi Rodrigues
Donos da Bola, Coletánea
Doutor Futebol, Adriana Brito and Patrícia Favalle
Fio de Esperança: Biografia de Telê Santana, André Ribeiro
Futebol Nation: The Story of Brazil Through Soccer, David Goldblatt
Futebol: The Brazilian Way of Life, Alex Bellos
Histórias da Bola, Paulo Roberto Falcão
Mário Travaglini: Da Academia à Democracia, Márcio Trevisan and
    Helvio Borelli

Matheus, O Senhor Corinthians, Marlene Matheus

Memória de Igarapé-Açu, Aluizio Moraes de Freitas

O Pais da Bola, Betty Milan

Recados da Bola, Jorge Vasconcellos

Sarriá 82: O que Faltou ao Futebol-arte?, Gustavo Roman and Renato Zanata

Sócrates, Tom Cardoso

Sócrates & Casagrande: Uma História de Amor, Casagrande and Gilvan Ribeiro

Sócrates Brasileiro, Kátia Bagnarelli with Regina Echeverria

Sócrates, Brasileiro: As Crônicas do Doutor em CartaCapital, Sócrates Brasileiro

Sócrates: O Filosofo da Bola, Aluizio Moraes de Freitas

Um Escolhido, João Roberto Basílio

Vicente Matheus: Quem Sai na Chuva é Para Se Queimar, Luiz Carlos Ramos

Zico Conta Sua História, Zico

Zico Uma Lição de Vida, Marcus Vinícius Bucar Nunes

The following documentary films were also useful:

Democracia em Preto e Branco

Football Rebels: Sócrates and the Corinthians' Democracy

Ser Campeão é Detalhe

Sócrates, O Doutor da Bola

Sócrates, O Gênio da Bola

ACKNOWLEDGEMENTS

I don't know if Sócrates ever met Garrincha, but I do know that for me at least there wouldn't be one without the other.

In 2004, five years after I had made my dream move to Brazil, I convinced a UK publisher to let me translate Ruy Castro's biography of Garrincha. The book was a success and so they asked me if I wanted to translate another. What's it about, I asked, and when the answer came back, 'It's a memoir written by Sócrates,' I almost jumped for joy. Who didn't love and admire Sócrates?

Sócrates' book was an unusual mixture of footballing memories, history, philosophy and cultural commentary, but it was never published, largely because of complicated rights issues.

I spoke with Sócrates several times about getting the project back on track or even of writing a book together and he was always enthusiastic. But we were never able to get going and it was only after the 2014 World Cup, three years after he passed away, that I finally found the time to think about writing the biography he so richly deserves.

When I decided to go ahead with the project, the first person I spoke to was Juca Kfouri, the dean of Brazil's sports writers. Kfouri was editor of sports magazine *Placar* at the time of

Corinthians Democracy and a close friend of Sócrates for 30 years.

The two men, I discovered, had been planning to write a book together since the 1990s and even spent hours recording interviews in 1999. Getting Kfouri's backing was important to me and he was a valuable source of stories, contacts and support. Handing over a transcribed copy of those conversations was a vital help as my project drew to a close. Without him this would have been infinitely more difficult and I owe him a massive debt of gratitude and admiration.

It goes without saying that my thanks go to all those who agreed to be interviewed. I interviewed more than 100 people and visited 14 different towns and cities and the number of people who refused to talk was mercifully small. The vast majority agreed that a biography of Sócrates was long overdue and they were keen to pitch in and help. The members of the legendary 1982 team were particularly accommodating, with all bar one of the starting side agreeing to be interviewed.

My early reporting was focused on Sócrates' home city of Ribeirão Preto. I visited Ribeirão 10 times and got to know people there well, including some of Sócrates' closest friends. Dr Said Miguel and Dr Aloisio Abud talked about his university years, Artur and Rodrigo helped me find old newspapers at the city's public archive, and Rogério Moroti at Botafogo was generous in passing on phone numbers of Sócrates' old team mates. João Moreira and Dario put me up on my trips and helped me navigate the city.

Special thanks go to Zé Bernardes, who was not just a great storyteller but also a respected physician who helped open many doors, and to Luiz Eduardo Rebouças, who was generous with his time and contacts. Most of all, my thanks go to Maurinho and Regina Saquy, two of the most generous people I have ever met who did not just give hours of their time, but also opened up their home and became great friends. Marinho's incredible memory shone colour and details on untold stories and Maritaca was a wonderful and welcoming source on Sócrates' earliest years at the club.

Rio de Janeiro, where Sócrates spent a frustrating few years, is where several of his international teammates now live. Leandro was one of the first people to embrace the idea of a biography and he, Junior and Zico were helpful.

Zé da Silva let me browse through his files, Armando de Paulo was generous and unguarded, and Márvio dos Anjos helped with contacts. Leila Sterenberg and Fernanda Cardoso at TV Globo gave me access to important stock footage, and Marcio MacCulloch at Flamengo passed on phone numbers that would otherwise have been hard to find.

Rocco Cotroneo; Gareth Chetwynd and Claudia Rodrigues; Brad Brooks; Flavia Lins e Silva and Nando Perdigão; and Lulu Garcia-Navarro and James Hider, all gave me a bed or a couch where I could lay my head.

I spent a week in Italy looking into Sócrates' year at Fiorentina and could not have managed without Lorenzo Marucci, whose contacts, translations and encyclopedic knowledge of the Tuscan side were invaluable.

Most of my work inevitably came in São Paulo. João Roberto Basílio and André Wanner at Corinthians and Felipe Espindola and Renata Lufti at SPFC both helped with names and numbers of Sócrates' former friends and teammates. In Santos, club historian Guilherme Guarche was helpful with contacts and stats, as were Kennedy and Milton Neves at Terceiro Tempo. During the months I spent going through old newspapers and magazines at the Mario de Andrade public library in São Paulo, Irinete and Emanuel were patient with my repeated search requests and Cesar Camasão patiently went through Sócrates' columns with the newspaper *Agora*.

Victor Rocha also did valuable work in researching news-paper archives and Corinthians expert Celso Unzelte was both brilliant and kind in helping me unravel the complexities of Brazilian football in the 1970s and 1980s (and his Almanaque do Corinthians app was an unbeatable resource for checking historical details). Former Corinthians director Sergio Scarpelli reached out to hard-to-pin-down colleagues, and both Ney and Alberto Helena Jr were as helpful as they were jovial when speaking about Sócrates' early years. Daniel Navas answered medical questions, Mario Naranjo provided research on Sócrates' time in Ecuador and authors Jorge Vasconcellos and Solange Cavalcante-Ferri were also very forthcoming. For old stats, the Rec.Sport.Soccer Statistics Foundation (RSSSF) is absolutely unbeatable.

Another big debt is owed to Sócrates' brothers Sóstenes, Raimundo and Raí, all of whom were generous with their time and their memories. Similarly, his ex-wives and partners Silvana, Simone, Adriana and Kátia all gave up their time to talk and were unguarded and generous. Rosemary agreed to chat after decades of silence and was vital in helping me resolve some chronological mysteries.

Thanks also go to Igor Ramos, Marcio Javaroni, André Dutra, Vinícius Alves de Souza, Gustavo and Sergio at Memofut, Karla Soares in Belém, Tony Danby, Ana Marcia Lopes, Fernando Beer and Carl Worswick in Colombia.

Tom Hennigan's feedback was important as the project inched forwards, and Dan Horch was always encouraging when my spirits flagged. James Young did a couple of interviews for me in Belo Horizonte and took a critical look at several early chapters. Thanks also go to Richard Lapper, Claire Rigby and Mauricio Savarese for talking over key points. Tim Vickery, Matthew Shirts and Alex Cuadros took some valuable time to run their eye over the final draft.

Thanks also to my agents David Luxton and Rebecca Winfield, and my editor Ian Marshall.

My biggest debt is to Brazil and Brazilians, who welcomed me with open arms almost 20 years ago and who have provided me with a happy home ever since. Brazil has been such a huge part of my life and the drama, colour, warmth and excitement far outweigh the frustrations. *Muito obrigado mesmo. Vocês não sabem como vou sentir sua falta.*

Most of all, my heartfelt thanks go to Mariane Kido. She was with me the moment the idea to write this book came into my head as we walked out the Hauptbahnhof in Duisburg in October 2014 and she never left my side the entire time since. She transcribed interviews, brought vital Brazilian context to areas that were unknown to me, and was always willing to discuss ideas and issues. Her insights were crucial and her support and love were unbeatable. *Te adoro. (Falei isso hoje?)*

INDEX

Brazilian players are indexed under the name by which they are commonly known.

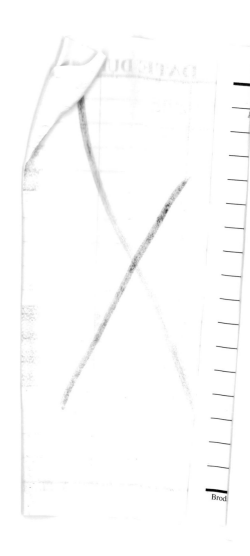